ALLISON
250 656 5425

MURDER BY THE BOOK

MURDER BY THE BOOK

Literary Mysteries from
Alfred Hitchcock Mystery Magazine
and
Ellery Queen's Mystery Magazine

Edited by Cynthia Manson

Carroll & Graf Publishers
New York

First edition 1995.

Carroll & Graf Publishers, Inc.
260 Fifth Avenue
New York, NY 10001

Library of Congress Cataloging-in-Publication Data is available

ISBN 0-7867-0250-8

Manufactured in the United States of America

95 96 97   5 4 3 2 1

CONTENTS

INTRODUCTION

Murder by the Book is a collection of short stories whose theme revolves around the literary world of writers, books, readers, rare book collectors, libraries, and even well-known characters taken from famous works. Our lineup of internationally known authors includes major talents such as James Thurber, Dorothy L. Sayers, Ruth Rendell, Michael Innes, Lawrence Block, and Julian Symons.

The range of subject matter reflects a broad spectrum of themes from the world of literature. For example, we include a story by Robert Barr about an inheritance hidden in the library of a private Lord's estate. Margaret Maron's story utilizes a map from Robert Louis Stevenson's classic *Treasure Island* to locate a secret treasure referred to in a will. Bill James's tale of a student murdered at a crime-writing class gives us an inside perspective on solving a murder. Crime writers are also the focus of Carl Martin's amusing story of a crime-writers club that plans a heist. A crime writers conference is at the center of Edward D. Hoch's story with sleuth Jeffrey Rand on the case. Both Robert Cenedella's and Donald Olson's stories feature writers contemplating a murder. Moving on to the reader angle, we have William Brittain's story about an avid fan of Dashiell Hammett and Michelle Knowlden's story, that pokes fun at Jane Austen lovers, while John Nelson's detective unravels the mysterious suicide of a man obsessed with Charles Dickens.

All of the stories included in this anthology are from *Ellery Queen's Mystery Magazine* and *Alfred Hitchcock Mystery Magazine*. For those readers who like a good mystery with literary twists and references, this anthology should prove most gratifying.

Cynthia Manson

MURDER BY THE BOOK

BILL JAMES

Body Language

ONE TUESDAY AFTERNOON, WHEN Professor Cameron Phelps was nearing the end of his lecture to a Contemporary Fiction class on The Detective Story in Modern Novel and Film, a man he certainly recognized from drinks parties given by the English Society a while back suddenly appeared in the doorway near him, stood for a moment scanning the undergraduates, then stepped forward, pointing some sort of handgun at Geraldine Marques, sitting two students in on the third row, and shot her through the head, shot her twice.

When the first bullet hit her, Geraldine's face did not disintegrate or explode, as that hanging melon does on screen during the famous target practice scene in *The Day of the Jackal*, but it certainly seemed to Cameron to lose all the conventional qualities and lineaments of a face. For what might have been a quarter of a second one of those looks of surprise, and yet at the same time of almost serene resignation, which in quite a few thrillers comes over the features of those about to be wasted, did register around Geraldine's eyes. That, though, must have been before the gun went off. Afterwards, nobody could have read anything in her expression because there was none, only this sudden dishevelment of the bone structure.

It was an old-fashioned lecture theatre, with long, curved, narrow mahogany benches going the full width of the room, except for the aisles, and steeply tiered to the back, where there was another door. Geraldine slipped down under the bench after the initial shot and, from his spot behind the lectern at the front, Cameron could not see much of her, only the whiteness of a cricket sweater she had regularly appeared in lately,

1

and the grey-streaked, fairish mass of her hair. The man with the pistol went to the aisle, stepped up two tiers, jumped onto the third bench, and walked a few steps along it, scattering the notebooks and papers of the couple of students between the aisle and Geraldine. He stood over the place where she lay and aimed the gun at her again.

"No," Cameron yelled. "Why? Oh, why?" He moved out from behind the lectern, the copy of *The Friends of Eddie Coyle*, from which he had been reading to illustrate irony, still in his hand. The man turned and stared at him for a moment. Her husband? Geraldine was a mature student with sons, from one of whom she might have borrowed the sweater. Didn't Cameron recall drinking Chianti with this man at some social evening for students and partners in her first year? A plumber? A roofer? "Mr. Marques," he shouted, "you'll never get away with this. Why don't we just talk it over like two sensible people?"

The man turned back, then bent down as if to get a better sighting of Geraldine on the floor. She must have rolled partway under the seat. In a moment he did something very extraordinary, which to Cameron carried a kind of sparkling symbolism. The attacker actually kneeled on the third bench, his back to Cameron, the gun pointed down in front of him at Geraldine. The contradiction seemed to Cameron heavy with meaning— this traditional attitude of subjection, even supplication, yet also this attitude of terrible dominance. In his teaching he always stressed the suitability of crime as a novelistic subject, because of its multitudinous complexities: hence today's look at irony, for instance.

The man fired again, and soon Cameron glimpsed a large, spreading red rectangle appear on the shoulder and back of the cricket sweater. Again that seemed to him significant: this garment of a rigidly formulated, indeed venerable, game now touched by deep disorder. He could smell what he knew must be cordite, sharp, pleasant, lingering. The man straightened, then walked swiftly, assuredly, back along the bench towards the door. Yes, perhaps a roofer. He had on what looked to Cameron like remarkably expensive brown fashion boots, possibly even Timberland. Roofers made a bomb, and plumbers. But how absurd, he thought, to be noticing such things when a woman lay dead and the murderer was escaping. Yet the mind was ungovernable, following its own streams of consciousness, not exactly regardless of events, but only contingent to them. He would diary his reactions with exactitude.

To his classes he had continually pointed out that action, action, and more action was the essence of crime writing: explicit philosophizing, even character analysis, had to be brief, if not actually sketchy, in the interest of pace. Yearly he quoted to his pupils that saying of—or was it about?—Len Deighton, the spy author, stipulating that if a narrative grew slack, the way to recover was to have somebody barge through the door holding a gun. And now it had really happened—and yes, by God, it worked: the whole tempo of things had changed. This lecture theatre's atmosphere no longer seemed even vaguely comparable with what it was when he had been skillfully elaborating on the fierce irony in the title of George V. Higgins's *The Friends of Eddie Coyle*—where "friends" meant the reverse. No question, it had been a well-prepared and genuinely felt lecture of very bright insights, but certainly the students had reacted much more vividly to the interruption by the armed man and the shooting of Geraldine. In fact, they were still tense, still white or flushed, many of them, some weeping.

So, then, action. The only relevant contribution he could think of now was pursuit of the gunman, who had left the room by the upper door, slamming it behind him. Cameron raced up the tiered floor after him. "No!" an undergraduate cried. "My God, Professor, he's armed. Let the police deal with it."

Yet that was not how these things were shaped at all. If some innocent bystander is drawn in during a crime, he is drawn in and has no choice but to become involved, though fearful. This crisis was what in Hemingway—an occasional practitioner of crime fiction—would be called "the moment of truth," and one could only put one's manliness on the line and hope it was of due quality. Cameron still carried the paperback George V. Higgins novel. Would he throw this at the gunman should he encounter him now? It was a paradigm situation: the pathetically ill-armed, run-of-the-mill, even insignificant man—one of life's ordinary Joes—willing to confront the violent brute, and able to offer against this threat only a farcically negligible missile, plus, though, his courage, determination, and the blessed instinct of good's resistance to evil. He remembered Fredric March coping with Bogart and other hoodlums in *The Desperate Hours.* Somehow and eventually this good and typical figure always won:

art's pressure towards tidiness ensured it. He felt wonderfully heartened as he ran, and considered it not foolhardy but obligatory to ignore the well-intentioned, frantic, yelled warning.

Then, as Cameron neared the door, it was flung open again and the man stood there once more, his gun raised. Jesus, had all that rubbish stuff about Hemingway and blessed instincts knackered this narrative so badly that the technique of an armed intruder bursting through the door had to be given such an immediate second run? Cameron stopped, horrified, and they stared at each other. This was the instant, wasn't it, when a fictional character would think lovingly of all those precious things that constituted the texture of existence—bird song, children's laughter, a modicum of Turkish delight, Mozart and/or Randy Crawford, plus, of course, the clean smack of a ball hit perfectly into the pool pocket.

"Why? You ask why?" the man cried in a strangely hollow, yet at the same time immensely powerful, voice.

"Yes, why?" Cameron answered. There could be a remarkable strength from repetition in dialogue: the strength of incantation.

"I'll tell you why. Oh yes, I'll tell you why." Perhaps this man attended evening creative writing classes and also knew about incantation.

One of the more promising students shouted: "What we are seeing here is violence as an outcrop of fundamental psychological disturbance. Character blazoned in action."

"Come," Cameron replied, leading down towards the lectern. He turned his back on the gun, knowing somehow that this was a gesture which could not provoke a shot. It would have been hopelessly outside the mode. "We are a university and everyone is entitled to his point of view. Tell me, are you Mr. Marques? Did we not take wine together, sir, on some earlier occasion?" Often elaborate politeness darkened prevailing menace even further, by showing the formalities of society in peril and so indicating their extreme fragility.

"It doesn't matter who I am."

"But may I call you Mr. Marques?"

"Call me what you will. See me simply as someone with a mission. I have fulfilled half of it."

"Half?"

Cameron felt a terrible fear grip him. If this were fiction it would have been an example of that storytelling trick of not giving the reader too much too soon: standard in crime writing, where narrative flair was the art of holding back. Lord, what was the other half of the mission? *Who* was the other half? As to halves, for half of half a term in Geraldine's second year Cameron had been banging her three or four times a week, after which she moved on to, he thought, Graham Liatt in the History of Political Ideas. The kind of ferocious sexual guilt that waylaid the hero in both *Presumed Innocent* and *Fatal Attraction* ravaged Cameron for a moment, though the actual circumstances in those tales were very different, naturally.

Marques followed him down to the lectern. Cameron replaced *The Friends of Eddie Coyle* on it and addressed the class: "This is Geraldine's, well, husband. Was. We're often left without a full statement of the murderer's point of view. Perhaps we get excessively preoccupied with the restoration of legitimacy, the efficacy of the detective as agent of civic recuperation. Today this can be corrected. I don't know whether Mr. Marques will agree to take questions later."

Cameron could see Geraldine's body again, exactly as it had been, except that the red rectangle on the sweater had grown. The greyness in her hair had almost put him off that liaison in her second year, and had ensured that he did not grieve irreparably when, after a few weeks, she grew restless for Liatt, or some other teaching ram. Perhaps he should have forgone even that short affair. Regret, vain second thoughts, incomprehensibility at one's own actions—these were the essence of the grippingly dramatic. Watching her, inert, he realized she was what Martin Amis in his novel *London Fields* would rather jokingly call the murder—the passive figure, to whom something is done, namely death: it could be significant that the term was applied to a woman, the exploited sex—feminist critics might like to mull that. Geraldine's body bellowed body language.

"She was moving away from me, losing me," Marques declared. "That's why I am here."

"Geraldine was?" Cameron asked.

"And so I decided to bring her to rest. She is mine again now, only mine, forever mine. Reclaimed at last." Passionately, his voice rose to even greater force, easily reaching people in the back row, with which Cameron himself sometimes had difficulty, and Marques lifted both hands in a kind of agonized yet victorious declaration.

He had placed the pistol on the copy of *The Friends of Eddie Coyle* on the lectern, within a couple of meters of Cameron. While

Marques was stretching like that it might have been possible to
snatch the gun. This did not seem at all the proper way things
should go, though. Instead, there ought to come a moment—a
moment when all the talking had been done, all the explanations
covered, all the overtones and wider issues hinted at—when
Marques would voluntarily surrender the weapon in a telling
gesture and Cameron would shake his hand, look once more
squarely into his eyes, seeing only agony and loneliness there,
and then take him regretfully but unswervingly to justice. It was
important to round off matters, hit a note of tragedy rather than
of banal force majeure. This kind of touch was what produced
resonances, lifted even brutal crime to a significant plane.

In any case, Cameron was not sure he would be able to manage
the automatic usefully even if he did grab it. It was of dark blue
metal, horribly like the tint of a bruise, Cameron thought—upset-
tingly so, disablingly so. But how wimpish a reaction! Was this
a sign of the essential impotence of the scholar and academic as
against the Man of Action—the Man of Action whom scholars
and academics battened on: historians with Attila or Wellington
or Rommel; himself—Cameron—in this particular course, with
murderers, bank robbers, roofers?

"How do you mean she's yours again now, only yours, forever
yours?" Kate Bilton called from the end of the back row. "How
can she be yours only yours? She's stone dead. This is surely
sloppy thinking. She's not anyone's now. Blast someone's skull
to establish possession? A bit roundabout, wouldn't you say?"

This kid Bilton had always suffered from a foul dose of liter-
alism. Why she was doing an English course at all Cameron
found it hard to tell. Realizing he had to say something to help
Marques out of his probably limited articulation, Cameron replied: "Death can supply a kind of resolution, surely, Kate. It has
its own awful, majestic neatness. Take the end of *Bonnie and
Clyde*—painful, yes, and yet in its oblique way triumphant."

"Oh, that's Emily Dickinson–type crap," Bilton said. "What
we've got here is a middle-aged, tireless shagger-around lying
broken up on the floor of room B117, knocked over by a husband
scared of scandal, AIDS, pox, and performance comparisons.
End of story."

Oh, how wrong she could be, with her rough, youthful common sense! The end of Geraldine, certainly, but not at all end
of story.

"Moving away from you?" Cameron asked him. "Do you

mean socially and educationally through her degree course here? Believe me, I do understand. This is a theme in so much bitter and fierce crime: the class battle localized in some terrible, emblematic love dispute. Her new cultural acquisitions—literature, scansion, critical theory, familiarity with the *Faerie Queen*—made you feel excluded and uncontrollably envious, yes? Shut out? I see. Social class—the root of almost all major conflict in the British novel, including the crime novel. Its motivating power not always easy to grasp for those in foreign cultures—the U.S.A. or Japan—yet so vital, for all that." Cameron turned sympathetically to him. "Yet being a roofer is a fine and noble trade, Mr. Marques, not to say indispensable." Then, after a moment, Cameron switched back to the undergraduates and gave a small, apologetic smile. "But, of course, you will have spotted that even as I enunciate this I sound patronizing, false, a slave of that very concept of social class. I don't even know this man's first name. Mr. Marques. That form of address indicates I am addressing a mere artisan."

"Roofer? Who's a fucking roofer?" Marques replied. "I'm in the Foreign Office, passed out second in Great Britain."

That use of the expletive really intrigued Cameron. He always gave two full lecture hours to the function of swearing in crime fiction. So often it could be used to compromise and amend the very class categorizations they were discussing here now, bringing magnificent ambiguity. It was exactly right for Marques to employ that demotic, briskly consonantal term when, at the same time, he was announcing himself virtually part of the establishment through his work and his, clearly, first-class intellect. Of course, the word had lost a good deal of its impact now through widespread use in prose of all genres. In the States, as Cameron told his classes, it had been necessary to augment its power a little by adding "mother:" "a motherfucking roofer?" might have had an extra punch about it, and created yet more fascinating uncertainties of the social ranking of the speaker.

"Moving away from you in which sense then?" Cameron asked.

"I couldn't satisfy her any longer."

Cameron immediately felt easier. He had failed to satisfy Geraldine Marques also, so if this was a jealousy job, her husband's rage should not fall on him. In fact, Geraldine had advised Cameron to try sex therapy, or some cock-specializing pseudo witch doctor she knew in one of the city's mean, multiracial, ghetto streets where a man might go who was not himself mean but who could not get it—or keep it—up. That standard weight of guilt was lifted and he no longer even vaguely thought of snatching the gun for self-protection. Was Marques after Liatt then? This was the second half of the mission? Cameron had heard Graham gave women as good as he got, in the current phrase, and then a bit more. Two girls in this class spoke rapturously of him, including the formidable Bilton.

Had Geraldine told Marques of Liatt? His extermination was to come next? Among the political ideas Liatt taught, he favoured radical, old-fashioned Toryism and wooed women with a mixture of haughty surliness and extravagant charm. The best eternal triangle plots always had some thematic, possibly stylistic, aspects, as well as the mere clash of rival lusts, and perhaps Marques was Social Democrat or even Labour. Then again, the sound of his surname—did it have yet further ambiguities: Marques, Marx? That also would distance him from Liatt. This could be altogether a marvellously layered situation.

Cameron wondered whether he should try to get a warning to Graham Liatt that he was about to have at least his face shot off and maybe worse. Yet there was a kind of unfolding inevitability about the way things were moving this afternoon. He felt it would be the behaviour of a philistine, even a vandal, to interfere. Matters had to take their somber course, hadn't they?

And then the upper-lecture-theatre door was flung open again. A man stood there. "Him!" Marques cried, in obvious, appalled recognition and anger.

It was not Liatt, but Albert Quant of French, bald, stooped, wet-nosed, filthy-jacketed, stained-trousered, greasy-breathed, loud-shirted, cheap-sandalled, who should have gone through early retirement years ago, but who somehow hung on and on and was now almost too late for late retirement. Alby (Froggyboy) Quant? It seemed unbelievable that he should have been giving it to Geraldine, or anyone else postwar. Alby, not Liatt, was the second half of the mission?

"I heard you were in the building," Albert remarked, in that hesitant way he always affected, the sod, pretending that English was unnatural to him because of his deep immersion in the cross-Channel parlance. "I am here."

"Bursting through the door like that. So, where's your bloody pistol?" Cameron asked.

"You told Geraldine she deserved to live among gods because she was so lovely," Marques cried. "Where did that leave me, even though I spent hundreds on these boots she admired?"

"I taught her the works of de Musset," Quant replied. "That is true. She seemed impressed by certain poems." He fell into that creepy, lopsided, reciting stance which could clear the senior common room. "One work in particular impressed her. It begins, *Regrettez-vous le temps?* I'll translate, shall I, very loosely, and I'll telescope? We enjoyed together those lines, Geraldine and I. They go like this: *Do you regret having missed that past period when the classical gods descended and inhabited this very earth? Our trouble is that we have come too late, you and I, into a world that is too old.*"

Marques cried: "That's it! She told me I was no use to her any longer, because I was of a hopelessly faded era. Damn it, she had come to regard you as a kind of supreme god—Zeus himself, for God's sake, as it were."

Alby dealt fingerwise with a string of snot that swung suddenly from one nostril. "I'm afraid this enhancement of my identity does happen now and then with women when we're into de Musset," he replied. "Especially mature women students. I don't encourage it."

"She said she had come to imagine you as a great, beautiful, thudding-winged swan," Marques complained. "Took the kids' white sweaters to mock up appropriate plumage and improve her attractiveness."

"As a swan Zeus did get it very effectively and significantly away on Leda," Quant replied. "I'm sure you know that. Yes, that was an example of when a god did indeed come on earth."

Cameron was delighted. "Oh, this is a murder with a definite classical flavour and, thus, right in the central British tradition. So many of our most distinguished crime-mystery stories are aimed at those with a thorough public school and Oxbridge humanities training. These books are intended, as the phrase goes, I think, for the fine mind momentarily at leisure, e.g., works by Dorothy L. Sayers. Classical, Biblical, archaeological references may abound, bringing a brilliant richness."

Marques reached out for the pistol, then replaced it on the lectern, as if the thought of doing Quant, with his special status, was preposterous, especially from a distance of more than thirty meters and up the slope.

"You must flee now," Quant remarked.

"No," Cameron said, aghast. "Things have surely come full circle. It is the juncture for retribution, for surrender, for completeness."

"Those considerations are the banalities of a merely terrestrial, law-and-order-obsessed, sickeningly tit-for-tat-orientated society. Go, Marques. Go now," Quant cried. "Run free, follow your impulses, as did the glorious gods of old."

"I do not deny the classics, Albert," Cameron replied, "and in fact I embrace one of their prime concepts: catharsis—the purging, the sacrifice. This now is due. This is the necessary culmination."

"Balls," Quant remarked.

Kate Bilton, looking from the lecture theatre window, said: "Too late, anyway. Our friends the cops are here, with flak jackets and dogs—using the term 'friends' ironically, of course. The porter must have been on the phone, hearing the shots. Marques is never going to get out."

"This just had to be the final chapter," Cameron said sadly, yet with satisfaction, gingerly confiscating the pistol. Then he leant forward to shake hands formally, meaningfully, almost mournfully with Marques. As he did so, some inadvertent pressure was applied to the trigger of the gun in his other hand and it went off. Marques fell. Dying, he gasped: "I am truly with her forever now." To Cameron, decorum seemed admirably present in this flourish of reconciliatory rhetoric. Blood welled.

"Christ, doesn't he spout, though?" Bilton said.

ROBERT CENEDELLA

Once a Writer . . .

WHEN EIC BESSEMER DECIDED to murder his wife, he felt quite smug about his chance of doing it with impunity.

Eric, after all, was the greatest murder-thinker-upper in the country. Not only did he bring out once every six months a mystery novel featuring Peter Ilyitch, Private Eye (whose fans disputed about whether he was called P.I. because those were his initials or because that was his profession)—but Eric also wrote monthly magazine stories about murders committed by people in ordinary pursuits of life (*The You or Me Murders 1*, or *2*, or *3*, or *16*, or *370*, these were numerically entitled); and finally, most popular and most numerous of all his endeavors, there was his weekly television series, *Murder in the First Degree*, the only such show still filmed in New York, and the only one ever whose remarkably ingenious killings were all devised by the same writer—Eric Bessemer—and all solved by Bessemer's remarkably perspicacious detective, Bernie Zuckerman, who each week in a final speech delivered straight into the camera's eye, revealed to Mr. & Mrs. America and all the ships at sea just who had committed this week's murder—and why.

�֍

WELL, BUT NOW CERTAIN developments made it necessary for Eric to kill his wife, Mildred.

He could remember the days when he had called Mildred Milly, and had kept his arm around her almost always; but those days were long gone. She was Mildred now, and whenever he could help it, which was usually, she was at least ten or twelve arms' lengths away from him.

From that distance, she complained. Constantly.

"All you think of is those mysteries," she whined. "Remember when we were married? Remember what you said then? You said you'd write political columns and commentaries and every four years help pick the next president."

"Know any columnist who makes as much money as I do?" Eric asked.

"Know any columnist who says *yessir* as much as you do?" Mildred countered. "*Ding-a-ling.* 'Hello,' says you. 'It's your editor,' says the phone. 'It's your producer,' says the phone. 'It's your publisher,' says the phone. 'It's your agent,' says the phone. 'Oh,' says you. 'Yessir,' says you. 'Anything you want,' says you. 'Different victim?' says you. 'New perpetrator?' says you. 'New clue?' says you. 'No problem,' says you. 'I'll get right to it,' says you. 'Hey Eric,' says me. 'Shut up, I'm busy,' says you. 'Gotta do this rewrite,' says you. 'Gotta have him stabbed with an icicle, and then the icicle melts,' says you. 'But listen, Eric,' says me. 'Get away, I'm busy,' says you. 'Eric, Eric,' says me, 'we've got tickets for Liza Minelli's new play tonight.' 'Get away,' says you. 'I'm busy,' says you. 'Rewrite,' says you. 'Deadline,' says you. Eric, Eric, why don't you tell them all to go to hell, them and their rewrites and their deadlines?!!"

"Well! Well!

That sort of imperviousness to the needs of a working man would itself be sufficient motive for murder—but Eric had lately come across another reason for doing away with the former Milly.

✳

THE NAME OF THIS NEW MOTIVE for Mildred's murder was Fifi Lovejoy, a name more fitting than even Eric himself had ever been able to dream up for any siren or cocotte or inamorata in even the most sizzling of his murder mysteries.

Fifi was the receptionist at the film studio's office, though she was usually not at her desk, but somewhere nearby, talking to . . . well, to Eric Bessemer, for one.

Fifi was two inches shorter than Eric's five feet ten, which put her wiggly blond hair just about at his hungry mouth; she walked toward him with her breasts waving *Hi there, you* and away from him with her rump weeping an up-and-down goodbye. If he said he was interested in baseball, she said, "Oh, really? Wonderful! I love baseball! All those little white pillows on the field and all those advertisements on the fences and those players' salaries and those hot dogs and everything!"

And, oh, yes, she thought Eric's films were great. She said so. She said, "Hey, I'm on page three of that new script of yours, and wow!" Page three. That was the page of each new script of his that she had just reached each time he came into the office. And she told him so—that is, after she had left the director or actor or gofer she was talking to at the time, and had come back to her desk to talk to Eric.

And by now, Fifi and Eric had gone out together—out of the office, that is, and into a nearby motel Fifi happened to know about—and there Fifi proved she loved him by allowing him to love her.

And love her he did.

After all, she did not, like Mildred, say things like, *When are you going to do something important? When are you going to stop letting those emforgodsakeployers make you work work work all the time?*

No. Fifi's way with him was much more admiring, as when, for example, she said that wow, she had happened to see the payroll accounts, and well, golly whiz, did Eric realize he earned as much as one of those there baseball players, one of those center basemen or second fielders or whatever, and wow golly, she loved him.

The day Fifi said that, they went again to the motel, but then afterward, she said with tears in her eyes that they couldn't do this anymore, it was an immoral sin, and oh, oh, wasn't there something he could do about it?

"Hmmm," he said.

"I'll try to figure something out," he said.

But he had a problem.

Long ago, when he was a boy, the stern tight-lipped mother who brought him up had taught him (and his father) that divorce was immoral.

So, well, okay, if he was to have blond hairs on his pillowslip for the rest of his life, there was nothing he could do but murder Mildred.

Therefore, he planned it. He used the expertise he had been

developing for years at his word processor, and oh, he was clever, oh, he was astute, because, for one thing, Mildred herself was going to give him an alibi.

And she did.

Oh, she did indeed.

She began helping him with this alibi as soon as he told her—with a straight face, mind you—that in the coming summer, he thought they should rent a beautiful cottage on the shore of, well, probably Westport, Connecticut, where various friends of Mildred's spent their vacations.

Mildred said immediately, "What? Oh! Hey! Wow!" And she went to the phone and sang into it: "Rachel? Oh, I've got a see-cret, I've got a see-cret . . ." And: "Sally? Guess where I'll be spending the summer vacation!?" And: "Debbie? I'm going to be your *neighbor* this summer!"

Good. Fine. Now all Eric had to do was to start setting up his alibi.

So: he started telling a number of people, every friend, every neighbor, and several workers at the publishing company and at the magazine and at the film studio, that on the coming Thursday, the day of the week when Mildred always had a date to play bridge with her friends, he would be going up to Westport, Connecticut, to look over some real estate. The evidence of all these people would confirm his alibi.

Okay. Fine as far as it went. What these individuals knew, or thought they knew, would lend credence to the more direct testimony of others that he had indeed been elsewhere when the murder was committed.

All right. Now he went to the bottom drawer of the desk in his study—a drawer into which he was in the habit of throwing useless old things, one of these being the extra key to the front door of the building next to his, a building in which he had lived until the money started rolling in and he had bought the condominium he and Mildred now lived in. He had forgotten to give this extra key to the landlord next door, who did not know of its existence, since Eric himself had had it made—and here it bloody well was in this drawer full of junk. Whee!

So at four in the morning, when no one would be likely to see him, he sneaked out of the bedroom he no longer shared with Mildred, went downstairs and out past the snoozing doorman, and up the three steps to the door of his former apartment building (which had no doorman at all) and tried the key. It worked. It still worked. It opened the door. Whee! Whee!

He returned then, sneaking past the still sleeping doorman in the lobby of his present residence, and went back up in the elevator to his top-floor condo.

He had not been seen.

He had not been heard.

And the key still worked.

He had only to wait now until next Thursday, the last day when Mildred would deface this otherwise lovely planet.

Next Thursday came. It did. It seemed to take about ten months for this to happen, but next Thursday did come.

He sat down to eat what would be his last breakfast ever with Mildred, and he listened to all her fulminations for what would be the very last time.

"Well," she said, "I'm glad you're going up to Westport. Find us a real nice house, okay? View of the beach. Two bathrooms. Comfortable, right? Oh—and don't sign any lease till I get up there and look at it, because I know you, all you'll care about is whether it's got an office for your word processor." She shook her head exasperatedly, then said: "Listen: you know what I don't understand?"

"What?"

"Why you worked all day yesterday on that script. I mean, you could have told them you were going up to Westport for *two* days."

"I had to get the script to them before five-thirty yesterday," said Eric. "A contract is a contract."

"A contract is a way of keeping you—*and* your wife—from having any fun," said Mildred. "Matter of fact, yesterday, with no bridge game, I could have gone with you. Er . . . think you'll be back by four? The bridge party doesn't start until then. Four, okay?"

"Not a chance," said Eric. "I'll be much later."

"Darn," said Mildred. "Darn! You could have gone yesterday and taken me, but oh, no! You preferred to punch that word processor."

"I had to finish the script and get it to them," said Eric.

"Script! Script! Short story! Mystery novel! It's all you think of! I bet you'll even be writing those things up there in Westport. You'll call it a vacation, but you'll work work work!"

Eric didn't argue with her. After today, he would never have to listen to her imprecations. Tomorrow he would be free, because this was it! This was the day!

✳

IT WAS 9:30 when he finished breakfast.

It was 9:38 when he took his car from the garage.

It was 10:09 when he parked the car in a space near the 125th Street railway stop.

It was 10:42 when a cab deposited him back downtown at Grand Central Station.

It was 10:44 when he got into a phone booth, called the mystery magazine, got the editor, and told him that oh gee whiz, he was at Grand Central Station, just about to take a train to Westport, but he had suddenly realized that he needed to make an important change in the story they were to be sending to the presses this week.

The editor said, "I thought the story was pretty good. What's this change?"

"Well, if the guy the murderess kills to get the property was the guy she'd been in love with in college, and she knew it, then she just couldn't pull the trigger. So I'm going to have him changed, have him get a plastic surgeon to make him, oh, humpbacked or something, and long-nosed and redheaded and swollen-cheeked, so he'll be pretty sure he's fooling her into giving this supposed innocent stranger the money for a half share in the estate that isn't his at all, whereas *she, not* recognizing him, kills him to get the whole estate that he doesn't own. And then she finds that out, and finds out that he's the man she loves, and she's killed him. Good, huh?"

"Well, yeah, yeah, I guess it is."

"But I've got to get it to you by tomorrow night, and here I am on my way to Westport, so look: can you send the story by messenger, fast fast, to the One-Twenty-Fifth-Street Station, and have him page me when my train stops there, and give me the manuscript?"

"Well ... gosh ... Look: how much time do we have?"

"The train will be there at eleven forty-five. And, hey, listen, maybe to hurry it up, you could send Ms. McIntyre, your secretary...."

"Hmm ... Well, yeah, sure. Yuh. Okay." And the editor was yelling for his secretary as he hung up.

That was it.

Beautifully plotted by the best murder-thinker-upper in the world.

So: Eric took the train to—supposedly—Westport.

It stopped at 125th Street.

From where he sat, in the most crowded car, he could hear Ms. McIntyre, two cars down, shouting: "Mr. Bessemer! Mr. Eric Bessemer!"

And he sat there waiting until she was nearly up to his car. Then he rose, and said loudly: "Is someone calling Mr. Eric Bessemer?"

A passenger said: "Eric *Bessemer?* The writer?"

"Yes, yes. That's me." (He did not add: *And you're a witness.*)

Ms. McIntyre entered the car at that moment, but did not at first see Eric Bessemer, because he was suddenly surrounded by passengers saying, *Uh, Mr. Bessemer . . . Autograph, please? . . . I love your stories, Mr. Bessemer . . .*

But Ms. McIntyre pushed through this small gang and handed Eric the package containing his manuscript.

"Whew!" she said. "Here's your story, Mr. Bessemer. Look, I'd better get off the train . . ."

"Gangway!" said Bessemer. "Let me help this lady off! And I've got to go up front anyhow. Gangway!"

And stuffing the manuscript into his briefcase, he followed her out of the railroad car.

She threw him a kiss and jumped off the train—and Eric waved, then continued through the next car, and got off it slowly, looking back along the platform toward Ms. McIntyre, who thank heaven was hurrying away from him toward the stairway to the street; and just to be on the safe side, he hid behind a post as the train started up and Ms. McIntyre started down.

In a matter of seconds, he was alone on the platform.

Whee! Everything had worked perfectly.

He waited, smiling, almost dancing, until Ms. McIntyre must surely be in a cab or a subway car, and then went downstairs and outside, found his car where he had parked it earlier, got into it, and drove it downtown.

He knew a public parking lot that not everyone else knew, a fairly small tucked-away section of Riverside Park, not many blocks from his Riverside Drive address—and sure enough, in that lot there was a space for his car.

He parked it; he took the revolver from under the seat and

hid it in his briefcase, under the bundle containing the manuscript Ms. McIntyre had given him.

And as he got out, he carried the briefcase.

He locked the car door.

And he walked out to Riverside Drive, and on up it toward
the scene-to-be of the most satisfying murder he had ever
plotted.

No one seemed to be coming out or going into his building,
or (even more importantly) the building next to his.

So: he went up the three steps, used the long-forgotten key
to the building he had once lived in, and took the elevator to
the roof. Both buildings were seventeen stories tall, since their
builders had built them at the same time—and only a short
stone wall stood between their roofs.

He scaled it.

And here he was, home, unseen by his doorman or anyone
else, one story above the scene of his coming liberation.

He nodded. He smiled. He went through the door to the
stairs, walked down one flight, took his apartment key from
his pocket, put it in the keyhole, and . . .

And stopped for a moment.

Smiled for a moment.

Reflected for a moment.

People could swear he had gone to Westport, and, indeed,
he would do so—by car—the moment his task was finished.
Ms. McIntyre could testify that he was on the train long since
gone. Some signature-seekers could confirm this. The real-
estate people in Westport would tell of his visits to them.

My God, he was a smart plotter!

He took the gun from his briefcase, putting it in his pocket,
then opened the door very very quietly.

Closed it, just as quietly.

Listened.

He heard Mildred's voice, speaking from somewhere toward
the back of the apartment, somewhere—yes, yes, from his office, where she was talking on the phone.

He crept closer, down the corridor, his hand on the revolver
in his pocket. She'd be through with this call in a minute, and
then . . .

Mildred's voice came to him quite clearly now.

"Well, no, Ms. Lovejoy . . . no . . ."

Ms. Lovejoy! Fifi!

"No, you see, Ms. Lovejoy, he's already left for Westport. . . . The company knew he was going there, didn't they? Well, there you are. You'll have to tell Mr. Sanford that he's gone already. . . . No, there's no way of reaching him. . . . What's that? Oh. Oh, well, what's this other writer's name? I see. . . . Yes, I have it. . . . I'll tell my husband when he returns tonight, Ms. Lovejoy. I'm sure he'll understand about the other writer. I mean, what else could you do with my husband out of town? Okay. Thank you. Goodbye."

Other writer!?

Eric pushed into the office. Mildred was just rising from the desk.

"What was all that about?" said Eric. "Other writer? What the hell . . . ?"

"Oh, where'd you come from, Eric?"

"Other writer?"

"Did you miss the train?"

"Never mind the verblungety train! What's this about another writer? *What* other writer, and for what reason?"

"Oh. Fella named Tom Altman. He's gonna rewrite your script, this week's script, because they have to do it in a hurry, they're shooting day after tomorrow, and with you in Westport today . . ."

"I'm not in Westport! Give me that phone!"

He pushed past her, grabbed the phone, dialed—and while she was crying out, *Don't! Don't call him! Let him think you're in Westport,* Eric said into the phone, "Mr. Sanford, please, emergency," then drummed his fingers on the desk while Mildred kept saying, *Westport!* and *Hang up! Don't bother with these people! Never mind Mr. Sanford! Don't do what he wants! Do what you want! Just hang up! Forget it! Let him think you're in Westport!*

Then came Eddie Sanford's voice on the phone: "Hello?"

"Eddie! Eddie, this is Eric Bessemer. I . . . Look, something wrong with the script? I mean . . ."

"Hey, Eric, I thought you were out of town someplace."

"Well, I'm not. Now, what's this about the script?"

"It needs work, Eric. Not your fault. Only, look, you laid it in Florida, and . . . Well, just guess what happened? Guess who we signed for it? Benny Quinlan! Benny Quinlan, hey, imagine that!"

"The Olympic ski champion?"

"Yeah! How's *about* that? *Box Office!*"

"Can he act?"

"He's *Box Office*! But, well, see, all those car chases down in Florida are gonna have to be changed to tricky breathtaking *ski* chases in the mountains of Vermont. So ... Well, we gotta rewrite."

"It's my script. Did you talk to Tom Altman yet?"

"No. I was just gonna call him."

"Well, don't. Now, look, I'll get it right away. Have it for you by tomorrow P.M. at the latest."

"Oh, wonderful! Wonderful! Look, Eric, we better say goodbye and you get busy, right?"

"Right." And they hung up.

Mildred was yammering at him as he turned to the smaller desk where he kept his word processor. He pulled it toward him and then rose to go to the closet, where he kept his reams of paper, Mildred all the time saying, *My God, aren't the real-estate people expecting you in Westport*, he all the time ignoring her as he got out paper, adjusted the desk light, and then, about the time she was saying, *Where's your sense of fitness? I mean, this instead of Westport, damn it*, he was saying to her, "Look, Mildred, there's something I want you to do ..." and he pulled from a drawer the story he had rewritten yesterday before he'd called Ms. McIntyre's boss and told him he'd rewrite it today. "Here," he said to Mildred. "Wait about two hours and then call Ms. McIntyre at the magazine. Tell her I decided to come back home and do this, it was so important— but she'll have to send a messenger, I'm too busy with another rewrite to bring it in myself, but it's all done, so a messenger, all right?"

"All right? All right? What the hell is all right around here? I just heard you say you'd be busy till late tomorrow, so you won't go to Westport tomorrow, either, right? Right? Right?"

"Right," said Eric. "Certainly not tomorrow."

"*Damn* you!" And out she went, slamming the door behind her.

Eric shrugged, then, turning to the word processor, he said half-aloud: "Let's see ... Scene One. FADE IN ON A MOUNTAIN IN VERMONT ..."

But then then phone rang. He picked it up and said, "Hello."

"Eric? Harry Willis here." His book publisher now. "Listen, Eric, your book is great except for the alibi you give your villain. I mean, nobody can vouch for him. He's a suspect, what good would it do for him to say he was someplace else at the time with no confirmation? They'd arrest him. He's gotta have witnesses backing him up."

"Wait a minute," said Eric. "I see your point, but look: suppose he goes on a train, see, and has a messenger deliver something to him at a stop—maybe just at One-Twenty-Fifth Street. Anyway, then he jumps off the train, commits the murder, and everybody thinks he's in Chicago or somewhere. Witnesses. And later he gets there by plane, under a different name, and people are testifying he was on the train. How's about that?"

"Great! Can you get it to be by Wednesday?"

"No problem." He hung up, and as he turned toward his word processor, the door opened again.

"I'll tell you this," Mildred said. "As long as you care about what all those editors and producers and publishers want you to do, you'll never do anything that you yourself really want."

And the door slammed again.

Eric sighed.

He took the revolver from his pocket, emptied it of its bullets, and threw them into the wastebasket.

"All right, where was I?" said Eric. Then: "Oh, yeah—Mountain in Vermont . . . ."

BILL PRONZINI

The Private Eye Who Collected Pulps

THE ADDRESS EBERHARDT HAD GIVEN me on the phone was a corner lot in St. Francis Wood, halfway up the western slope of Mt. Davidson. The house there looked like a baronial Spanish villa—a massive two-story stucco affair with black iron trimming, flanked on two sides by evergreens and eucalyptus. It sat on a notch in the slope 40 feet above street level and it commanded an impressive view of Lake Merced and the Pacific Ocean beyond. Even by St. Francis Wood standards—the area is one of San Francisco's moneyed residential sections—it was some place, probably worth half a million dollars or more.

At four o'clock on an overcast weekday afternoon this kind of neighborhood is usually quiet and semi-deserted; today it was teeming with people and traffic. Cars were parked bumper to bumper on both fronting streets, among them half a dozen police cruisers and unmarked sedans and a television camera truck. Thirty or 40 citizens were grouped along the sidewalks, gawking, and I saw four uniformed cops standing watch in front of the gate and on the stairs that led up to the house.

I didn't know what to make of all this as I drove past and tried to find a place to park. Eberhardt had not said much on the phone, just that he wanted to see me immediately on a police matter at this address. The way it looked, a crime of no small consequence had taken place here today—but why summon me to the scene? I had no idea who lived in the house; I had no rich clients or any clients at all except for an

22

appliance outfit that had hired me to do a skip-trace on one of its deadbeat customers.

Frowning, I wedged my car between two others a block away and walked back down to the corner. The uniformed cop on the gate gave me a sharp look as I came up to him, but when I told him my name his manner changed and he said, "Oh, right, Lieutenant Eberhardt's expecting you. Go on up."

So I climbed the stairs under a stone arch and past a terraced rock garden to the porch. Another patrolman stationed there took my name and then led me through an archway and inside.

The interior of the house was dark, and quiet except for the muted sound of voices coming from somewhere in the rear. The foyer and the living room and the hallway we went down were each ordinary enough, furnished in a baroque Spanish style; but the large room the cop ushered me into was anything but ordinary for a place like this. It contained an overstuffed leather chair, a reading lamp, an antique trestle desk-and-chair, and no other furniture except for floor-to-ceiling bookshelves that covered every available inch of wall space; there were even library-type stacks along one side. And all the shelves were jammed with paperbacks, some new and some which seemed to date back to the 1940s. As far as I could tell every one of them was genre—mysteries, Westerns, and science fiction.

Standing in the middle of the room were two men—Eberhardt and an inspector I recognized named Jordan. They both turned when I came in. Eberhardt said something to Jordan, who nodded and immediately started out. He gave me a nod on his way past that conveyed uncertainty about whether or not I ought to be there. Which made two of us.

Eberhardt was my age, 51, and he seemed to have been fashioned of an odd contrast of sharp angles and smooth blunt planes: square forehead, sharp nose and chin, thick and blocky upper body, long legs and angular hands. He was chewing on the stem of a battered black briar and wearing his usual sour look; but it seemed tempered a little today with something that might have been embarrassment. And that was odd, too, because we've been friends for 30 years, ever since we went through the Police Academy together after World War II and then joined the San Francisco police force. In all that time I had never known him to be embarrassed by anything while he was on the job.

"You took your time getting here, hotshot," he said.

"Come on, Eb, it's only been half an hour since you called. You can't drive out here from downtown in much less than that." I glanced around at the bookshelves again. "What's all this?"

"The Paperback Room," he said.

"How's that?"

"You heard me. The Paperback Room. There's also a Hard-cover Room, a Radio and Television Room, a Movie Room, a Pulp Room, a Comic Art Room, and two or three others I can't remember."

I just looked at him.

"This place belongs to Thomas Murray," he said. "Name mean anything to you?"

"Not offhand."

"Media's done features on him in the past—the King of the Popular Culture Collectors."

The name clicked then in my memory; I had read an article on Murray in one of the Sunday supplements about a year ago. He was a retired manufacturer of electronic components, worth a couple of million dollars, who spent all his time accumulating popular culture—genre books and magazines, prints of television and theatrical films, old radio shows on tape, comic books and strips, original artwork, Sherlockiana, and other such items. He was reputed to be one of the foremost experts in the country on these subjects, and regularly provided material and copies of material to other collectors, students, and historians for nominal fees.

I said, "Okay, I know who he is. But I—"

"Was," Eberhardt said.

"What?"

"Who he *was*. He's dead—murdered."

"So that's it."

"Yeah, that's it." His mouth turned down at the corners in a sardonic scowl. "He was found here by his niece shortly before one o'clock. In a locked room."

"Locked room?"

"Something the matter with your hearing today?" Eberhardt said irritably. "Yes, a damned locked room. We had to break down the door because it was locked from the inside and we found Murray lying in his own blood on the carpet. Stabbed under the breastbone with a razor-sharp piece of thin steel, like a splinter." He paused, watching me. I kept my expression stoic and attentive. "We also found what looks like a kind of dying message, if you want to call it that."

"What sort of message?"

"You'll see for yourself pretty soon."

"Me? Look, Eb, just why did you get me out here?"

"Because I want your help, damn it. And if you say anything cute about this being a big switch, the cops calling in a private eye for help on a murder case, I won't like it much."

So that was the reason why he seemed a little embarrassed. I said, "I wasn't going to make any wisecracks; you know me better than that. If I can help you I'll do it gladly—but I don't know how."

"You collect pulp magazines yourself, don't you?"

"Sure. But what does that have to do with—"

"The homicide took place in the Pulp Room," he said. "And the dying message involves pulp magazines. Okay?"

I was surprised, and twice as curious now, but I said only, "Okay." Eberhardt is not a man you can prod.

He said, "Before we go in there you'd better know a little of the background. Murray lived here alone except for the niece, Paula Thurman, and a housekeeper named Edith Keeler. His wife died a few years ago and they didn't have any children. Two other people have keys to the house—a cousin, Walter Cox, and Murray's brother David. We managed to round up all four of those people and we've got them in a room at the rear of the house.

"None of them claims to know anything about the murder. The housekeeper was out all day; this is the day she does her shopping. The niece is a would-be artist and she was taking a class at San Francisco State. The cousin was having a long lunch with a girl friend downtown, and the brother was at Tanforan with another horseplayer. In other words three of them have got alibis for the probable time of Murray's death, but none of the alibis is what you could call unshakable.

"And all of them, with the possible exception of the housekeeper, have strong motives. Murray was worth around three million, and he wasn't exactly generous with his money where his relatives are concerned; he doled out allowances to each of them but he spent most of his ready cash on his popular-culture collection. They're all in his will—they freely admit that—and each of them stands to inherit a potful now that he's dead.

"They also freely admit, all of them, that they could use the inheritance. Paula Thurman is a nice-looking blonde, around twenty-five, and she wants to go to Europe and pursue an art career. David Murray is the same approximate age as his brother, late fifties; if the broken veins in his nose are any indication he's an alcoholic as well as a horseplayer—a literal loser and going downhill fast. Walter Cox is a mousy little guy who wears glasses about six inches thick; he fancies himself an investments expert but doesn't have the cash to make himself rich—he says—in the stock market. Edith Keeler is around sixty, not too bright, and stands to inherit a token five thousand dollars in Murray's will; that's why she's what your pulp cops call 'the least likely suspect.' "

He paused again. "Lot of details there, but I figured you'd better know as much as possible. You with me so far?"

I nodded.

"Okay. Now, Murray was one of these regimented types— did everything the same way day after day. Or at least he did when he wasn't off on buying trips or attending popular-culture conventions. He spent two hours every day in each of his Rooms, starting with the Paperback Room at eight a.m. His time in the Pulp Room was from noon until two p.m. While he was in each of these Rooms he would read or watch films or listen to tapes, and he would also answer correspondence pertaining to whatever that Room contained—pulps, paperbacks, TV and radio shows, and so on. Did all his own secretarial work—and kept all his correspondence segregated by Rooms."

I remembered these eccentricities of Murray's being mentioned in the article I had read about him. It had seemed to me then, judging from his quoted comments, that they were calculated in order to enhance his image as King of the Popular Culture Collectors. But if so, it no longer mattered; all that mattered now was that he was dead.

Eberhardt went on, "Three days ago Murray started acting a little strangely. He seemed worried about something but he wouldn't discuss it with anybody; he did tell the housekeeper that he was trying to work out 'a problem.' According to both the niece and the housekeeper he refused to see either his cousin or his brother during that time; and he also took to locking himself into each of his Rooms during the day and in his bedroom at night, something he had never done before.

"You can figure that as well as I can: he suspected that somebody wanted him dead, and he didn't know how to cope with it. He was probably trying to buy time until he could figure out a way to deal with the situation."

"Only time ran out on him," I said.

"Yeah. What happened as far as we know it is this: the niece came home at 12:45, went to talk to Murray about getting an advance on her allowance, and didn't get any answer when she knocked on the door to the Pulp Room. She became concerned, she says, went outside and around back, looked in through the window and saw him lying on the floor. She called us right away.

"When we got here and broke down the door, we found Murray lying right where she told us. Like I said before, he'd been stabbed with a splinterlike piece of steel several inches long; the outer two inches had been wrapped with adhesive tape—a kind of handle grip, possibly. The weapon was still in the wound, buried around three inches deep."

"Three inches?" I said. "That's not much penetration for a fatal wound."

"No, but it was enough in Murray's case. He was a scrawny man with a concave chest; there wasn't any fat to help protect his vital organs. The weapon penetrated at an upward angle and the point of it pierced his heart."

I nodded and waited for him to go on.

"We didn't find anything useful when we searched the room," Eberhardt said. "There are two windows but both of them are nailed shut because Murray was afraid somebody would open one of them and the damp air off the ocean would damage the magazines; the windows hadn't been tampered with. The door hadn't been tampered with either. And there aren't any secret panels or fireplaces with big chimneys or stuff like that. Just a dead man alone in a locked room."

"I'm beginning to see what you're up against."

"You've got a lot more to see yet," he said. "Come on."

He led me out into the hallway and down to the rear. I could still hear the sound of muted voices; otherwise the house was unnaturally still—or maybe my imagination made it seem that way.

"The morgue people have already taken the body," Eberhardt said. "And the lab crew finished up half an hour ago. We'll have the room to ourselves."

We turned a corner into another corridor and I saw a uniformed patrolman standing in front of a door that was a foot or so ajar; he moved aside silently as we approached. The door was a heavy oak job with the bolt slides into a locking plate was splintered as a result of the forced entry. I let Eberhardt push the door inward and then followed him inside.

The room was large, rectangular—and virtually overflowing with plastic-bagged pulp and digest-sized magazines. Brightly colored spines filled four walls of floor-to-ceiling bookshelves and two rows of library stacks. I had over 6000 issues of detective and mystery pulps in my Pacific Heights flat, but the collection in this room made mine seem meager in comparison. There must have been at least 15,000 issues here, of every conceivably type of pulp and digest, arranged by category but in no other particular order: detective, mystery, horror, macabre, adventure, Western, science fiction, air-war, hero, love. Then and later I saw what appeared to be complete runs of *Black Mask* and *Dime Detective* and *Weird Tales* and *The Shadow* and *Western Story*; of *Ellery Queen's Mystery Magazine* and *Alfred Hitchcock's Mystery Magazine* and *Manhunt*; and of titles I had never even heard of.

It was an awesome collection, and for a moment it captured all my attention. A collector like me doesn't often see anything this overwhelming; in spite of the circumstances it presented a certain immediate distraction. Or it did until I focused on the wide stain of dried blood on the carpet near the back-wall shelves, and the chalk outline of a body which enclosed it.

An odd queasy feeling came into my stomach; rooms where people have died violently have that effect on me. I looked away from the blood and tried to concentrate on the rest of the room. Like the Paperback Room we had been in previously, it contained nothing more in the way of furniture than an overstuffed chair, a reading lamp, a brass-trimmed rolltop desk set beneath one of the two windows, and a desk chair that had been overturned. Between the chalk outline and the back-wall shelves there was a scattering of magazines which had evidently been pulled or knocked loose from three of the shelves; others were askew in place, tilted forward or backward, as if someone had stumbled or fallen against them.

And on the opposite side of the chalk outline, in a loosely arranged row, were two pulps and a digest, the digest sandwiched between the larger issues.

Eberhardt said, "Take a look at that row of three magazines over there."

I crossed the room, noticing as I did so that all the scattered and shelved periodicals at the back wall were detective and mystery; the pulps were on the upper shelves and the digests on the lower ones. I stopped to one side of the three laid-out magazines and bent over to peer at them.

The first pulp was a 1930s and 1940s crime monthly called *Clues*. The digest was a short-lived title from the 1960s, *Keyhole Mystery Magazine*. And the second pulp was an issue of one of my particular favorites, *Private Detective*.

"Is this what you meant by a dying message?"

"That's it," he said. "And that's why you're here."

I looked around again at the scattered magazines, the disarrayed shelves, the overturned chair. "How do you figure this part of it, Eb?"

"The same way you're figuring it. Murray was stabbed somewhere on this side of the room. He reeled into that desk chair, knocked it over, then staggered away to those shelves. He must have known he was dying, that he didn't have enough time or strength to get to the phone or to find paper and pencil to write out a message. Bt he had enough presence of mind to want to point *some* kind of finger at his killer. So while he was falling or after he fell he was able to drag those three magazines off their shelves; and before he died he managed to lay them out the way you see them. The question is, why those three particular magazines?"

"It seems fairly obvious why the copy of *Clues*," I said.

"Sure. But what clues was he trying to leave us with *Keyhole Mystery Magazine* and *Private Detective*? Was he trying to tell us how he was killed or who killed him? Or both? Or something else altogether?"

I sat on my heels, putting my back to the chalk outline and the dried blood, and peered more closely at the magazines. The issue of *Clues* was dated November 1937, featured a Violet McDade story by Cleve F. Adams, and had three other, unfamiliar authors' names on the cover. The illustration depicted four people shooting each other.

I looked at *Keyhole Mystery Magazine*. It carried a June 1960 date and headlined stories by Norman Daniels and John Collier; there were several other writers' names in a bottom strip, a couple of which I recognized. Its cover drawing showed a frightened girl in the foreground, fleeing a dark menacing figure in the background.

The issue of *Private Detective* was dated March, no year, and below the title were the words "Intimate Revelations of Private Investigators." Yeah, sure. The illustration showed a private eye dragging a half-naked girl into a building. Yeah, sure. Down in the lower right-hand corner in big red letters was the issue's feature story: "Dead Man's Knock" by Roger Torrey.

I thought about it, searching for connections between what I had seen in here and what Eberhardt had told me. Was there anything in any of the illustrations, some sort of parallel situation? No. Did any of the primary suspects have names which matched those of writers listed on any of the three magazine covers? No. Was there any well-known fictional private eye named Murray or Cox or Thurman or Keeler? No.

I decided I was trying too hard, looking for too-specific a connection where none existed. The plain fact was, Murray had been dying when he thought to leave these magazine clues; he would not have had time to hunt through dozens of magazines to find particular issues with particular authors or illustrations on the cover. All he had been able to do was to reach for specific copies close at hand; it was the titles of the magazines that carried whatever message he meant to leave.

So assuming *Clues* meant just that, clues, *Keyhole* and *Private Detective* were the sum total of those clues. I tried putting them together. Well, there was the obvious association: the stereotype of a private investigator is that of a snooper, a keyhole peeper. But I could not see how that would have anything to do with Murray's death. If there had been a private detective involved, Eberhardt would have figured the connection immediately and I wouldn't be here.

Take them separately then. *Keyhole Mystery Magazine.* Keyhole. That big old-fashioned keyhole in the door?

Eberhardt said abruptly, "Well? Got any ideas?" He had been standing near me, watching me think; but patience had never been his long suit.

I straightened up, explained to him what I had been ruminating about, and watched him nod: he had come to the same conclusions long before I got here. Then I said, "Eb, what about the door keyhole? Could there be some connection there, something to explain the locked-room angle?"

"I already thought of that," he said. "But go ahead, have a look for yourself."

I walked over to the door, and when I got there I saw for the first time that there was a key in the latch on the inside. Eberhardt had said the lab crew had come and gone; I caught hold of the key and tugged at it, but it had been turned in the lock and it was firmly in place.

"Was this key in the latch when you broke the door down?" I asked him.

"It was. What were you thinking? That the killer stood out in the hallway and stabbed Murray through the keyhole?"

"Well, it was an idea."

"Not a very good one. It's too fancy, even if it was possible."

"I guess you're right."

"I don't think we're dealing with a mastermind here," he said. "I've talked to the suspects and there's not one of them with an IQ over a hundred and twenty."

I turned away from the door. "Is it all right if I prowl around in here, look things over for myself?"

"I don't care what you do," he said, "if you end up giving me something useful."

Slowly I wandered over and looked at one of the two windows. It had been nailed shut, all right, and the nails had been painted over some time ago. The window looked out on an overgrown rear yard—eucalyptus trees, undergrowth, and scrub brush. Wisps of fog had begun to blow in off the ocean; the day had turned dark and misty. And my mood was beginning to match it. I had no particular stake in this case and yet because Eberhardt had called me into it I felt a certain commitment. For that reason, and because puzzles of any kind prey on my mind until I know the solution, I was feeling a little frustrated.

I went to the desk beneath the second of the windows, glanced through the cubbyholes: correspondence, writing paper, envelopes, a packet of blank checks. The center drawer contained pens and pencils, various-sized paper clips and rubber bands, a tube of glue, a booklet of stamps. The three side drawers were full of letter carbons and folders jammed with facts and figures about pulp magazines and pulp writers.

From there I crossed to the overstuffed chair and the reading lamp and peered at each of them in turn. Then I looked at some of the bookshelves and went down the aisles between the library stacks. And finally I came back to the chalk outline and stood staring down again at the issues of *Clues*, *Keyhole Mystery Magazine*, and *Private Detective*.

Eberhardt said impatiently, "Are you getting anywhere or just stalling?"

"I'm trying to think," I said. "Look, Eb, you told me Murray was stabbed with a splinterlike piece of steel. How thick was it?"

"About the thickness of a pipe cleaner. Most of the 'blade' part had been honed to a fine edge and the point was needle-sharp."

"And the other end was wrapped with adhesive tape?"

"That's right. A grip, maybe."

"Seems an odd sort of weapon, don't you think? I mean, why not just use a knife?"

"People have stabbed other people with weapons a hell of a lot stranger," he said. "You know that."

"Sure. But I'm wondering if the choice of weapon here has anything to do with the locked-room angle."

"If it does I don't see how."

"Could it have been *thrown* into Murray's stomach from a distance, instead of driven there at close range?"

"I suppose it could have been. But from where? Not outside this room, not with that door locked on the inside and the windows nailed down."

Musingly I said, "What if the killer wasn't in this room when Murray died?"

Eberhardt's expression turned even more sour. "I know what you're leading up to with that," he said. "The murderer rigged some kind of fancy crossbow arrangement, operated by a tripwire or by remote control. Well, you can forget it. The lab boys searched every inch of this room. Desk, chairs, bookshelves, reading lamp, ceiling fixtures—everything. There's nothing like that here; you've been over the room, you can tell that for yourself. There's nothing at all out of the ordinary or out of place except those magazines."

Sharpening frustration made me get down on one knee and stare once more at the copies of *Keyhole* and *Private Detective*. They had to mean something, damn it, separately or in conjunction. But what? What?

"Lieutenant?"

The voice belonged to Inspector Jordan; when I looked up he was standing in the doorway, gesturing to Eberhardt. I watched Eb go over to him and the two of them hold a brief, soft-voiced conference. At length Eberhardt turned to look at me again.

"I'll be back in a minute," he said. "I've got to go talk to the family. Keep working on it."

"Sure. What else?"

He and Jordan went away and left me alone. I kept staring at the magazines and I kept coming up empty.

Keyhole Mystery Magazine.

Private Detective.

Nothing.

I stood up and prowled around some more, looking here and there. That went on for a couple of minutes—until all of a sudden I became aware of something Eberhardt and I should have noticed before, should have considered before. Something that was at once obvious and completely unobtrusive, like the purloined letter in the Poe story.

I came to a standstill, frowning, and my mind began to crank out an idea. I did some careful checking then, and the idea took on more weight, and at the end of another couple of minutes I had convinced myself I was right.

I knew how Thomas Murray had been murdered in a locked room.

Once I had that, the rest of it came together in short order. My mind works that way; when I have something solid to build on, a kind of chain reaction takes place. I put together things Eberhardt had told me and things I knew about Murray, and there it was in a nice ironic package: the significance of *Private Detective* and the name of Murray's killer.

When Eberhardt came back into the room I was going over it all for the third time, making sure of my logic. He had the black briar clamped between his teeth again and there were more scowl-wrinkles in his forehead. He said, "My suspects are getting restless; if we don't come up with an answer pretty soon, I'm going to have to let them go on their way. And you too."

"I may have the answer for you right now," I said.

That brought him up short. He gave me a penetrating look, then said finally, "Give."

"All right. What Murray was trying to tell us, as best he

could with the magazines close at hand, was how he was stabbed and who his murderer is. I think *Keyhole Mystery Magazine* indicates how and *Private Detective* indicates who. It's hardly conclusive proof in either case but it might be enough for you to pry loose an admission of guilt."

"You just leave that part of it to me. Get on with your explanation."

"Well, let's take the 'how' first," I said. "The locked-room angle. I doubt if the murderer set out to create an impossible crime situation; his method was clever enough, but as you pointed out we're not dealing with a mastermind here. He probably didn't even know that Murray had taken to locking himself inside this room every day. I think he must have been as surprised as everyone else when the murder turned into a locked-room puzzle.

"So it was supposed to be a simple stabbing done by person or persons unknown while Murray was alone in the house. But it wasn't a stabbing at all, in the strict sense of the word; the killer wasn't anywhere near here when Murray died."

"He wasn't, huh?"

"No. That's why the adhesive tape on the murder weapon— misdirection, to make it look like Murray was stabbed with a homemade knife in a close confrontation. I'd say he worked it the way he did for two reasons: one, he didn't have enough courage to kill Murray face to face; and two, he wanted to establish an alibi for himself."

Eberhardt puffed up a great cloud of acrid smoke from his pipe. "So tell me how the hell you put a steel splinter into a man's stomach when you're miles away from the scene."

"You rig up a death trap," I said, "using a keyhole."

"Now look, we went over all that before. The key was inside the keyhole when we broke in, I told you that, and I won't believe the killer used some kind of tricky gimmick that the lab crew overlooked."

"That's not what happened at all. What hung both of us up is a natural inclination to associate the word 'keyhole' with a keyhole in a door. But the fact is, there are *five other keyholes* in this room."

"What?"

"The desk, Eb. The rolltop desk over there."

He swung his head around and looked at the desk beneath the window. It contained five keyholes, all right—one in the rolltop, one in the center drawer, and one each in the three side drawers. Like those on most antique rolltop desks, they were meant to take large old-fashioned keys and therefore had good-sized openings. But they were also half hidden in scrolled brass frames with decorative handle pulls; and no one really notices them anyway, any more than you notice individual cubbyholes or the design of the brass trimming. When you look at a desk you see it as an entity: you see a *desk*.

Eberhardt put his eyes on me again. "Okay," he said, "I see what you mean. But I searched that desk myself and so did the lab boys. There's nothing on it or in it that could be used to stab a man through a keyhole."

"Yes, there is." I led him over to the desk. "Only one of these keyholes could have been used, Eb. It isn't the one in the roll top because the top is pushed all the way up; it isn't any of the ones in the side drawers because of where Murray was stabbed—he would have had to lean over at an awkward angle, on his own initiative, in order to catch that steel splinter in the stomach. It has to be the center drawer then, because when a man sits down at a desk like this, that drawer—and that keyhole—are about on a level with the area under his breastbone."

He didn't argue with the logic of that. Instead he reached out, jerked open the center drawer by its handle pull, and stared inside at the pens and pencils, paper clips, rubber bands, and other writing paraphernalia. Then, after a moment, I saw his eyes change and understanding come into them.

"Rubber band," he said.

"Right." I picked up the largest one; it was about a quarter-inch wide, thick and strong—not unlike the kind kids use to make slingshots. "This one, no doubt."

"Keep talking."

"Take a look at the keyhole frame on the inside of the center drawer. The top doesn't quite fit snug with the wood; there's enough room to slip the edge of this band into the crack. All you'd have to do then is stretch the band out around the steel splinter, ease the point of the weapon through the keyhole, and anchor it against the metal on the inside rim of the hole. It would take time to get the balance right and close the drawer without releasing the band, but it could be done by someone with patience and a steady hand. And what you'd have then is a death trap—a cocked and powerful slingshot."

Eberhardt nodded slowly.

"When Murray sat down at the desk," I said, "all it took was for him to pull open the drawer with the jerking motion people always use. The point of the weapon slipped free, the rubber band released like a spring, and the splinter shot through and sliced into Murray's stomach. The shock and impact drove him and the chair backward, and he must have stood up convulsively at the same time, knocking over the chair. That's when he staggered into those bookshelves. And meanwhile the rubber band flopped loose from around the keyhole frame, so that everything looked completely ordinary inside the drawer."

"I'll buy it," Eberhardt said. "It's just simple enough and logical enough to be the answer." He gave me a sidewise look. "You're pretty good at this kind of thing, once you get going."

"It's just that the pulp connection got my juices flowing."

"Yeah, the pulp connection. Now what about *Private Detective* and the name of the killer?"

"The clue Murray left us there is a little more roundabout," I said. "But you've got to remember that he was dying and that he only had time to grab those magazines that were handy. He couldn't tell us more directly who he believed was responsible."

"Go on," he said, "I'm listening."

"Murray collected pulp magazines and he obviously also read them. So he knew that private detectives as a group are known by all sorts of names—shamus, op, eye, snooper." I allowed myself a small wry smile. "And one more just as common."

"Which is?"

"Peeper," I said.

He considered that. "So?"

"Eb, Murray also collected every other kind of popular culture; that's something we've overlooked in this dying message thing. One of those kinds is prints of old television shows. And one of your suspects is a small mousy guy who wears thick glasses; you told me that yourself. I'd be willing to bet that some time ago Murray made a certain obvious comparison between this relative of his and an old TV show character from back in the fifties, and that he referred to the relative by that character's name."

"*What* character?"

"Mr. Peepers," I said. "And you remember who played Mr. Peepers, don't you?"

"Well, I'll be damned," he said. "Wally Cox."

"Sure. Mr. Peepers—the cousin, Walter Cox."

�֍

AT EIGHT O'CLOCK THAT NIGHT, while I was working on a beer and reading a 1935 issue of *Dime Detective*, Eberhardt rang up my apartment. "Just thought you'd like to know," he said. "We got a full confession out of Walter Cox about an hour ago. I hate to admit it—I don't want you to get a swelled head—but you were right all the way down to the Mr. Peepers angle. I checked with the housekeeper and the niece before I talked to Cox, and they both told me Murray called him by that name all the time."

"What was Cox's motive?" I asked.

"Greed, what else? He had a chance to get in on a big investment deal in South America and Murray wouldn't give him the cash. They argued about it in private for some time, and three days ago Cox threatened to kill him. Murray took the threat seriously, which is why he started locking himself in his Rooms while he tried to figure out what to do about it."

"Where did Cox get the piece of steel?"

"Friend of his has a basement workshop, builds things out of wood and metal. Cox borrowed the workshop on a pretext and used a grinder to hone the weapon. He rigged up the slingshot this morning—let himself into the house with his key while the others were out and Murray was locked in one of the Rooms."

"Well, I'm glad you got it wrapped up and glad I could help."

"You're going to be even gladder when the niece talks to you tomorrow. She says she wants to give you some kind of reward."

"Hell, that's not necessary."

"Don't look a gift horse in the mouth—to coin a phrase. Listen, I owe you something myself. You want to come over tomorrow night for a home-cooked dinner and some beer?"

"As long as it's your wife who does the home cooking," I said.

After we rang off I thought about the reward from Murray's niece. Well, if she wanted to give me money I was hardly in a financial position to turn it down. But if she left it up to me to name my own reward I decided I would not ask for money at all; I would ask for something a little more fitting instead. What I really wanted was Thomas Murray's run of *Private Detective*.

MICHELLE KNOWLDEN

The Jane Austen Murder

I WAS DYING SLOWLY. Cholera was seeping into my blood. My fever hot eyes blurred the print on the paper before me, and the pulse raced beneath my clammy skin. A voice on the intercom was only so much noise.

Shaking, I pressed the switch. "Not now, Millie. Send them away." I slipped back in my chair into a stupor.

A moment later the door flew open. An expanse of purple linen filled the small office. A large angry face appeared, topped by a white hat. Large manicured hands slapped the desk with white gloves. I winced and checked *Biddle's Medical Encyclopedia* opened at cholera—yes, noise sensitivity was a symptom of the disease.

"How dare you send me away!" The purple blur swelled with indignation.

The secretary behind her was asking me if I wanted Security. I waved my hand languidly. "It's all right, Millie. I'll take care of this."

The woman in purple sat heavily in the chair facing me. She was still fuming, but now wordlessly.

I wiped my damp brow. "What do you want, Aunt Helena?" I asked her wearily. "As you can see, I'm not feeling well and would like to go home."

She looked at me suspiciously. "What's wrong with you?"

"Cholera."

She snorted. "Don't be ridiculous. No one gets cholera in Wisconsin."

"I think I caught it from the missionary at church last week." Too late, I remembered she had made one of her infrequent appearances at church at the same service I attended. Which had probably reminded her that it was time to check up on me.

"The missionary from Alaska? Don't be a fool, Michaela." Her eyes narrowed. "Six months ago you were dying of cancer. A year ago it was bronchial pneumonia. Before that you were bedridden with angina. What game are you playing?"

I closed my eyes. I was dying alphabetically. Slowly my immune system was working its way through *Biddle's Medical Encyclopedia*, whether it was the paperback version in my suitcase, the two-volume set in my office (always opened to the current malady), or the leather-bound edition near my bed.

Aunt Helena was still talking. "Your malingering is endangering your monthly check from your uncle's trust. As the executor of his trust, I will execute his wishes to the best of my ability. One of his wishes was that no money would be given to any niece or nephew who was not gainfully employed."

"I am fully aware of the terms . . ."

She swept on as if I had not spoken. "I think it is time to check the books of your detective agency. Except for the occasional murder case I find for you, I doubt you've done a single investigation."

"The agency has been busy with a number of investigations, Aunt Helena. Gary LaMare is backlogged on a number of insurance cases. Robyn's assisting him, along with managing several research projects in our literary investigations department. The agency is doing fine."

"I was not inquiring about your partner's or your assistant's workload. I want to know what you have been doing. You're the one in charge of criminal investigations for your agency. What are you working on now?"

As I slipped further and further into the sickness, the recent past was turning into color-bright images moving with a dreamlike quality. Aunt Helena was assuming some of these same qualities. Only her booming voice came through clearly.

I mopped at my brow again and took a sip of water. My throat felt like splintered wood. "I was offered the Simons' stolen jewelry case last month."

She leaned eagerly forward. "I read about it in the newspaper. I know it's the gardener. Have you pinned it on him yet?"

"I couldn't take the case. I was recuperating from chicken pox last month."

Her expression was apoplectic. I was past caring. The room was beginning to spin in slow circles.

"This has gone too far! The trust will no longer tolerate your hypochondriacal obsessions. Either you take a case immediately, or your funds will be stopped."

"Aunt Helena—no one has called in a case for over a week. The doctor's given me medication for the cholera. I'll go home, sleep, and maybe even recover. Next week I may be well enough to take a case."

She sniffed. "That is not acceptable. It appears I must once again bring you a case. Have you heard of the Emma Harris murder case?"

I frowned. The pounding in my head was worse. "In Mansfield Park? Husband reported her missing on Monday? Body found by a friend yesterday in friend's house? Looked as if she had interrupted a burglary?"

Aunt Helena nodded in a self-satisfied way. "Emma's godmother is one of my dearest friends. She and I started a chapter of the Jane Austen Literary Club and Tea Hour here three years ago. This has all been such a dreadful trial for her. Emma was a sweet girl."

Not like me. "What has this to do with me?" I asked wearily.

"Joan would like you to take this case. She has already told the police she will be hiring you. You have to find Emma's murderer for Joan's sake and for the trust. We'll take the evening train. I'll pick you up from the office in one hour. We'll stay at Emma's home. Pack for a week."

After the staccato of commands, she marched out of my office. I rested my head in my arms for a moment. Then I pressed the intercom. "Robyn, Aunt Helena just left. Pack a bag. We leave in an hour."

❋

AUNT HELENA'S SECRETARY, Gregory, was waiting at the train station for us with our tickets. The train left the station moments after we arrived. Aunt Helena did not like to wait and timed her arrivals to coincide with the instant of her departures. Gregory was another of Aunt's projects—a thin, sad-eyed poet who had never been published. He, his fish tanks, and cartons of overdone verses lived in an apartment above Helena's garage.

Helena sat next to me. Gregory sat as far from me as possible. No matter what Aunt Helena said, Gregory believed in all my diseases. He sat on the other side of Robyn Cardex, a cousin of mine also subject to the terms of our uncle's trust and an assistant investigator at the agency. She had a degree in Victorian literature and was grateful for a position that satisfied the conditions for the monthly checks. She was working on her master's degree at the local university. I enjoyed introducing her as "my assistant Robyn Cardex, a colleague cousin attending Cutter College." As I rested my head against the seat and the countryside whipped by us, I was suddenly struck with the thought that soon she would be finished with her degree and ruin my alliteration exercise. I opened my eye and fixed her with it.

"You will go for your doctorate next," I said. She and Helena exchanged a startled look. I closed my eye.

It was a three hour train ride. With my usual skill and two of Dr. Stout's pills, I managed to sleep through most of it. Whenever I was awake, I could hear Helena telling Robyn about poor, dear Joan and how distraught she must be over her godchild's death. How poor, dear Joan had survived middle class destitution in an unfortunate marriage after she had been raised in a fine and literate home. Her grandfather had been the founder of Wisconsin's Jane Austen Literary Club and Tea Hour—a rival to the prestigious Jane Austen Society. He had even seen the back of the great lady in London as a child. Of lesser note, he had also been one of the richest men in the country. At one time, the Williams family had owned much of the county. He had influenced the naming of the town and much of the surrounding environs with his love of Austen. An eleven-year marriage to a bookkeeper with an affinity for professional bowling had been purgatory for poor, dear Joan. She was now living in a small apartment in town, not far from her childhood home, Northanger Abbey. Her father had given the Abbey to Emma when Emma (christened after Austen's heroine, of course) married.

Upon arriving in Mansfield Park, Helena swept out of the train, the rest of us following. I walked a little tentatively, as my cholera had reached the stage of intestinal cramping. I planned to skip the more distasteful symptoms fortified with more of Dr. Stout's pills. The interesting, less repulsive effects of the disease I could enjoy to the fullest.

Joan Williams was waiting at the station for us. Gregory,

Robyn, and I stood by silently while Aunt Helena and Joan exchanged sounds of bereavement. Finally Aunt Helena introduced us and eagerly asked about the state of the police investigation. Joan smiled at me. "Poor," she said. "They are nothing but fools. But as her genius, Jane Austen, says, 'It soon flies over the present failure and begins to hope again.'"

Aunt Helena nodded sagely. "Austen's *Sense and Sensibility*, of course."

"Actually, it's *Emma*, dear. But come—it is late. The car is just this way."

As we left the train station, I saw Joan eyeing me in the rear view mirror and assumed she was concerned over my wan demeanor. "I've had cholera for a week now," I said conversationally. She rolled down her window. I discussed my symptoms and the doctor's treatment with some enthusiasm for the rest of the journey. Gregory held a tissue in front of his nose. Aunt Helena read a book, and Robyn dozed.

Mansfield Park was a small village in a rural section of east Wisconsin. Joan gave us a brief history of the area with evident pride. The Harris estate was four miles from the outskirts of town, on a hill overlooking the village. A small sign on a wrought-iron fence named the estate Northanger Abbey. The building did not look like an abbey; it was more of a colonial palace.

Although it was late, a retinue of servants and Martin Harris waited for us. Harris looked as if he too was enduring a bout of cholera. The young widower was pale and trembling. I would have wagered Aunt Helena did not have a maternal bone in her, yet she went all motherly at the sight of him. She and Joan ushered him into the house, clucking sentimental nonsense. We entered a parlor filled with antiques and wing back chairs. Carved oak bookcases lined the walls from floor to ceiling. When Joan and Aunt paused for breath, I shook his hand and introduced myself and Robyn to him. "This is my assistant, Robyn Cardex, a colleague cousin attending Cutter College, and I'm Micky Cardex, sometime sleuth. Excuse my appearance—I have cholera." Gingerly, he removed his hand from mine.

In the shadows of the room sat a large desk. My eye was caught by a movement, and as I stared, a lanky man unfolded himself from the chair and walked over to us. I recognized him immediately as one of the local police, detective variety.

He had that official air of arrogance and a bulge at his side. Harris hastened to introduce Lieutenant John Neeling to us. Neeling barely glanced at Robyn or Aunt Helena. He glared at me. "Ms. Mickey Cardex. I've heard of you and what you did to the Rostanovich case in Watertown. I can't prevent Mrs. Williams from wasting her money on you, but I will give you this warning. Mess with this case and I will have your head."

He turned on his heel and slammed out of the house, leaving a curious silence behind. "Well," Joan said uncertainly. I shook my head to clear travel and fever fuzz. Although everyone in the room was shifting in and out of focus, I was aware that they were staring at me. Harris cleared his throat twice but said nothing. I looked at the servant who seemed most like a housekeeper and suggested "Bed" in a croaking voice. The others remained in the parlor while I followed the housekeeper to the bedrooms above.

※

THE MORNING BROUGHT breakfast and a country, sunlit day. I filled my plate with invalid-mild food—a plain omelette, fresh fruit, and a slice of coffee cake. I lined up my bottles of medication between my almond-flavored coffee and apricot nectar. As I gazed out the window, I saw Robyn jog by. Because of the cholera, I had to forgo my early morning run. Pity.

A moment later Martin Harris joined me at the breakfast table. After a few halting attempts at pleasantries, he asked what my plans for that day would be.

I sorted through my pill bottles. "First thing—we need to see where the body was found."

"I'll call the Allans, Stan and Dee, and tell them to expect you. It's the second woodhouse on New Haven Court."

"Woodhouse?"

Harris smiled. "Sorry. Joan's term. She disparages anything not made of stone or brick. Look, I'm driving out that way anyway. Stan's gardener has some cuttings for me. May I drive you?"

We agreed to go immediately after breakfast and applied ourselves to the food.

Later I waited in the front hall for Harris, leaning against the door. My head was throbbing. I had sent Robyn to the Mansfield Park coroner's office and the local newspaper to gather information. As I glanced at my watch, Aunt Helena sailed through. She was pulling on her gloves and adjusting her hat. I straightened up apprehensively.

"Where are you going, Aunt Helena?"

"To solve the case, of course. With you moping about the place, someone must take matters into her own hands. I have studied the clues thoroughly and determined that the murderer can only be one person. I'm off to uncover the final bit of evidence, and then I'll have him."

"Who is the murderer?"

"Of course you'd like to know. Letting your elderly aunt dash about, going hither and yon, doing all your investigation . . ."

"Never mind, Aunt Helena. Have fun. I'll see you when you get back."

She leaned towards me, confidentially. "It's Stan Allan. I have conclusive evidence that it is him." She gave me a brisk nod and left the house with a wilted Gregory following.

After dropping me off at the front door of a small country estate, Harris drove around to the back of the house. Stan and Dee Allan were waiting at the door for me. They were a couple in their late twenties, slim, dark, and well-dressed. I quickly discovered that Stan had an unbreakable alibi. He had been in Europe with his partner, in constant company with either his German colleague or his partner while there. Dee, Emma's friend, had been the one to find Emma's body. She was still upset about it and reluctant to enter the kitchen where the body had been found.

She dabbed her watering eyes. In a faltering voice she described Emma's exemplary life. She was known for her business sense and her attention to detail. She was a volunteer for her church's food fund and a member of the town's ladies' Rotary. Everyone had liked her pleasant husband. She had been a member of every committee and club except the literary ones. She was a bit dull there, not even interested in the Austen influence in the village.

Dee had been staying with her parents the week Stan was in Germany. Martin Harris had called her at her parents' on Tuesday to tell her that Emma had disappeared. She had been very concerned. This was not like Emma, a model of predictability. When she heard again from Stan early Thursday morning that Emma was still missing, she was determined to return home to see if Emma had called and left a message. She entered through the kitchen—the door was never locked. She found Emma's body just inside the door. Her skull had been crushed and an arm turned at an impossible angle. Dee called the police and then had been sick in the kitchen sink.

I was to gather three important pieces of information in the course of my questioning: one, the gardener had been in Wyoming that week for a brother's funeral; two, Dee had been at her parents' house, a two hour drive, since Sunday evening; three, Emma had invested a tidy sum in Stan's business.

After Harris took me home, I found Helena and Robyn in the parlor having a midmorning respite of coffee and cake. I dragged my fever-ridden body to a chair and joined them. Helena was staring discontentedly into space. Robyn told me in undertones that Helena had found out about Stan Allan's alibi. Robyn gave me the background on another player in this case. The police report had been sketchy regarding Charles Hubbard, Emma's last appointment on the day she was murdered. Hubbard had been engaged to Emma before she met and married Harris. Although the broken engagement had been bitter on Hubbard's part, local gossip said he was over it and was engaged to marry next month. He ran his own travel agency in Briar Heights, a neighboring village. Emma had also invested in Hubbard's travel agency. When I murmured something about Lady Bountiful, Helena bridled.

Joan entered the room at this point and seemed pleased that Stan Allan had been cleared of suspicion. When I asked her about Hubbard, she looked thoughtful.

"Chuck was a dear boy—biddable and constant. I was hoping that he and Emma would marry, but Emma had a mind of her own."

Aunt leaned forward, her nose quivering, intent on the hunt. "It is imperative we see this man. We will go at once. Joan, have you anything to give us to trap him?"

" 'I have nothing to send by my love.' "

"Ah," said Helena triumphantly. "*Northanger Abbey*, of course."

"No, dear. *Persuasion*."

We found Charles Hubbard at his travel agency, still distraught over Emma's death. As a suspect, he was not in the running. He too had been in Europe, escorting a small tour group through the haunts of Eliot and Dickens. Europe appeared to be filled with people who had not killed Emma.

He talked about Emma's sweet, common-sense nature and how lovingly she had ministered to Joan after the breakup of Joan's marriage. For almost a month, Emma had let her godmother stay at Joan's childhood home before helping the poor woman move to the apartment in town. She was known for her charity work in the village. With friends, she was generous with both educated business advice and seed money for new ventures. Martin was another matter. He was weak in character, with a liberal arts degree and no job skills. He had wormed his way into the steady relationship that Hubbard had enjoyed with Emma and caused Emma to break off with Charles. In their few years of marriage, Martin had lived off his wife's fortune.

Back at Emma's, we worked our way through a sumptuous lunch. I was reviewing Robyn's notes on Marie Linder, a neighbor who had heard "strange noises" at the Allans' on Tuesday. She had seen a tall, shadowed figure walking slowly past the backlit window. As Linder was also known as the local crackpot, her call had been written into the police report and ignored. It was not mentioned in the newspaper. I glanced up from the notes to see Aunt's gleaming eyes resting on Martin. Hoping to distract her, I asked Joan about Linder. She meditated a moment on her sherbet. " 'Her opinions are all romantic,' " she said.

"Wonderful book," Aunt Helena said with enthusiasm. "*Pride and Prejudice*, of course."

"Actually, that was from *Sense and Sensibility*, dear."

The distraction did not work. Aunt's attention was focused on Martin for the rest of the meal. As we left the dining hall, she hissed at me that she was off on a new lead. Gregory threw me a hunted look as he followed her out the door. I closed my eyes as a wave of dizziness passed through me. When I opened my eyes, they were gone.

I spent the rest of the afternoon on the sofa in the library. My pills were arrayed on the table next to me, and servants came periodically to refill the coffeepot and cookie plate. Between worries over what Aunt was doing and staying close enough to the fire to allay the fever chills, I did manage to finish Robyn's notes. Neeling's report had contained some scurrilous remarks about Martin's work ethics and financial status. The brevity of his interview with Hubbard was explained by Robyn's marginal note. Charles was presently engaged to Neeling's sister. She had also included an interesting phone call transcription between Emma and her lawyer about the possibility of placing a lien against the Allans' home. Robyn then diagrammed notes on Austen's books and characters to assist me in translating Joan's allusions.

I was perusing Jane Austen's *Emma* when Martin and Joan joined me for pre-dinner drinks. I had just sent Robyn to the phone upstairs to try discreetly to locate Aunt when there was a commotion at the door. Aunt Helena entered triumphantly with the police detective, John Neeling, in tow. Neeling immediately walked over to Martin and read him his rights. I stood up weakly, and asked the lieutenant on what grounds he was making the arrest.

"Your aunt has found the murder weapon—a mallet was discovered in the corner of his garage. It still had traces of hair and blood on it: his wife's hair and blood." He manacled Martin, who was pale and shaken. "Ms. Cardex, your aunt has done a great thing for our community."

Aunt preened herself modestly while arranging herself on a chair. I sat down slowly, frowning. The food here was excellent and the surroundings commodious. I had hoped to draw this case out longer, but I disliked seeing an innocent man imprisoned.

"It was not Martin who killed Emma," I said to Neeling. Martin nodded and voiced a vigorous agreement. Joan shook her head sadly and turned to Neeling.

"What could plainly speak of guilt, but a husband's protestation of innocence?"

"What I don't understand," I mused, "is why he would take the body to the Allans'? Why not just leave it in the garage?"

John Neeling and Aunt exchanged a pitying look. "To divert attention from himself, of course," Helena said. "Really, Michaela, one would think you were new to the detection business."

"I rather think her body was left there as an ironic note," Joan offered kindly. We stared at her blankly. "Because it was in a woodhouse, of course."

Aunt nodded. "Joan, you are a rare one. Jane Austen's *Emma* was Emma Woodhouse. A brilliant deduction, dear."

I mumbled under my breath, "I detest murders with a theme."

As Neeling urged the wan and protesting Martin to the door, I pulled myself out of the chair again. "Sir, it was not her husband who killed Emma Harris, but her godmother, Joan Williams."

In the ensuing pandemonium, I picked up Robyn's notes on the case. I cleared my throat, and it was suddenly quiet. "This house did not originally belong to Emma Harris but had been built by Joan's grandfather as a memorial to his favorite author, Jane Austen. Joan's father gave it to Martin and Emma Harris when they married with the provision it would revert back to Joan if Emma predeceased her. It would have been difficult to see her family home occupied by those who did not care for Jane Austen or her books."

Joan had sat frozen since I named her Emma's murderer. Now she spoke. "She was poorly named. The real Emma was spirited and intelligent. Emma Harris cared for nothing but her money. This was my home, not theirs."

John Neeling walked over to her and took her arm gently. "I'm sorry, ma'am, but I must ask you to come with me."

Martin Harris shook my hand gratefully as they took Joan away. "When did you discover it was Joan?"

I smiled at him apologetically. "I knew before I arrived here. 'You may be wondering why all this was not told you last night. But I was not the master enough of myself to know what could or ought to be revealed.'" I sighed. *"Pride and Prejudice,"* I said. "And this case has had too much of both."

Later that evening, on the way to the train station, Aunt Helena glared at me. "I may never forgive you for this. Who will chair the Club refreshment committee now? No one could do it as well as Joan."

"Better yet—who will be paying us?" asked Robyn gloomily.

"Taken care of," I assured her, downing my daily draught of diarrhea inhibitor. "Martin was relieved enough with the results of our investigation to offer payment and a small bonus."

On the train, Aunt Helena sulked in her seat. Robyn frowned over her case notes while Gregory stared out the window, heaving melancholy sighs. My fever had finally broken, and I was feeling the euphoria peculiar to the newly well. I sifted happily through *Biddle's Medical Encyclopedia.* One never knew what lay around the corner—intrigue, betrayal, madness, or murder. It was enough to content myself with the structure of planned goals and familiar risks. So with a sense of well-being and a finger tucked in *Biddle's*, I looked up at my companions.

"So what's next? Something parasitic, perhaps?"

JAMES THURBER

The Macbeth Murder Mystery

"IT WAS A STUPID MISTAKE TO MAKE," said the American woman I had met at my hotel in the English lake country, "but it was on the counter with the other Penguin books—the little six-penny ones, you know, with the paper covers—and I supposed of course it was a detective story. All the others were detective stories. I'd read all the others, so I bought this one without really looking at it carefully. You can imagine how mad I was when I found it was Shakespeare." I murmured something sympathetically. "I don't see why the Penguin-books people had to get out Shakespeare plays in the same size and everything as the detective stories," went on my companion. "I think they have different-colored jackets," I said. "Well, I didn't notice that," she said. "Anyway, I got real comfy in bed that night and all ready to read a good mystery story and here I had *The Tragedy of Macbeth*—a book for high school students. Like *Ivanhoe*." "Or *Lorna Doone*," I said. "Exactly," said the American lady. "And I was just crazy for a good Agatha Christie, or something. Hercule Poirot is my favorite detective." "Is he the rabbity one?" I asked. "Oh, no," said my crime-fiction expert. "He's the Belgian one. You're thinking of Mr. Pinkerton, the one that helps Inspector Bull. He's good, too."

Over her second cup of tea my companion began to tell the plot of a detective story that had fooled her completely—it seems it was the old family doctor all the time. But I cut in on her. "Tell me," I said. "Did you read *Macbeth*?" "I had to read

51

it," she said. "There wasn't a scrap of anything else to read in
the whole room." "Did you like it?" I asked. "No, I did not," she
said, decisively. "In the first place, I don't think for a moment
that Macbeth did it." I looked at her blankly. "Did what?" I
asked. "I don't think for a moment that he killed the king," she
said. "I don't think the Macbeth woman was mixed up in it, either. You suspect them the most, of course, but those are the ones
that are never guilty—or shouldn't be, anyway." "I'm afraid," I
began, "that I—" "But don't you see?" said the American lady. "It
would spoil everything if you could figure out right away who did
it. Shakespeare was too smart for that. I've read that people never
have figured out *Hamlet*, so it isn't likely Shakespeare would have
made *Macbeth* as simple as it seems." I thought this over while I
filled my pipe. "Who do you suspect?" I asked, suddenly. "Macduff," she said, promptly. "Good God!" I whispered, softly.

"Oh Macduff did it, all right," said the murder specialist.
"Hercule Poirot would have got him easily." "How did you
figure it out?" I demanded. "Well," she said, "I didn't right
away. At first I suspected Banquo. And then, of course, he was
the second person killed. That was good right in there, that
part. The person you suspect of the first murder should always
be the second victim." "Is that so?" I murmured. "Oh, yes,"
said my informant. "They have to keep surprising you. Well,
after the second murder I didn't know *who* the killer was for
a while." "How about Malcolm and Donalbain, the king's
sons?" I asked. "As I remember it, they fled right after the
first murder. That looks suspicious." "Too suspicious," said the
American lady. "Much too suspicious. When they flee, they're
never guilty. You can count on that." "I believe," I said, "I'll have
a brandy," and I summoned the waiter. My companion leaned
toward me, her eyes bright, her teacup quivering. "Do you know
who discovered Duncan's body?" she demanded. I said I was
sorry, but I had forgotten. "Macduff discovers it," she said, slipping into the historical present. "Then he comes running downstairs and shouts, 'Confusion has broken open the Lord's
anointed temple' and 'Sacrilegious murder has made his master-
piece' and on and on like that." The good lady tapped me on the
knee. "All that stuff was rehearsed," she said. "You wouldn't
say a lot of stuff like that, offhand, would you—if you had found
a body?" She fixed me with a glittering eye. "I—" I began.
"You're right!" she said. "You wouldn't! Unless you had prac-

ticed it in advance. 'My God, there's a body in here!' is what an innocent man would say." She sat back with a confident glare.

I thought for a while. "But what do you make of the Third Murderer?" I asked. "You know, the Third Murderer has puzzled *Macbeth* scholars for three hundred years." "That's because they never thought of Macduff," said the American lady. "It was Macduff, I'm certain. You couldn't have one of the victims murdered by two ordinary thugs—the murderer always has to be somebody important." "But what about the banquet scene?" I asked, after a moment. "How do you account for Macbeth's guilty actions there, when Banquo's ghost came in and sat in his chair?" The lady leaned forward and tapped me on the knee again. "There wasn't any ghost," she said. "A big, strong man like that doesn't go around seeing ghosts—especially in a brightly lighted banquet hall with dozens of people around. Macbeth was *shielding somebody*!" "Who was he shielding?" I asked. "Mrs. Macbeth, of course," she said. "He thought she did it and he was going to take the rap himself. The husband always does that when the wife is suspected." "But what," I demanded, "about the sleepwalking scene then?" "The same thing, only the other way around," said my companion. "That time *she* was shielding *him*. She wasn't asleep at all. Do you remember where it says, 'Enter Lady Macbeth with a taper'?" "Yes," I said. "Well, people who walk in their sleep *never carry lights*!" said my fellow-traveler. "They have a second sight. Did you ever hear of a sleepwalker carrying a light?" "No," I said, "I never did." "Well, then, she wasn't asleep. She was acting guilty to shield Macbeth." "I think," I said, "I'll have another brandy," and I called the waiter. When he brought it, I drank it rapidly and rose to go. "I believe," I said, "that you have got hold of something. Would you lend me that *Macbeth*? I'd like to look it over tonight. I don't feel, somehow, as if I'd ever really read it." "I'll get it for you," she said. "But you'll find that I am right."

✳

I READ THE PLAY OVER CAREFULLY that night, and the next morning, after breakfast, I sought out the American woman. She was on the putting green, and I came up behind her silently and took her arm. She gave an exclamation. "Could I see you alone?" I asked, in a low voice. She nodded cautiously and followed me to a secluded spot. "You've found out something?" she breathed. "I've found out," I said, triumphantly, "the name of the murderer!" "You mean it wasn't Macduff?" she said. "Macduff is as innocent of those murders," I said, "as Macbeth and the Macbeth woman." I opened the copy of the play, which I had with me, and turned to Act II, Scene 2. "Here," I said, "you will see where Lady Macbeth says, 'I laid their daggers ready. He could not miss 'em. Had he not resembled my father as he slept, I had done it.' Do you see?" "No," said the American woman, bluntly, "I don't." "But it's simple!" I exclaimed. "I wonder I didn't see it years ago. The reason Duncan resembled Lady Macbeth's father as he slept is that *it actually was her father!*" "Good God!" breathed my companion, softly. "Lady Macbeth's father killed the king," I said, "and, hearing someone coming, thrust the body under the bed and crawled into the bed himself." "But," said the lady, "you can't have a murderer who only appears in the story once. You can't have that." "I know that," I said, and I turned to Act II, Scene 4. "It says here, 'Enter Ross with an old Man.' Now, that old man is never identified and it is my contention he was old Mr. Macbeth, whose ambition it was to make his daughter queen. There you have your motive." "But even then," cried the American lady, "he's still a minor character!" "Not," I said, gleefully, "when you realize that he was also *one of the weird sisters in disguise!*" "You mean one of the three witches?" "Precisely," I said. "Listen to this speech of the old man's. 'On Tuesday last, a falcon towering in her pride of place, was by a mousing owl hawk'd at and kill'd.' Who does that sound like?" "It sounds like the way the three witches talk," said my companion, reluctantly. "Precisely!" I said again. "Well," said the American woman, "maybe you're right, but—" "I'm sure I am," I said. "And do you know what I'm going to do now?" "No," she said. "What?" "Buy a copy of *Hamlet*," I said, "and solve *that!*" My companion's eye brightened. "Then," she said, "you don't think Hamlet did it?" "I am," I said, "absolutely positive he didn't." "But who," she demanded, "do you suspect?" I looked at her cryptically. "Everybody," I said, and disappeared into a small grove of trees as silently as I had come.

EDWARD D. HOCH

The Spy at the Crime Writers Congress

THEY'D HELD THE RETIREMENT PARTY for Jeffery Rand on the previous Friday night, but he was still around the office four days later, clearing out a decade's accumulation of trifles and trinkets from his desk at Double-C. Though he was not yet 50, a number of factors had converged in recent months to convince him that retirement from British Intelligence was the proper course for him to follow.

For one thing, there was his forthcoming marriage to Leila Gaad, who'd shared his adventures in Egypt before moving to England to be near him. The wedding date was only a month away, and Leila deserved a husband who wouldn't be up half of the night trying to crack an intercepted cipher, or worse, yet, programming a computer to crack it.

Then, too, there'd been the death of Taz. His Russian archrival had come out of retirement to handle one more Kremlin assignment—only to meet a grisly death on a street in Switzerland. Rand didn't want to end up that way.

So he was going off with Leila and leaving the Department of Concealed Communications in the hands of Parkinson and the others—men more skilled than himself in the new technology of codebreaking. Only one assignment remained for that afternoon, something wished on him by Hastings in the month prior to his retirement.

"You're retiring, Rand. You're the perfect one for it," Hastings had insisted.

Rand was dubious. "Talk to a roomful of crime writers about ciphers?"

"That's what they want. They're having an International Congress for three days at the Piccadilly Hotel, and they asked to hear a talk on codes and ciphers. They've already lined up Scotland Yard men, locksmiths, crime reporters, and firearms experts, in addition to a good many authors."

"I'm no speaker," Rand insisted.

"That's no problem. Your segment of the program will be chaired by Chancy O'Higgins, the mystery writer and television host. If you should falter he'll get you going with the proper questions."

Along with most other Britons, Rand had watched O'Higgins on Weekend television, seated with an hourglass and a flickering candle while he spun ghost stories, interviewed witches, and created an eerie atmosphere that was uniquely his own. The prospect of sharing the program with O'Higgins persuaded Rand to accept.

And so on this Tuesday afternoon in early October, Rand journeyed up to the Piccadilly Hotel. He remembered with some amusement Leila's comment when he'd told her about it. "A good thing! You'll meet some publishers and they'll ask you to do a book about your experiences. We must live on something after you retire."

Oddly enough, the first person he met in the hotel lobby turned out to be a publisher. Rand approached him when he saw the silver sheriff's badge that identified him as a member of the Organizing Committee. "Pardon me, are you with the Crime Writers?"

"I certainly am. Don't have my name tag on, but I'm George Bellows. I do some writing, but mainly I'm with Bellows Brothers, the publisher."

"Jeffery Rand. I'm one of the afternoon's speakers."

"Rand of Double-C! Of course we've all heard of you. Anxious to hear your talk. Come along—this way." He led Rand to the elevator, pausing on the way to introduce him to Edgar Wallace's daughter, Penelope Wallace, the Congress Director. "She's done a fine job," Bellows said when they had squeezed in among the others on the elevator. "And so has Jean Bowden, our Chairman Jean was out to Heathrow Saturday morning to meet the American delegation. The opening sessions have gone very well."

"Are many here from America?"

"Over a hundred. They're the ones with white name tags. The British and Canadians have red tags, the Scandinavians yellow—you'll see a great many of those—and the other Europeans are blue."

Rand turned to a white-haired woman crowded into his corner of the elevator. "You must be American," he said, glancing at her name tag. The name on it was Gretta Frazer.

"That I am, from Chicago and Washington. I write paperback Gothics. It may not be literature, but it's fun and it pays the bills." The elevator jolted to a stop and they found themselves deposited in a reception area adjoining the conference rooms. A bar ran along one wall and many of the delegates had a drink in hand. "I hope we can chat more later," Gretta Frazer said before she was swept away by a couple of friends."

"That's Pat McGerr," Bellows said, "another writer from Washington. And the fellow with the black beard is H. R. F. Keating. Perhaps you've read some of his books."

Bellows steered him expertly through the crowd, aiming toward a large familiar figure who was the center of attention near the bar. He recognized Chancy O'Higgins at once from his weekly appearances on the television screen. He was not quite so fat as he appeared on camera, but he'd still be hard to miss. His sandy hair flew off in all directions like some latter-day Dylan Thomas, and his jacket didn't quite come together across his bulging abdomen.

"Rand!" he thundered in his familiar television voice. "I was just telling Michael Gilbert I hope we can start the session promptly at two. The publishers sponsored a cruise on the Thames this morning and people are just getting back from it. But I think we'll have enough to begin. Anyway, it's good to meet you. I think we'll have a lively session."

Rand followed him into a large meeting room, past rows of chairs to the speaker's table. Already placed on it were the twin props from the O'Higgins television show, the hourglass and the candle. The bulky author eyed his watch until the hands showed exactly two o'clock, then he upturned the hourglass so that the sand would start its descent. "Come on, everyone!" he boomed out. "Take your seats, please."

He lit the candle, as he did at the beginning of each TV show, and opened with a glowing recitation of Rand's accomplishments during his years with Double-C. Rand saw the American woman, Gretta Frazer, slip in and take a seat next to Penelope Wallace. George Bellows was down front in the first row.

O'Higgins concluded his opening by turning to Rand. "Now then, Mr. Rand, what can you tell an assembly of crime writers about codes and ciphers that we don't already know?"

Rand stood up, gazing out at the sea of expectant faces. "Thank you for your kind introduction, Mr. O'Higgins. It's indeed a pleasure to meet you and the other crime writers assembled here from all over the world. Your work, of course, is what keeps people interested in my work. In truth, communications today between governments or agents of a government are more likely to be concealed by electronic technology than by the traditional book codes or Vigenere ciphers. I want to go into some of these things in detail—though naturally I won't be telling you anything that hasn't already been hinted at in the public press."

He paused for a sip of water, then continued. "Sometimes communications are concealed merely by the geography of the situation. For example, staff cars and limousines in the Moscow area have long communicated with the Kremlin and each other by radiotelephone. The Americans had a secret spy satellite with an antenna system so highly sophisticated it could listen in on those conversations as the satellite passed slowly over Moscow."

He went on like this a bit longer, then switched to an account of his own experiences, ending with the story of Taz's recent death in Switzerland. A few in the audience headed for the doors then, but most remained for a brief question-and-answer period.

Finally, as the last of the sand trickled through the hourglass, Chancy O'Higgins rose to end the session. Rand glanced at his watch and saw that it was exactly three o'clock. "Accurate hourglass you have there."

O'Higgins smiled. "It has to be, for television."

He bent to blow out the candle as the audience streamed toward the doors. At that instant, as if by some bizarre cause-and-effect relationship, a muffled boom shook the building.

George Bellows came instantly alert. "That was a bomb—in the hotel!"

"Damned I.R.A.!" someone else muttered. The bombings of London hotels and restaurants, apparently the work of an Irish

Republican Army splinter group, had grown to epidemic proportions that autumn. Barely a week passed without some new outrage and a new list of casualties.

Bellows and some others ran to the stairs, and Rand was left standing with O'Higgins and Gretta Frazer. "It was a fine, interesting talk," she complimented him. "This is my first meeting with a real spy."

"I'm hardly that," Rand protested.

They were still chatting and moving toward the door when George Bellows returned. "Terrible thing!" he told O'Higgins. "It was a bomb, all right, and it killed Tom Wager."

O'Higgins was shocked. "Not Tom!" He turned to Rand. "Did you know him? He was a journalist who turned to writing spy thrillers."

"Afraid I don't read much in the field. But where did the bomb go off?"

"Down in the lobby. Couple of other people were injured. I suppose Tom was on his way up here when it happened."

"I'd better go right down," O'Higgins said. They started for the stairs and Rand trailed along, though he noticed the American woman stayed behind. Perhaps she was squeamish.

When they reached the lobby it was a scene of turmoil. Firemen, police, and Scotland Yard men mingled with doctors and ambulance attendants. The blast seemed to have gone off near the center of the small lobby, leaving a large scorched spot in the carpeting. Every window and glass partition in sight was shattered.

Rand sidestepped a uniformed bobby trying to clear the lobby and found his old friend Inspector Stephens standing with two bomb-squad experts. "Hello, Rand. What are you doing here?"

"Speaking to the Crime Writers International Congress. I'd just finished when we heard the blast."

"It was one of their chaps who got killed. Fellow named Wager."

"More Irish terrorists?"

Inspector Stephens hesitated. "Probably. Who else sets off bombs in hotel lobbies these days?"

"But you're not sure?"

"Too soon to tell."

Rand could sense that something was wrong. "What's the rub?"

"Bomb wasn't planted in the lobby. It was in the briefcase Wager was carrying."

"You think he was bringing it in to plant it?"

"Doubtful. He must have known all the hotels run spot searches these days. More likely it was planted without his knowledge."

"That makes it premeditated murder," Rand said.

"It's a possibility," Stephens admitted.

❊

RAND HAD EXPECTED TO LEAVE the hotel at once, letting Scotland Yard deal with the bombing, but that was not to be. George Bellows caught him at the door and urged him back. "You can do us a great service, Mr. Rand, if you'll talk to Tom Wager's widow."

"That's a bit out of my line. Perhaps a clergyman—"

"She heard you speak upstairs. She won't talk to anyone else."

A bit puzzled, Rand followed the publisher to a room just off the lobby. A tall slim woman, a bit younger than he'd expected, awaited him with dry eyes. "You're Mr. Rand. I'm Joyce Wager, Tom's wife."

"A terrible thing about your husband," he said, taking her hand.

"Tom was fated to die violently. He often said so himself. I've no tears to shed for him."

Rand made no comment.

"But that doesn't mean I intend to let his killer go unpunished. He was a good man, for all his faults."

"I don't see how I fit in," Rand said. "I'm not with the police, and I've just retired from British Intelligence."

"Tom's new book is a factual one—about a writer who worked with the Germans during the war, writing propaganda for them while serving as a correspondent in Switzerland. The truth about the man never came out after the war, and he's had a successful writing career since that time."

"The man's name?"

"Tom's manuscript, to be published next month, only identifies him by the code name of Lucky."

"He never told you who Lucky was?"

She shook her head. "That's what I want you to find out. I think Tom was killed by this man Lucky. Tom told me he met someone for lunch while I was on the boat ride this morning, and that he was meeting him again in the lobby at five minutes after three."

"Who's publishing the book?" Rand asked, glancing at Bellows.

"Not me, old chap. Red Lion is his publisher."

"Will you help?" Joyce Wager asked Rand.

"I'll ask a few questions. I can't do more than that."

Inspector Stephens entered the room and indicated that Mrs. Wager was needed. When she'd left, Rand said, "The woman's composure astounds me. Her husband hasn't been dead a half hour."

"They were not terribly close," the publisher admitted.

Wager's body had been removed and a crew was busy cleaning up the lobby. Rand and Bellows crossed to the hotel lounge with its shattered windows and found a number of the delegates talking in hushed tones about the tragedy. He was getting quite skilled at reading name tags now, and he identified Michael Gilbert standing with Nigel Morland and Josephine Bell. A number of American writers, including Robert L. Fish and Stanley Ellin, were seated at a table close to the door. Hillary Waugh and Franklin Bandy stood nearby, looking serious.

Chancy O'Higgins was holding court at a round center table, his booming voice only slightly softened by the tragedy. He motioned Rand to join him and said "I've often thought crime writers would make the perfect murderers. What do you say, Rand?"

"Do you think one of the crime writers killed Tom Wager?"

"It's a possibility, isn't it? Just as likely as the I.R.A., heaven knows!"

"You're only saying that because you're Irish," the American woman, Gretta Frazer, said.

"I'm a Scotsman and there's quite a difference," O'Higgins corrected her with a smile. "But really, wouldn't we make the perfect murderers?"

George Bellows joined them with a drink from the bar. "We'd be forever killing our victims with icicles in locked rooms."

After another round of drinks and some comments by Christianna Brand and Desmond Bagley, Rand excused himself and went outside for a taxi. As he glanced in both directions, a familiar black limousine glided to the curb. "This is an honor," Rand said, climbing into the back seat with Hastings.

"Part of the service for retired personnel. How was your talk?"

"Seemed well-received. Until the bombing, that is."

"Ah, yes. Poor Tom Wager."

Rand smiled. "I gather you have an interest in him."

"We have an interest in a book he's written."

"You know about that?"

"It's no secret. His publisher issued a press release a month ago. We asked to see galley proofs as a matter of routine."

"What do you think?"

Hastings shrugged. "It reads like fiction but it could be fact. If so, it could be dangerous for someone trying to live down his past. The bombing just doesn't feel like an I.R.A. job."

"I'm retired, remember? Where do I fit in?"

Hastings snorted. "You'll never really retire, Rand. This business is in your blood."

"All right, what do you want?"

"If this Lucky—the fellow in the book—did kill him, it was because he feared Wager would start naming names. I want you to go back to tomorrow's sessions and see what you can find out."

The limousine passed Rand's apartment and circled the block. "I can do that," Rand admitted. "But I might not find Lucky. He might be pure fiction, or he might have been Wager himself. Did anyone ever call him Lucky Wager?"

"Not that I know of. But he *was* in Switzerland during the war."

"There's no doubt the dead man is really Wager?"

"His wife identified him."

"Could she have killed him for his book royalties?"

"That's highly unlikely as a murder motive. He'd only received a small advance from his publisher."

This time around the block Rand signaled the driver to stop. "All right," he said, getting out. "I'll be in touch."

Rand took the elevator to his apartment and unlocked the door. It was nearly dark, and only the last of the twilight filtered through his mesh curtains. But when he saw the curtains closed he knew he had a visitor. "Leila?" he called.

A light by the sofa snapped on, and then he saw her.

It was Gretta Frazer and she was pointing a gun at him.

✳

"SIT DOWN," she said, lowering the weapon. "I won't shoot you."

"Getting in the mood for one of your Gothics?" he asked the American woman.

"Not exactly."

"I thought I left you back at the hotel."

"You did. You must have taken the long way home."

"I was chatting with a friend. What's the gun for?"

"I didn't know how you might react to finding me here. I'm a bit old for a housebreaker."

"What are you, usually?"

The white-haired woman opened her purse and tossed him her wallet. "Inside pocket, under the calendar."

He found an ID card and recognized it at once. "National Security Agency in Washington. I'd like to read one of your Gothics someday."

"The novels are a sideline. I've worked in N.S.A.'s Communications Section for the past twenty years."

"Then my talk this afternoon was nothing new to you."

"I've heard it all before, if not in so public a forum. The information about our spy satellites was especially distressing."

"It's all been in print."

"Nevertheless, we don't like that sort of information turning up in every other spy novel."

Rand smiled. "I understand N.S.A. is even more computerized than we are. Is it true you have a machine programed to read every cablegram sent to or from the country, and to print out any messages containing key words like 'oil' or 'Mideast' or 'Russia'?"

"We have something like that," she conceded. "I'll give you a tour next time you're in Washington."

"What do you want of me now?"

"I came to talk about Tom Wager's death."

"It seems to be a popular subject today."

"His book is popular at N.S.A. I drew the assignment of coming here because my writing gives me a perfect cover at an International Convention like this. My mission was to contact Wager and offer him money to reveal the identity of Lucky."

Rand nodded thoughtfully. "You may have supplied the motive I've been searching for. If Wager went to Lucky and demanded more money than you offered, it could have got him killed."

"We think that's what happened, and that's why I'm here. We need someone familiar with operations during the Second World War, and I understand you were in intelligence work back then."

"As a *very* young man," Rand assured her. "But I'll do what I can for you!" *And* for Hastings, *and* for Joyce Wager, he added silently. He'd never been so much in demand when he was head of Double-C.

He just wondered how he was going to satisfy any one of them, let alone all.

※

RAND SPENT MUCH OF Wednesday morning at his old office, looking through microfilmed records of the war years. Tom Wager certainly had been a correspondent in Switzerland for a time, but there was no hint he'd committed any of the acts he had ascribed to Lucky. Working from a list of delegates to the Crime Writers International Congress, Rand attempted to pin down any sort of trail leading back to the war years.

But there was nothing.

The closest he came was a cross-indexed note on publisher George Bellows, who'd served as a P.O.W. interrogator for Army Intelligence. There was nothing on Chancy O'Higgins. When he struck out with the other names as well, he began to wonder about different nationalities—but he decided the task was fruitless. He had no real evidence that the mysterious Lucky was a crime writer.

A little before noon he went back to the hotel.

The first person he saw in the lobby was an American novelist, Richard Martin Stern, who directed him to a downstairs meeting room where a panel discussion on mystery writing was about to begin. Stern himself was on the panel, along with Eric Ambler, Gavin Lyall, and Stanley Ellin. Rand stood near the back of the room, listening to the introductory remarks offered by moderator Dick Francis, then walked over to where Gretta Frazer was standing. "Hello," she greeted him. "I understand we missed a very good demonstration by the Police Dog Squad yesterday afternoon. The dogs sniffed out hidden drugs."

"Dogs that could sniff out explosives would be more to the point."

"The police have those too."

Chancy O'Higgins appeared, along with Mrs. Wager, and Rand drifted over to catch their conversation. "I can't put you on the show to talk about spies and your husband's murder," the wild-haired writer was saying, "much as I'd like to. I tell ghost stories. The public—my public—doesn't want reality. There are enough talk shows on the BBC for that."

Joyce Wager turned to Rand for help. "Can't you convince him? I need all the help and publicity I can get to bring Tom's killer to justice."

"We're all doing the best we can," Rand assured her.

When she walked away to join a group of Swedish writers, O'Higgins muttered, "Damn woman's trying to promote his book on my show."

They listened to the rest of the discussion, and when it broke up the writers scattered about the room in small groups, chatting informally while photographers snapped pictures. Rand watched Gretta Frazer deep in conversation with Ruth Rendell and Celia Fremlin. Then, as she moved away toward the door, a uniformed bellman appeared. He was paging someone, and Gretta Frazer motioned to him. He handed her an envelope and moved on.

"... and I did line up a few people for my show," O'Higgins was saying. "C. P. Snow was here for our opening dinner Sunday night, and Kingsley Amis was on the boat ride yesterday. Both of them have written mysteries, you know, and I thought—"

Gretta Frazer tore open the flat of the envelope.

There was a flash and a roar of an explosion.

Rand leaped forward, but it was too late.

�֎

INSPECTOR STEPHENS WAS UNHAPPY. "Letter bomb," he told Rand. "A favorite terrorist weapon, though fortunately one that isn't used too often. A flat piece of plastic explosive with a detonator that went off when the envelope was opened."

"How many injuries in all?"

"Gretta Frazer was killed almost instantly, and three people near her were taken to the hospital. A few others have minor cuts. We're lucky there weren't more."

"Gretta Frazer wasn't lucky," Rand said. "Have you traced the letter?"

"It was left at the desk upstairs, with a note to deliver it down here after the discussion. The clerk didn't see who left it." Stephens shook his head. "I can't see any reason for singling out this American woman."

"There may have been a reason," Rand confided. "She worked for N.S.A. in Washington. She was sent here to buy information from Tom Wager."

"So the same killer disposed of them both?"

"Looks like it. He may not have been sure how much Wager told her before he died."

Rand left Stephens and moved among the others, aware of the shock etched deep on their faces. Though they wrote about murder, this was the closest most of them had ever been to one. He spotted O'Higgins talking with the American writer William P. McGivern, and when they separated Rand cornered the Scotsman and asked, "Are you staying here at the hotel?"

The stout man nodded. "I live in Cambridge and each night after the TV show I enjoy a late drink with fellow writers who live more than an hour's train journey away. I'm here till tomorrow."

"I'd like to talk to you about these killings. Could I come up to your room?"

"Certainly, old man. Room 334. I'll be there in half an hour." He glanced around at the others. "The closing dinner tonight will be more like a wake, I'm afraid. And the press isn't helping any. They seem to think mystery writers can solve crimes as well as write about them."

Rand found Joyce Wager trying to comfort some of the dead woman's American friends. Once more he was amazed at her calm in a crisis. When she was alone he asked her, "Was your husband ever called Lucky?"

"You mean like in his book? Certainly not, Mr. Rand. Tom wasn't writing about himself."

"But he was in Switzerland at the time he described."

"So was Lucky. That was how Tom learned about him."

"Why would he wait thirty years to tell about it?"

"I have no idea." She stared at the knot of policemen clustered around the spot where Gretta Frazer had died. "Do you know who did it yet? Who killed Tom and that woman?"

"I think I do," Rand told her. "Even if I have no evidence, I can't risk waiting for another bomb and another death."

�֎

CHANCY O'HIGGINS GREETED HIM at the door and showed him to an overstuffed chair, adjusting the cushions as Rand sat down. His ubiquitous hourglass and candle stood on the low coffee table between them, though the candle was unlit.

O'Higgins turned over the hourglass as he sat down opposite Rand. "Have to keep track of the time. In an hour I must start dressing for tonight's dinner."

"I heard there was some talk of canceling it."

"Just talk. If the bombs are the work of the I.R.A. we can't buckle under that easily. We went through the blitz, after all, so I guess we can survive a few bombs."

"The bombs aren't the work of the I.R.A.," Rand said. "They're the work of this man named Lucky, a ghost from thirty years ago."

Chancy O'Higgins frowned. "Have you discovered who he is?"

"I think it's you, O'Higgins. I think you killed Tom Wager and Gretta Frazer."

"Oh, come now!"

"His wife is certain Lucky exists."

"His wife! Have you considered the possibility that *she* killed him?"

"I'm sure she'd have put on a more grief-stricken act if she were the murderer. And she'd have had no motive for killing Gretta Frazer, who'd hardly be interested in the Wagers' marital problems. No, I'm betting on you, O'Higgins."

The stout man remained calm, tapping the tips of his fingers together. "Even if Joyce Wager didn't kill her husband, she might have lied about the identity of the dead man. Wager could still be alive, and behind the whole thing himself."

"I considered that too, but it doesn't hold up. The bomb went off in the lobby of a hotel where scores of people who knew Wager were attending a convention. Anyone might have caught a glimpse of him just before the explosion. Anyone might have said, 'No, the dead man isn't Tom Wager.' Hardly the sort of risk a clever murderer would take. The victim had to be Wager, and it's highly unlikely his wife was involved.

After all, wives can find far less risky ways to kill their husbands."

O'Higgins was still frowning. "So we're back to me as Lucky—correct?"

"Correct. You see, Wager was supposed to meet his killer in the lobby at 3:05. The meeting was necessarily in the lobby to make certain Wager didn't wander into the session where I was talking and endanger so many people—or if he did enter the session room, that he'd leave before the bomb went off. It also had to be in the lobby because you hoped the explosion would be blamed on the I.R.A. Now I asked myself, why was the time set at 3:05 instead of three o'clock? Since the killer didn't intend to keep his appointment anyway, what difference could five minutes make?

"But if Wager knew Lucky had to be somewhere else until three, the odd timing is explained. Where did Lucky have to be? At my talk, of course. But not as a spectator, because any of them could have left early. Only one person besides myself *had* to stay until three o'clock, and that was you. To convince Wager you really meant to meet him, you had to set the time for a few minutes *after* three."

"What sort of proof is that?" O'Higgins scoffed. "If Wager was meeting me, he would have come upstairs where he knew I was."

"I'm sure you persuaded him against it. According to his wife he'd already had a luncheon meeting with Lucky— when I suppose you managed to hide the bomb in his brief-case—and the later meeting could have been arranged so you'd pay him the money he demanded. You could easily have convinced him that the money shouldn't be passed up-stairs, in view of hundreds of delegates who knew you both. You no doubt suggested meeting in the lobby and then strolling up Piccadilly."

"Anything else?"

"Oh, yes, Wager's book exposed a man he named Lucky. Your name, Chancy, is the Scottish word for Lucky, isn't it?"

Chancy O'Higgins was still smiling, but now—in a move-ment too fast for Rand to follow—his right hand held a small Beretta automatic. "Keep talking, Rand. You have until the sand runs through this hourglass, and then you will die."

"Oh?"

"You are seated on the last of my little infernal machines.

When I adjusted the cushion for you, I tripped the timer so it would explode in one hour. Watch the sand. It is your life draining away."

Rand shifted uneasily. He was certain the man was serious. "Do you intend to remain here until it explodes?"

"Of course. My bombs are carefully made. It will destroy you and the chair. I will shield my face and body and suffer a few minor burns at worst. Just enough to place me above suspicion."

The sand was already a quarter of the way through the glass. "Why don't you light your candle too," Rand suggested, "and really set the scene?"

O'Higgins flicked a lighter with his left hand and leaned over to touch the wick. "I'll do just that. It pleases me that you're not afraid to die."

"Forty-five minutes is a long time."

"No one will rescue you, if that's what you're thinking. I used the hour timer to give you a chance for your life. If you hadn't accused me you could have walked out of here alive without ever knowing about the bomb in the chair."

Rand reached out and pushed the candle close to the hourglass.

"*Don't touch that!* Another movement and I'll shoot you! The bomb will easily hide the traces of a bullet wound."

"Sorry. I just wanted a little more light on my life slipping away. While we're waiting you can tell me about Gretta Frazer. I understand that you killed Wager to silence him, but why did you kill the American woman?"

"Because Wager told me of her money offer, and I couldn't be sure I'd killed him before he talked. When she left the lounge immediately after you yesterday, I followed her to your apartment. I knew you were both after me then, and I couldn't risk leaving her alive. The letter bomb was carefully made to kill only her."

The sand was now halfway through the hourglass, and Rand imagined he could feel the outline of the bomb under his cushion. "Well—thirty minutes to live, more or less. What shall we talk about? Your years in Switzerland?"

O'Higgins sighed. "I was a young man then, too young for the assignment, I suppose. Reporting the war from a neutral country like Switzerland was a bore at best. I fell in with some people from the German Embassy and it was the first excitement I'd had. I imagined writing a book about it later, but of course I never did. Tom Wager wrote the book."

"He waited thirty years."

"He waited until I was a successful author and television personality. Then he came to me for money. When I refused him, he threatened me with the book. My only mistake was in not killing him at once. I waited, and too many people became interested in the book—people like you and Gretta Frazer."

He fell silent for a moment, and Rand focused his eyes on the hourglass. Only a quarter of the sand remained in the upper part now. He watched the candle flame flickering next to it and asked, "But why use bombs? Why injure innocent people?"

"The Germans got me interested in explosives and bomb-making while I was writing propaganda for them. Later I kept it up, as a hobby. On weekends I'd go off to the fields outside Cambridge and set off little bombs. If I say so myself, I'm now quite an expert on the technique. I've never had a bomb that failed."

"If I die you'll never get away with it, O'Higgins. Too many people know what I'm working on."

Chancy O'Higgins shook his head. "Nobody knows. People in your line of work are secretive."

Rand's eyes were on the sand. "You can't kill me like this!"

"You're retired, Rand. Your life is over anyway."

"At forty-nine?"

"It's you or me." He raised the pistol an inch. "Don't move and don't try kicking the table."

They sat in silence, facing each other, as the last of the sand trickled away. Still holding the gun steady, the stout man rose and stepped behind his chair, shielding his lower face with an upturned arm.

Rand watched the sand.

Just a few grains more, and then—

The sand was finished. The hour was up.

Nothing happened.

"Your bomb is a bit late," Rand remarked.

"It *couldn't* be late! That timer is foolproof!" He glanced at his watch but that did him no good, since he hadn't checked it at the beginning of the hour.

They waited another minute. Rand could feel the sweat running down his back.

Nothing happened.

"It's not going to explode," Rand said. "It's a dud."

O'Higgins motioned with his gun. "Get out of the chair and stand facing the wall! No tricks!"

Rand did as he was told and the stout man moved forward, clawing at the cushion with his left hand.

That was when the bomb went off.

※

HASTINGS FOUND RAND in the emergency ward at the hospital, having some lacerations on his back treated by a young nurse. "Wait till Leila hears of this!"

Rand smiled through a lip he'd cut when his face hit the wall. "I hope you won't tell her. Is O'Higgins dead?"

Hastings nodded. "Dead on arrival. So he was our bomber?"

"*And* the mysterious Lucky. I'll tell you all about it."

"Stephens already told me you were sitting on a bomb. How'd you turn the tables?"

"He was timing it with his hourglass. When it didn't go off on schedule he had to have a look. Said he'd never had one fail. But I'd gotten him to light his damned candle, and I shoved it up right next to the glass. Among Sixteenth Century seamen it was called 'warming the glass.' In order to shorten their watch they put the hourglass near a lantern or lamp. The glass expanded from the heat and the sand ran through faster. It was a flogging offense on most ships."

"So the hour wasn't really up when O'Higgins thought it was."

"Luckily for me! I didn't really know if my hourglass stunt would work, but it was the only chance I could think of."

"He should have known better than to go examining an unexploded bomb."

"He had too much pride. He couldn't believe it when it didn't explode on schedule."

"By God, Rand, you can't retire! What will we do without you?"

Rand turned over as the nurse finished dressing his wounds. "You'll get by. There'll be others a good deal better than me."

"I'm betting you'll be back within six months," Hastings said.

Rand remembered what had happened to the Russian, Taz, when he came out of retirement. That had been a bomb too, only Taz hadn't been as lucky as Rand.

"No," he told Hastings, "don't bet on it."

❈

EDITORIAL NOTE: No, you *can* bet on it. Rand will be back!

MARGARET MARON

Lieutenant Harald and the Treasure Island *Treasure*

"I THOUGHT YOU LIKED PUZZLES," argued Oscar Nauman's disembodied voice.

"I do," Lieutenant Sigrid Harald answered, balancing the telephone receiver on her shoulder as she struggled with a balky can opener. "That's one of the reasons I joined the NYPD. I get paid for it, Nauman. I don't have to waste a free weekend."

"But this is a real buried treasure. One of my former students is going to lose her inheritance if it isn't found soon, and I told her we'd help."

As one of the America's leading abstract artists, Oscar Nauman could have sold one or two paintings a year and lived in comfortable retirement on some Mediterranean island. Instead, he continued to chair the art department at Vanderlyn College over on the East River where Sigrid first met him during a homicide investigation. The end of the case hadn't been the end of their acquaintance, though. He kept walking in and out of her life as if he had a right there, lecturing, bullying, and keeping her off balance. Her prickly nature seemed to amuse him, and Sigrid had quit trying to analyze why he persisted.

Or why she allowed it.

"We can drive up tonight," said Nauman. "Unless," he

added craftily, knowing her aversion to sunrises, "you'd rather leave around six tomorrow morning?"

"Now listen, Nauman, I don't—" The can opener slipped. "Oh, damn! I just dumped soup all over the blasted stove."

"Throw it out. I'll pick you up in thirty minutes and we'll have dinner on the way."

"I am *not* going to Connecticut," she said firmly, but he had already hung up.

✳

FOURTEEN HOURS LATER, she sat on the terrace of Nauman's Connecticut house and placidly bit into a second Danish. A good night's sleep had removed most of her annoyance at being dragged from the city and hurtled through the night at Nauman's usual speed-of-sound driving. The sun was shining, the air was warm, and she had found an unworked double-crostic in an elderly issue of the *New York Times*.

She looked contented as a cat, thought Nauman. Her long dark hair was pinned at the nape more loosely than usual, and her faded jeans and cream-colored knit shirt were more becoming than those shapeless pantsuits she wore in town. Thin to the point of skinniness, with a mouth too wide for conventional beauty and a neck too long, her cool gray eyes were her best feature, but these were presently engrossed in her paper.

He'd been up for hours and was so impatient to be off that he swept cups, carafe, and the remaining sweet rolls back onto the large brass tray and carted it all away without asking Sigrid if she'd finished.

"I thought your friend wasn't expecting us before ten," she said, following Nauman to the kitchen where she retrieved her cup and refilled it while he loaded the dishwasher.

"It'll take us about that long to walk over." He took her cup and poured it in the sink.

"*Walk?*" Sigrid was appalled.

"Less than a mile as the crow flies. You walk more than that every day."

"But that's on concrete," she protested. "In the city. You're talking about trees and snakes and briars, aren't you?"

"It used to be an Indian trading path," Nauman coaxed, leading her out through the terrace gate. "It'll be like a walk through Central Park."

"I hate walking in Central Park," Sigrid muttered, but she followed him across a narrow meadow to a scrub forest. As Nauman disappeared behind a curtain of wild grapevines, she hesitated a moment, then took a deep breath and plunged in after him.

Ten minutes later, sweaty, her ankles whipped by thorns, a stinging scratch on her arm, she was ready for mutiny. "No Indians ever walked through this jungle."

"Not this part. We're taking a shortcut. The path is just past those tall oaks."

"If it isn't, I'm going back."

But it was; and once they were on it, the walk became more pleasant. Sigrid was used to covering twenty-five or thirty city blocks at a stretch, but she was deeply suspicious of nature in the raw. Still, it was cooler under the massive trees in this part of the forest. The path angled downward and was so broad that no branches caught at her clothing. She began to relax. They crossed a small stream on stepping stones and the path rose gently again.

As Nauman paused to re-tie his sneaker, a large black bird lazily flapped along overhead in their general direction.

"That crow of navigational fame, no doubt," said Sigrid.

Her smiles were so rare, thought Oscar, that one forgot they transformed her face. She was more than twenty-five years younger than he and nearly as tall and she photographed badly, but perhaps a painting? He hadn't attempted a portrait since his student days.

"Hi, Oscar!" came a little voice from the top of the path. "Welcome to Treasure Island."

To Sigrid, Jemima Bullock looked like a thoroughly nice child as she ran down to meet them in cut-off jeans. She was sturdily built, athletic rather than buxom, with short reddish-blonde hair, an abundance of freckles on every inch of visible skin, and an infectious grin as Nauman effected introductions.

"Jemima's the art world's contribution to oceanography."

"What Oscar means is that he's eternally grateful I didn't stay an art major at Vanderlyn," Jemima explained cheerfully. "My technical drawing was good, but I bombed in creativity."

"At least you had the native wit to admit it," Nauman said.

�֎

AT THE TOP OF THE PATH, they rounded a hummock of wisteria and honeysuckle vines to find an old cottage of undressed logs. A wide porch ran its length and gave good views of rolling woodlands and of Jemima's battered VW van, which was parked on the drive beneath an enormous oak.

"My uncle was caretaker for the Rawlings estate," said Jemima, leading them up on the porch and pulling wicker chairs around a bamboo table. "The main house is farther down the drive, but no one's lived there for years. Uncle Jim mostly had the place to himself.

What looked like a small telescope on a tripod stood at the far end of the porch. "He called this Spyglass Hill but that's really a surveyor's transit."

"Nauman said his hobby was Robert Louis Stevenson," said Sigrid. "Is that why you welcomed us to Treasure Island?"

"Partly, but Uncle Jim was nutty about only one of Stevenson's books: *Treasure Island*. He was my mother's favorite uncle, see, and their name was Hawkins; so when he was kid, he used to pretend he was Jim Hawkins in the book. Mom named in Jemima Hawkins Bullock after him, and, since he never married, we were pretty close. I used to spend a month up here every summer when I was growing up. He's the one who got me interested in oceanography, though it started off with treasure maps. Every summer he'd have a new one waiting for me."

She darted into the house and reappeared a moment later with a book and a large leather-bound portfolio of charts which she spread out on the porch table.

"This is a survey map of the area," she said. Her finger stabbed a small black square. "Here's this cottage." She traced a short route. "Here's Oscar's house and the path and stream you crossed. See the way the stream comes up and intersects the creek here? And then the creek runs back down and around where a second stream branches off and merges again with the first stream."

"So technically, we really are on an island," said Sigrid, obscurely pleased with that idea.

"A body of land surrounded by water," Nauman agreed. He pulled out his pipe and worked at getting it lit.

"The freaky thing is that it's actually shaped like the original Treasure Island," said Jemima. She flipped the book open to an illustration. To Sigrid's eyes, the two were only roughly similar, but she supposed that wishful thinking could rationalize the differences.

"Uncle Jim made all these treasure maps for me. So many paces to a certain tree while I was small; later he taught me how to use a sextant and I'd have to shoot the stars to get the proper bearing. He didn't make it easy, either. It usually took two or three days and several false starts to find the right place to dig. It was worth it, though."

Sigrid leafed through the sheaf of hand-drawn charts. Although identical in their outlines, each was exquisitely embellished with different colored inks: tiny sailing ships, mermaids, and dolphins sported in blue waters around elaborate multi-pointed compasses. Latitude and longitude lines had been carefully lettered in India ink, along with minute numbers and directions. Sigrid peered closely and read, "Bulk of treasure here."

"He never made much money as a caretaker," said Jemima, "but the treasures he used to hide! Chocolates wrapped in gold and purple foil, a pair of binoculars I still use, maps and drawing pads and compasses so I could draw my own." There was a wistful note in her voice as of a child describing never-to-come-again Christmas mornings.

"Tell her about the real treasure," Nauman prompted, bored with the preliminaries.

"I'm coming to it, Oscar. Be patient. She has to understand how Uncle Jim's mind worked first—the way he liked making a mystery of things. It wasn't only his maps," she told Sigrid. "He never talked freely about his life, either. He'd trained as a surveyor but seldom held a steady job till after his leg was hurt—just bummed around the world till he was past thirty. I guess he might've seen or done some things he didn't want to tell a kid; but when he was feeling loose, he'd talk about a treasure he brought home from England during World War II. Nothing direct, just a brief mention. If you asked too many questions, he'd cut you off. I used to think it might be gold, then again it'd sound like jewels. Whatever it was, he got it in London. He was on leave there and the building he was in was hit by a buzz bomb. Crushed his left leg.

"That London hospital was where he really got into the *Treasure Island* thing. The nurses kept bringing him different editions of the book. Because of his name, you see. He'd always had a flair for precision drawing—from the surveying—and when he started mapping the wards on scrap paper, they brought him sketch pads and pens and he was off to the races. I think they made a pet out of him because they knew his leg would never heal properly. Anyhow, he let it slip once that if the nurses hadn't liked him, he never would have recognized the treasure when it appeared."

She looked at Sigrid doubtfully through stubby sandy lashes. "That doesn't sound much like gold or diamonds, does it?"

"He never revealed its nature?"

"Nope. Anyhow, Uncle Jim knew it takes an M.S. to get anywhere in oceanography. That means an expensive year or two at some school like Duke, and I just don't have the money. In fact, I haven't been able to get up here much these last four years because I've had to work summers and part time just to stay at Vanderlyn. Uncle Jim said not to worry, that he was going to give me the treasure for graduation and I could sell it for enough to finance my postgraduate work.

"When he called three weeks ago to make sure I was coming, he said he was drawing up a new map. The heart attack must have hit him within the hour. I drove up the next morning and found him slumped over the table inside. He'd just finished sketching in the outline. It was going to be our best treasure hunt."

An unembarrassed tear slipped down her freckled cheek, and she brushed it away with the back of her hand.

"The trustees for the Rawlings estate have been very understanding, but they do need the cottage for the new caretaker. Uncle Jim left everything to me, so they've asked if I can clear out his things by the end of the month. You're my last hope, Lieutenant Harald. Oscar said you're good at solving puzzles. I hope you can figure out this one 'cause nobody else can."

Sigrid looked at Nauman. "But I don't know a thing about sextants or surveyor's transits, and anyhow, if he died before he finished the map—"

"Nobody's asking you to go tramping through hill and dale with a pickax," Nauman said, correctly interpreting her horrified expression. "Jemima doesn't think he'd buried it yet."

"Come inside and I'll show you," said the girl.

In essence, the cottage was one big room, with kitchen equipment at one end and two small sleeping alcoves at the other end separated by a tiny bath. A shabby couch and several comfortable looking armchairs circled an enormous stone fireplace centered on the long rear wall. A bank of windows overlooked the porch, and underneath were shelves crammed with books of all shapes and sizes. Most were various editions of—"What else?" said Jemima—*Treasure Island*. In the middle of the room was a round wooden table flanked by six ladderback chairs, one of which was draped in an old and worn woollen pea jacket with heavy brass buttons. A rusty metal picnic cooler sat beside one chair with its lid ajar to reveal a porcelain interior.

"Things are pretty much as Uncle Jim left them. That cooler was our treasure chest because it was watertight. As you can see, there was nothing in it."

Sigrid circled the table, carefully cataloguing its contents: an uncapped bottle of India ink, a fine-nibbed drawing pen, a compass, a ruler, four brushes, a twelve-by-eighteen-inch block of watercolor paper with the top half of the island sketched in, a set of neatly arranged watercolors and a clean tray for mixing them. Across from these, a book was opened to a reproduction of the map Robert Louis Stevenson had drawn so many years ago, and several more books formed a prop for two framed charts. Sigrid scanned the cottage and found the light oblongs on the whitewashed walls where a chart had hung on either side of the stone chimney.

"Uncle Jim often used them as references when he was drawing a new map," explained Jemima. "The right one's a copy of the survey map. It's the first one he drew after he took the job here and realized that the streams and creek made this place an island almost like the real Treasure Island. The other one's the first copy he made when he was in the hospital. I guess he kept it for sentimental reasons even though the proportions aren't quite right."

Sigrid peered through the glass at the sheet of yellowed watercolor paper, which was frayed around the edges and showed deep crease lines where it had once been folded into quarters. It, too, was minutely detailed with hillocks, trees, sailing ships, and sounding depths although, as Jemima had noted, it wasn't an accurate copy.

She turned both frames over and saw that the paper tape that sealed the backings to the frames had been torn.

"We took them apart," Jemima acknowledged. "A friend of mine came over from the rare book library at Yale to help appraise the books, and he thought maybe the treasure was an autographed letter from Stevenson or something like that which Uncle Jim might've hidden inside the matting."

"None of the books is rare?" asked Sigrid. That had seemed the most likely possibility.

"He thought they might bring a few hundred dollars if I sold them as a collection," said the girl, "but individually, nothing's worth over forty dollars at the most. And we thumbed through every one of them in case there really was a letter or something. No luck."

Sigrid's slate gray eyes swept through the large, shabby room. Something jarred, but she couldn't quite put her finger on the source.

"Not as simple as a double-crostic, is it?" Nauman asked.

Sigrid shrugged, unnettled by his light gibe. "If a treasure's here, logic will uncover it."

"But we've *been* logical!" Jemima said despairingly. "Last week my mom and I and two cousins went over every square inch of this place. We looked behind knotholes, jiggled every stone in the fireplace, checked for loose floorboards, and examined mattress seams and cushion covers. Nothing. And my cousins are home ec majors," she added to buttress her statement.

"Mom even separated out all the things Uncle Jim might have brought from England." She gestured to a small heap of books stacked atop the window case. "Luckily he dated all his books. My Yale friend says none of those is worth more than a few dollars."

Sigrid lifted one. The blue cloth binding was familiar, and when she read the publication date—1932—she realized it was the same edition of *Treasure Island* as the one her father had owned as a boy and which she had read as a child herself. Memories of lying on her stomach on a window ledge, munching toasted cheese sandwiches while she read, came back to Sigrid as she paused over a well-remembered illustration of Jim Hawkins shooting Israel Hands. Inscribed on the flyleaf was *A very happy Christmas to our own Jim Hawkins from Nurse Fromyn and staff.* Underneath, a masculine hand had added *12/25/1944.*

The other four books in the heap carried dates which spanned the early months of 1945. "Mom said he was brought home in the summer of '45," said Jemima, peering around Sigrid's shoulder.

"What else did he bring?"

"That first map he drew," she answered promptly, "a shaving kit, that jacket on the chair, and Mom thinks that leather portfolio, too." She fetched it in from the porch and carefully removed the charts it held before handing it over. It measured about eighteen by twenty inches.

The leather was worn by forty years of handling, but when Nauman turned it over, they could still read the tooled letters at the edge of the case. "Bartlelows," he said. "They're still the best leather goods shop in London. And the most expensive."

Sigrid found a worn spot in the heavy taffeta lining. Carefully, she slipped her thin fingers inside and worked the fabric away from the leather. Had any slip of paper been concealed there, her search should have found it. Nothing.

The shaving kit and threadbare pea jacket were equally barren of anything remotely resembling treasure. "My cousins thought those heavy brass buttons might be worth five dollars apiece," Jemima said ruefully. She looked around the big shabby room and sighed. "If only Uncle Jim hadn't loved secrets so much."

"If he hadn't, your childhood would have been much duller," Oscar reminded her sensibly. He knocked his pipe out on the hearth. "You promised us lunch, and I for one am ready for it. Food first, ratiocination afterwards. Lead us to your galley, Jemima Hawkins, and if it's water biscuits and whale blubber, you'll walk the plank."

"It's cold chicken and fresh salad," Jemima giggled, "but we'll have to pick the greens ourselves. Uncle Jim's garden is just down the drive."

Sigrid looked dubious and Oscar grinned. "Don't worry. I know you can't distinguish lettuce and basil from poison oak and thistles. You stay and detect; we'll pick the salad."

※

LEFT ALONE, Sigrid circled the room again. Although spartan in its furnishings, the area itself was so large that another thorough search was impractical. One would have to trust the home ec cousins' expertise. As a homicide detective with her own expertise, she had told Nauman that logic would uncover a treasure if it were there to be found, but perhaps she'd spoken too soon.

If there were a treasure . . .

She stared again at the forlorn table where Jemima's uncle had died so peacefully. At the drawing paraphernalia and the uncompleted map. At the empty chest on the floor, its lid ajar to receive a treasure as soon as old Jim Hawkins had mapped its burial site. She lingered over the two framed charts and a sudden thought made her measure the older one against the leather portfolio.

Jemima said this had been the very first *Treasure Island* map her uncle had attempted and that he'd kept it for sentimental reasons. But what if this were the map Robert Louis Stevenson had drawn himself? Wouldn't that be a real treasure? And what better place to hide it than in plain sight, passed off as Hawkins' own work?

She strode across the rough-planked floor and pulled two likely books from the shelves beneath the windows. One was a fairly recent biography of Stevenson, the other a facsimile copy of the first edition of *Treasure Island*. Both contained identical reproductions of the author's map, and the biography's version was labeled *Frontispiece of the first edition as drawn by RLS in his father's office in Edinburgh*.

She carried the books over to the table, but there was no denying the evidence of her eyes: the embellishments were different and the map Hawkins had brought home from London was misproportioned. The uncle's island had been drawn slightly longer and not quite as wide as Stevenson's original version.

Disappointed, Sigrid returned the books to their former slots and continued circling the room. Surely that expensive portfolio had something to do with the treasure. Or was it only a bon voyage gift from the nurses when Hawkins was shipped home?

She paused in the door of the tiny bath and inspected the battered shaving kit again. Had such a homely everyday pouch once held diamonds or gold?

Nothing about the cottage indicated a taste for luxury. Devising modest treasures and drawing exquisitely precise maps for his young namesake seemed to have been the caretaker's only extravagance. Otherwise, he had lived almost as a hermit, spare and ascetic, still making do with an ancient pea jacket whose eight brass buttons were probably worth more than everything else in his wardrobe.

She paused by the chair which held the jacket and again tried to make herself take each item on the table top separately and significantly.

And then she saw it.

❊

WHEN JEMIMA AND OSCAR REENTERED the cottage, hilarious with the outrageous combination of herbs and salad greens they had picked, they found Sigrid standing by the window with her finger marking a place in the blue clothbound book she'd read as a child. Jemima started to regale her with their collection, but Oscar took one look at Sigrid's thin face and said, "You found it."

Her wide gray eyes met his and a smile almost brushed her lips. "Can you phone your expert at Yale?" she asked Jemima.

"Sure, but he checked all the books before. Or did you find a hidden one?"

Sigrid shook her head. "Not a book. The map." She pointed to the older of the framed charts.

"What's special about Uncle Jim's map? It's not the original, if that's what you're thinking. Charlie told me that one was auctioned off in the forties and he's pretty sure the same person still owns it."

Nauman had found a reproduction of the original and silently compared it to the faded chart on the table. "Look, Siga, the proportions are wrong."

"I know," she said, and there was definite mischief in her eyes now. "That's precisely why you should call him, Jemima."

"You mean the books are all wrong?" asked the girl.

Sigrid opened the blue book to the forward. "Listen," she said. With one hand hooked into the pocket of her jeans, she leaned against the stone chimney and read in a cool clear voice Stevenson's own version of how he came to write *Treasure Island*; of how, in that rainy August of 1881, he and his stepson "with the aid of pen and ink and shilling box of water colours," had passed their afternoon drawing.

On one of these occasions, I made a map of an island . . . the shape of it took my fancy beyond expression . . . and I ticketed it "Treasure Island" . . . the next thing I knew, I had some papers before me and was writing out a list of characters.

Sigrid turned the pages. "The next is familiar territory. The story was written, serialized in a magazine and then was to be published in book form." She read again,

I sent in my manuscript, and the map along with it . . . the proofs came, they were corrected, but I heard nothing of the map. I wrote and asked; was told it had never been received, and sat aghast. It is one thing to draw a map at random, set a scale in one corner of it . . . and write up a story to the measurements. It is quite another to have to examine a whole book, make an inventory of it, and, with a pair of compasses, painfully design a map to suit the data. I did it; and the map was drawn in my father's office . . . but somehow it was never Treasure Island to me.

Sigrid closed the book. "If you'll look closely, Jemima, you'll see the handwriting on that map's a lot closer to Stevenson's than to your uncle's."

Oscar compared the maps with an artist's eye, then lifted the phone and wryly handed it to Jemima. "Call your friend."

It took several calls around New Haven and surrounding summer cottages to chase Jemima's expert to earth. While they waited, Oscar created an elaborate dressing for their salad and sliced the cold chicken. Lunch was spread on the porch and Sigrid was trying to decide if she really approved mixing basil and parsley together when Jemima danced through the open doorway.

"He's going to call Sotheby's in New York!" she caroled. "And he's coming out himself just to make sure; but if it's genuine, he says it'll bring thousands—enough to pay for at least two years in any M.S. program in the United States!"

Oscar removed an overlooked harlequin beetle from the salad bowl and filled Jemima's plate. "Admit it, though," he said to Sigrid. "It was the coincidence of remembering that passage from your childhood book that made you suspect the map, not logic."

"It was logic," she said firmly, forking through the salad carefully in case more beetles had been overlooked. She was not opposed to food foraged in a garden instead of in a grocery, but Nauman was entirely too casual about the wildlife.

"Show me the logic," Oscar challenged, and Jemima looked at her expectantly, too.

"All right," said Sigrid. "Why would your uncle acquire an expensive portfolio if not to bring home something special?"

"It didn't have to be that map."

"No? What else was the right size?"

"Even so," objected Oscar, "why not assume he was

taking pains with it because it was the first copy he'd drawn himself?"

"Because it's been folded. You can still see the crease lines. If he'd ever folded it up himself, why buy a leather case to carry it flat? We'll probably never know exactly how the map disappeared in the 1880's and reappeared during the blitz, but I'd guess one of the publisher's clerks misfiled it or maybe an office boy lifted it and then was afraid to own up."

"So that it rattled around in someone's junk room until it caught a nurse or corpsman's eye and they thought it would cheer up their Yank patient? Maybe," Oscar conceded. He cocked a skeptical eye at Sigrid. "So, on the basis of some old crease marks, you instantly deduced this was the original Stevenson-drawn *Treasure Island* map?"

"They helped. Made it seem as if that paper hadn't been carefully handled from the beginning." She peered at a suspicious dark fleck beneath a leaf of spinach. "Too, he'd told Jemima that if it hadn't been for the nurses, he wouldn't have recognized the treasure when it appeared. Lying there in bed, he would have read the book they'd given him from cover to cover, wouldn't he? Including the foreword about the missing map? I'm sure it would have interested him because of his own mapping skills. That's really what made me look twice: the map was all wrong.

"Jemima's uncle was far too skillful to have miscopied a map with the book right there in front of him. I don't care how sentimental he might later have been over a first attempt, I couldn't see him framing and hanging a misdrawn, ill-proportioned copy.

"And *that*," she concluded triumphantly as she presented Oscar with a potato beetle done in his dressing, "is logic."

JOHN NELSON

Magwitch Returns

HE WAS MY FIRST SUICIDE VICTIM. I had only been on the force two weeks when my partner Allan Hyath and I got the call. A neighbor in an apartment across the hall heard the shot. He rushed out into the hall and pounded on the door, but there was no response. The door was locked and he was about to break it down when the landlord, who had also heard the shot, came panting up the stairs. The landlord unlocked the door and they discovered the body sprawled in an overstuffed chair, a bullet in his head, and a .22 pistol on the floor near the body.

When we arrived, the two men were trying to keep curious neighbors out of the doorway. They had thrown a coat over the trunk and head of the body. Allan and I worked our way through the crowd and into the room. Allan said nothing to the two waiting men, but strode to the body, jerked off the coat, and studied the corpse carefully.

I took one look at the bloody head and turned away. I couldn't understand how Allan could look at it so closely without emotion. But then there was much about Allan I couldn't understand. He was a small man with watery brown eyes and short-cropped, dishwater-blond hair with at least three cowlicks and no natural part. In two weeks of working with him daily, I had never seen him comb his hair or even look in a mirror. He was always quite clean, but otherwise he seemed oblivious to his personal appearance. He never took part in any of the normal precinct camaraderie, and the other cops rarely noticed him. Yet when they did, they treated him with a surprising degree of respect. On our patrols, between the family fights, the car accidents, the robbery reports, and the other oddly mundane aspects of police work, Allan talked almost totally of books, everything from the latest mystery thriller (he found it tedious) to the latest works on evolution, a field he found fascinating.

While Allan studied the room, I tried to clear the hall of onlookers. Then I turned back for a look at the place myself. It was a small living room with a sliding glass door in the far wall that opened onto a patio. To my left was a tiny dining table and, beyond a bar that formed a half wall, a narrow passageway between the appliances that served as a kitchen. To the right a hall extended to what I assumed was the bedroom. Looking again at the living room, I was struck by the rows of bookshelves that filled nearly every wall. Other furnishings were sparse. With the exception of the chair the victim occupied, the only other piece of furniture in the room was a crowded metal desk. On one side of it sat a small bust of Charles Dickens, in the middle was a typewriter with paper still in it, and between and around these were at least a dozen neatly stacked piles of books and papers. Behind the desk was a break in the wall of books, a space nearly overwhelmed by a large radio receiver.

Allan was now openly admiring several of the deceased's books, and I decided it was time to take a closer look at the body. Prepared for it as I was by then, I still couldn't look at it long. Even a small caliber gun can make quite a mess when fired at point blank range into the side of a man's head. The body was that of a man in his late sixties, partly bald, frail, and too thin to have been in good health. I turned to the landlord. "What was this guy's name?"

"Andrew Thornton."

I glanced back at the body. "Any idea why he might do this?"

He shook his head. "None at all."

"I do." The across-the-hall neighbor, still standing near the doorway, turned to face me. "Two weeks ago Andy discovered he had Parkinson's disease. He'd been pretty depressed since then. He told me his doctor said that with exercise and medication they could slow the progress of the disease. But Andy couldn't face the idea of the inevitable results."

"Were you two close friends?" I asked.

The neighbor shook his head. "No, not really. Although to be honest, I may have been his only friend. In two years I never knew him to have a visitor. He didn't seem to mind, though. He had a couple of interests that kept him busy."

"Dickens and criminology." It was the first time Allan had spoken, and he caught us both by surprise. I turned to see him studying a book that had been lying beside the typewriter.

Allan continued. "He has quite an impressive library here in both areas." He looked at me. "Did you notice the radio frequency?"

I gave him a puzzled look. In reply he switched on the radio. The room was immediately filled with the crackle of a police radio, broken by the voice of Lydia Smith, one of our dispatchers. Allan switched it off. "What about the note?" He nodded towards the typewriter.

"Note?" Fighting a rising sense of foolishness, I strode to the desk and read the paper still rolled in the typewriter. " 'I've lived the best of times, I've lived the worst of times, but I never anticipated this. I hope those who came after me observe the twists in their own lives more carefully.' "

I met Allan's gaze, but I was not prepared for his next comment. "I've checked the patio door. It's locked from the inside. You want to check the windows for me?" Without waiting for a reply, he turned to the neighbor and the landlord. "Did either of you pass anyone in the hall or hear any sound coming from this room before the gunshot?"

The neighbor's head shot up as if he had been slapped. "Of course not. You don't mean that you think ... What are you talking about? This is clearly a suicide. The door was locked, the gun is next to him, there's a suicide note in the typewriter." He stopped abruptly and shook his head in obvious disgust.

Allan nodded, then turned back to me. "Go to the car and call in the detectives. This may not be a suicide."

I stared at him blankly. "I don't understand, Allan. What are you thinking about?"

In reply he leaned over the desk and tapped a daily appointments calendar and then the book nearest the typewriter. "Look at these."

The appointment calendar was blank for today's date. I flipped the page. In large block letters were the words, "Don't miss the first spirit." I looked up at Allan, but he simply shrugged. I picked up the book. It was a copy of *Great Expectations*. I thumbed through it. Twenty pages in was a sales slip, apparently doing duty as a placemark. I looked at it closely and then back at Allan.

He nodded. "It's now ten forty-two A.M. The date on that sales slip is today. Can you tell me why a man would buy a four-hundred-and-forty-page book literally minutes before he was going to kill himself?"

�֎

WE TOOK OUR LUNCH AT TWELVE THIRTY in a Taco Shack on Eighty-third. It was a run-down greasy spoon operated by an Italian with no sense of irony. For reasons he never made clear, it was one of Allan's favorites. Halfway through lunch we were joined by Joe Martin, one of the detectives who had relieved us earlier that morning. Joe squeezed his two hundred twenty pounds into the seat beside me and gave us a crooked smile. "I saw your car out front and thought I'd stop and fill you in on what we found," he said. "You know, it sure is lucky you spotted that sales slip, because without it this thing would certainly have gone down as a simple suicide."

I glanced at Allan and wondered what he thought about his "luck."

Joe continued. "Anyway, we went to the bookstore and asked around. Now get this. When Thornton bought that book this morning, he said he was taking a long trip and needed something to read. But he didn't say where he was going, his neighbors don't seem to know, and we can't find any tickets or anything else in the apartment to tell us where he was going. We did find one thing, though, the name of his lawyer, Charles Teller of Teller, Brown and Hopkins."

Allan's eyes lit up. "Rather high-priced lawyers for a man who lives in a cheap apartment on Forty-fifth."

Joe nodded. "That's what I thought. Anyway, I'll see him this afternoon and see what he can tell me. I also talked to Thornton's doctor this morning, and that bit about Parkinson's disease checks out."

Allan nodded as if he'd known it would. "Anything else?"

Joe shook his head. "Just the lousy routine stuff next, checking every blasted travel agent in town to see if Thornton had reservations with any of them. You don't have any ideas to help me there, do you?"

Allan cut him off with a wave of his hand. "Hold on a

second, Joe." He slid out of his chair and returned a moment later with a phone book. Flipping it open to the yellow pages' listing for travel agents, he ran his fingers down the names while he spoke. "What do we know about this Thornton fellow? He's a police bluff, he's also a fanatic Dickens reader. In fact, the book he bought this morning was *Great Expectations* and—" He paused and then started laughing. "Try this one." He pushed the phone book across the table to Joe and jabbed his finger at a listing. "Pip's Travel Service."

Joe shook his head. "Why there?"

"Pip is the protagonist in *Great Expectations*."

Joe shook his head. "If you ask me, that's stretching things. But," he smiled, "you really *are* good at that. I'll check it out." He stood up to leave. "If you come up with any other great ideas, let me know."

Allan laughed. "Sure thing. Do me a favor, though. Let me know what the lawyer says."

As Joe took his large frame out the door, I turned to Allan. "Well, what do you think?"

Allan raised his palms as if to say "Who knows?" "I'm still trying to figure out why a man with two copies of *Great Expectations* would buy a third."

We finished our lunch in silence. Allan seemed preoccupied, and I was hesitant to disturb him. The rest of the day was routine. At four-thirty we heard from Joe. Allan had picked the right travel agent. Thornton was scheduled on a flight to Perth, Australia, on June ninth, almost three months away. From Perth he was taking a bus south to a small town named Busselton. He had made the reservation just that morning.

Joe had also met the lawyer, Charles Teller. Teller knew nothing about a trip, but he did have some interesting comments about Thornton's will. Apparently Thornton had no relatives, was something of a recluse, and lived off investment income. Where he had originally picked up the money, Teller didn't know, but Thornton's estate was worth over a quarter of a million dollars. Finally, it was left entirely to the city university to improve its English literature department. But there was one catch: the will was valid only if another agency did not lay claim to the estate within twenty-four hours of Thornton's death.

When we returned to our car, Allan sat behind the wheel for nearly a minute before starting the engine. Then abruptly he turned to face me. "Let's take another look at that apartment," he said.

When we arrived, Allan began to study the shelves. "What exactly did that note say again?" he asked.

I shook my head. "Short of going back to the station and re-reading it, I can't tell you exactly. But it was something like 'I've seen the best of times, I've seen the worst, but I never expected this' or something like—hold on. I see what you're after." I turned to a bookshelf and began to skim through the titles. I quickly spotted a copy of *A Tale of Two Cities*, opened it, and began to read the first page aloud. " 'It was the best of times, it was the worst of times, it was the age of wisdom, it was the age of foolishness.' " I thumbed through the rest of the book. There were no marks, and nothing was inserted. I looked up at Allan, puzzled. "Does he have any more copies of this book?"

Allan nodded. "Yes, I've spotted at least two others, but I wonder. How did that note end?"

"Sometimes about how he couldn't foresee the twists in his life."

"Bingo!" Allan had pulled out another book. It, too, held a sales slip. He held up the book so that I could see the spine. *Oliver Twist*. Then he handed me the sales slip. "A book wasn't the only purchase Thornton made this morning," he said. "He also rented a meat locker for the next six months."

On the way back to the station, Allan asked me to review the facts for him. I took a moment to collect my thoughts, then began. "Well, we have what appears to be a suicide, but with some weird twists." Allan chuckled, and I shook my head. "No pun intended. Thornton was a police buff and a Dickens fanatic. He leaves a suicide note quoting *A Tale of Two Cities* and making an oblique reference to *Oliver Twist*. He has reservations to fly to Australia and take a bus to someplace called Busselton. He has an appointment tomorrow with the first spirit, whatever that means, and he rented a meat locker this morning before killing himself, besides buying a book that he already had two copies of." I paused. "I guess that's it. And if it makes any sense to you, you're one up on me."

Allan slowed for a stop light, glanced at me, and grinned. "I'm not sure I've got it all worked out yet, but when I do I'll call you. Are you going to be busy tonight?"

His question surprised me. "No, why? What do you mean, you're not sure what it means *yet*?'

Allan ignored my second question. "Can you meet me at the station at twelve-thirty?"

"Twelve-thirty! Tonight? For heaven's sake why?"

"I'll tell you tonight, when I'm sure."

I shrugged. "Okay, Allan. I don't have the foggiest what you're up to, but I'll be there."

Allan never called me, but when I arrived at the police station at twelve thirty-five, I found him and Joe Martin waiting. Joe was as curious as I, but all Allan would say was that we were going to the bus station. We arrived there at twelve fifty-three. As we climbed out of Allan's car, he headed straight for the entrance, but Joe and I held back. Allan stopped and looked back at us impatiently. "Well?" he asked.

Joe coughed. I knew we were thinking the same thing. "Look, Allan," I said, "I know you've got some great surprise here, and I hate to ruin it, but as you well know, being a cop isn't the safest job in town. Before we go waltzing into something that involves an investigation of a possible murder, we—"

"There was no murder. Andrew Thornton committed suicide, a carefully planned suicide."

"Then why did he buy a book, rent a meat locker, and make plane reservations?" Joe was skeptical.

"I'll tell you in a minute. But we must go now or our beloved police department may be out of a great deal of money." With that, Allan turned and strode to the bus station entrance without looking back.

We followed him through the doorway and down the line of storage lockers until he came to Number 69. He stopped, checked his watch, and scanned the surprisingly crowded depot. A bus had just arrived, and several dozen people were milling around, claiming luggage, and greeting relatives. When Allan spotted a slender, middle-aged man in a three-piece suit, he nodded. As the man joined us, Joe looked at him dumbfounded. "Charles Teller?"

Allan nodded and turned to me. "I would like you to meet the first spirit."

Teller smiled and drew a key out of his vest pocket.

"That is the key to locker number 69, I assume," Allan said. Teller nodded, and Allan continued. "And in that locker is an updated will, leaving some of Thornton's estate to a law enforcement agency, most likely ours."

Teller nodded again; then he unlocked the door and withdrew a brown folder. "To be specific," he said, "it leaves half of his estate, roughly one hundred twenty-five thousand dollars, to the local police department for updating its equipment and for additional officer training. The remainder of the estate goes to the university, as stated in the first will."

Joe looked from Teller to Allan and shook his head. "How did you know?" I asked Allan.

Allan smiled, relishing his accomplishment. "It wasn't too difficult once I fully accepted the obvious, that Andrew Thornton killed himself and there was no murder. As long as we suspected murder, we were looking for clues to lead us to a murderer, or at least to a motive. But none of the evidence did that. Yet if Thornton killed himself, then all the clues were left intentionally for only one purpose, to lead us somewhere he didn't want to tell us about directly. In other words, a sort of game.

"Now what were those clues? A reservation on a flight to Australia, an appropriate destination since the clue that led us to the travel agency came from *Great Expectations* and the benefactor in *Great Expectations* was sent to Australia. But why didn't he stop there? Why the bus to Busselton? Clearly, something was important about the bus, hence this." He looked around him at the depot. "Next, the meat locker. Renting the locker, again, made no sense at all unless you looked at it in terms of a clue in a game. Combine it with our bus and what do you have? *Meet locker bus.* So here we are, meeting at a locker in the bus station. But which locker and at what time? The locker is the same number as the date Thornton was scheduled to fly to Australia, June ninth, or 6-9, but more important, it's the date of Dickens' death. June 9, 1870. And the time. His appointment for today was to meet the first spirit. By now it was clear the clue would come from Dickens. What else could it refer to but the three spirits in *A Christmas Carol*, and what was the only group of three persons in this case?" He nodded at Teller, then answered his own question. "Teller, Brown and Hopkins. And like the first spirit, he appeared at one A.M."

Joe broke in. "And of course the earlier will told you that the locker would probably contain a new will. Since he had two interests and his original will left everything to the furthering of only one of those two interests—"

"Exactly." It was Teller. "I wasn't sure what Mr. Thornton was planning when he had this new will drawn up and left directions for it to be used only if a policeman met me here at one A.M. on the day after his death, but I didn't realize that he was planning suicide. In hindsight, I guess I should have. Anyway, once he did I felt I should go along with his last wishes."

I began to laugh. "In other words, the police force had to prove itself worthy of the money, or it would all have gone to the university. Well, Allan, if you don't get a promotion out of this, I'll be stumped. What other cop can claim he saved the department a hundred and twenty-five thousand dollars?"

Allan gave me an ironic smile. "You know, I'm not so sure. I wonder if there isn't a final joke in this on us all. Remember, the original key to almost all of this was the book *Great Expectations*. But the benefactor in that book, a character named Magwitch, was also a convict who returned illegally from Australia. Consequently, all his money was forfeited to the Crown. I almost hate to look, but if we do some digging in Thornton's past—"

Allan was interrupted by a rotund man in a plain blue business suit. "Excuse me, but I have a strange message from Edward Thornbush, alias Andrew Thornton, that I was to meet a lawyer named Charles Teller here." He looked at each of us questioningly. "My name is Howard Albus, and I work for the IRS."

MICHAEL Z. LEWIN

The Hit

THE MAN WALKED SLOWLY ALONG THE AISLE and then stopped. "Excuse me," he said.

The woman looked up from her book. "Yes?"

"Is this seat taken?" He pointed to one of two empty seats across the table she was resting her elbows on.

"No," she said, without betraying her annoyance. The carriage was by no means full. Elsewhere there were empty pairs of seats, even another table. Oh well, it happens. She could always move to another seat herself. Unfair. A pain. A fact of life.

The woman picked her book up.

Inevitably the man spoke again. "Are you enjoying it?" The woman said nothing. The man, however, persisted. "The book. Is it good?"

"Fine," the woman said without raising her eyes.

The man said, "It's just that I have been waiting my whole career for this moment."

Still not raising her eyes, and despite her expectations, the woman felt a flicker of curiosity as she digested what he had said. She said, "Oh yes?" in a way that could equally be the prelude for a go-away-and-leave-me-alone outburst.

"My whole career," the man repeated easily. "It's been sort of a dream. A career target. And now it's happened."

The woman put her book down. "What *are* you talking about?" she said.

"I wrote what you are reading," the man said.

"You ..." She looked at the cover of the book.

With a modest laugh, the man said, "I am Clive Kessler. I've

95

always hoped that one day I would see someone reading one of my books on the train and now it's happened. I suppose it's a rite-of-passage event for a writer. A coming of age." He grinned good-naturedly.

The woman smiled. "You're Clive Kessler?" she asked, and once the question was out, she felt stupid to have asked it.

Kessler reached across the table, asking to shake hands. In a mock-American voice he said, "And you are my one millionth customer, so you win the grand prize."

The woman shook hands. "What prize?"

"A cuppa coffee and a Briddish Rail donut. D'ya take sugar?"

"Yes," the woman said.

"I'll be right back," the man said.

※

BY THE TIME KESSLER RETURNED with two coffees and two jam donuts the woman had read what little there was about the author on the cover of her paperback thriller.

"I didn't know how much sugar to bring," he said. "If one of these mingy little packets isn't enough you can always scrape some off a donut. Here, use mine." He began to scrape sugar onto a serviette.

"No no," she laughed. "This is plenty."

"If you're sure," he said. "As my one millionth customer, I want to see you're treated right."

"I must say," she said, "you're younger than I would have expected, for having written eight novels."

"And you're younger than I expected my millionth reader to be," Kessler said quickly. "No, in fact I am older than I look."

"Are you?"

"Thirty-four. Do I look thirty-four?"

She shook her head. Although his hair was beginning to recede, she would have guessed late twenties. Not an unpleasant-looking man, and when he joked his face lit up.

"And you're what? About forty-five?"

"Thank you *very* much."

"Fifty? Fifty-five? It's just that my publisher tells me I particularly appeal to the older reader."

"Really?" she asked.

"So I was told."

"I'm surprised."

"I will fax my publisher immediately and have my image corrected," he said. "Conductor? Conductor? I want to send a fax. Where *is* the conductor? They're never around when you need one. So, how old are you? It's not that I would ask on my own account, but if I am to prove my point with the publisher . . ."

"Twenty," she said.

"Twenty," he repeated. "And lovely with it. And did your parents give you a name, or do they just call you what mine used to call me. 'Oy, you. Come here. Clean this mess. No, I don't believe your brother did it.' I was fifteen before I realised that my name wasn't 'Oy, you.' "

"Really?" she asked.

"All those years thinking I was Japanese. Sounds Japanese, doesn't it? 'Oy, you.' People teasing me because I lost the war. I never understood."

"You're joking, aren't you?" she said.

"Let's just say that I lead a rich fantasy life. But of course I have to, don't I?"

"Where do your ideas come from, then?"

"From the very air we breathe. They're all around us."

"No, really."

"Really? Well, as you're a prize-winning reader, I'll tell you. They come from paying attention to what I see and what I read and what happens to me. And then I try to think of different ways it might have happened."

"Different ways?"

"If I do it the same way everybody else does it, then there's no point, is there? If I write the three little pigs, who cares? But if I write a story called the three little wolves, then I'm on my way. See?"

"I think so," she said.

"So," Kessler said. "Do you have a name?"

"Catherine. But people call me Cat."

"So, Cat, are you married? Do you have children?"

"Give us a chance!" she said.

"I keep forgetting. You're not one of my typical readers. You're my one-millionth reader."

"Am I? Really?"

"I hereby pronounce you Clive Kessler's official one millionth reader. If you accept this official position, you must shake my hand again."

They shook hands again but this time the man did not release the woman immediately. "You have nice hands," he said quietly. "But I expect everybody tells you that." He released her.

She said, "No, they don't."

"Well, they should. Because you do. And that's official, too. But to make your hands official we must shake books on it." He picked up her book. Instinctively she grabbed it, too. He shook the book up and down. "There," he said, "we've shaken books on it, so it's settled."

"You're weird," she said.

"I'm sorry," he said quietly. "I didn't mean to upset you."

"You didn't upset me," she said.

"I was just a bit lonely. I saw you reading the book. And, well, the rest is history."

"Lonely?" she said.

"A writer's life is a lonely one," he said. "You have to do it by yourself."

"Oh, I see."

"And you never meet any of the people you do it for," he said. "They may buy the book, and eventually the publisher tells you how many you've sold. But normally you never meet anybody who ever reads them. The people who, after all, are the people you wrote the book for."

"I never thought of that," she said.

"Did you ever meet a writer before?"

"Only in school. They had a poet come in. It was in primary school and most of the kids thought her jokes were pretty naff. I kind of liked her, though."

"And so you continue to read. And here you are, on the train today, reading one of mine. So, where are you going?"

"To Reading. I'm visiting my dad's mum."

"Do you like her?"

"Not much."

"So, it's a duty visit?"

"Yeah. I go about every couple of months."

"You're a very good granddaughter, Cat."

She laughed. "Dad gives me a tenner and pays the train fare."

"And you make an old woman happy."

"She doesn't usually know who I am, to tell the truth. But it's a day out."

"I'm going to Reading, too," the man said.

"What for?"

"Research."

"Oh."

"For my next book. I'm going to have a look at Reading Gaol."

"The jail. What for?"

"Because famous people have been incarcerated there. Oscar Wilde, for instance."

"Yeah?"

"And Stacey Keach. He's an American actor. Played Mike Hammer on the tele."

"What was he in jail for?"

"Drugs."

"Oh."

"He's out now, though."

"Who's Mike Hammer?"

"Mickey Spillane's psychotic, misogynistic private eye."

"Oh."

"Not your thing, private eyes?"

"They're okay, but I like books with more romance in them better."

"And sex?"

She smiled. "Don't mind."

"Like my books?"

She hesitated.

"You haven't got to the sexy bits then?" He nodded at the open book on the table between them.

"What sexy bits?" she asked.

"I don't want to spoil them by telling you," he said easily. "Surprise, unexpectedness . . . They make sex so much more exciting, don't you think?"

She frowned at him across the table.

"I'm sorry if I've upset you by referring to sex," he said gently. "You said you didn't mind. I didn't mean to offend you. All I mean to do is chat." He raised one of his hands and counted off on his fingers. "One, chat. Two, see Reading Goal. Three, invite you for a meal after you see your gran. Four, walk around the park. *Then*, if we get to the thumb, then maybe we can talk about sex before the last train home. Something like that."

The man spoke lightly, playfully. But the woman's mood

had become hard. He saw it, recognized it, and said, "What's wrong, Cat?"

She picked the book up. "I've read this book before."

"A real fan. That's great. Do you want me to sign it?"

She pulled the book to her chest. "There are no sexy bits in it."

"There aren't?"

"None."

"It's hard to believe that someone can write a book, can spend all the time and energy it takes to convert blank sheets of paper into something interesting, and then not remember what he's written."

"Yes. It is hard to believe."

"It happens, though."

"So tell me the story of the book."

"The story?"

"What is it about?"

"You can write a book," the man said, "and then once you start on another you can't remember a single thing about the first. Not a single thing."

The woman was not impressed with this insight about writers. She and the man looked at one another for a number of seconds.

Then the man said, "I *am* a writer."

"Congratulations."

"My name is John Leigh. I'm twenty-seven years old. I've written three novels, and finally one of them got published last summer. Actually published. That's quite a big deal these days. It was called *Winter Rain*. It came out in June. It went back in again in July. I've written another novel since then, but the publishers don't even want to read it. I have always wanted to be a writer, since I was about twelve. I have always wanted to be on a train or a plane and see a beautiful woman reading one of my books. I've wanted to know what it would be like to introduce myself and to see what she felt about what she was reading. Because when I write, the way I do it is by writing as if it's a letter to a woman I love, by writing as if I am making love to her."

So you lie to the women you make love to, the woman thought. She said, "And so you made all that stuff up."

"Yes. To find out what it would feel like. To see if it was

worth my continuing to write. To see if it was worth keeping on trying."

"And is it?"

"It was very nice while we were talking, while we were getting along. Extremely nice. I liked it."

"Even though you were lying through your teeth."

"You wouldn't have talked to me otherwise, would you?"

"No."

"I have no regrets," he said.

"How did you know there was nothing in the book about the real Clive Kessler?"

"I study the book racks in railroad stations. I make a list of books with no picture of the author and nothing saying he's sixty-five, gay, and a leper."

"You make a list?"

"I'm a very organized person."

"Did you really write a book called *Winter* ... whatever it was?"

"*Winter Rain.*"

"Yeah."

"No," he said. "I've never written a book. But I'm only twenty-four. I have time."

"Never written a book," she said, "but you have picked up girls this way before."

"Yes," he said.

"Really?"

"No," he said. "In fact, this is the first time I've tried it. I was in Taunton station and I saw you buy a copy and so I looked at another copy and there was nothing about the author, and then I saw you sitting alone." His voice trailed away.

She smiled and raised one eyebrow as she watched him think.

"You said you'd read it before."

"Yes."

"But you bought a new copy."

"I read a library copy," she said, "but I wanted one of my own."

"Oh," he said.

"Or I read a mate's copy, and wanted one of my own. Or I lost my first copy. Or I just wanted two."

He stared at her.

"No more questions? I thought authors were always full of questions."

"*Have* you read it before?"

"Of course not." She laughed.

"Oh," he said.

"And I don't have a grandmother."

"You don't?"

"I am going to Reading to meet my boyfriend."

"You are?"

"To tell you the absolute truth," she said, "he and I are going to sort out how we can get rid of his wife."

"I don't believe you," the man said. "You're just getting back at me."

"It is the truth," the woman said. "And it's such an exquisite relief to be able to tell someone, someone who can't possibly hurt me."

"I can't?"

"For one thing, you're a complete stranger. For another, you're a liar and a fantasist. Nobody would ever believe you. I feel really good for having said it out loud now. Not that I am getting cold feet. I'm not. My boyfriend—well, he's a little old to be called that—but he's exactly what I have always wanted in a man. He's mature. He's exciting. And he is extremely rich, or at least he will be if his wife dies by accident. My only worry is that he'll chicken out, so chances are I'll have to do it myself. I won't mind that. She's a bitch and a ball-breaker. She deserves to die. I figure I'll run her over. She jogs, so it shouldn't be hard. God, I hate joggers. Don't you?"

"You're making all this up," he said.

Her look at him was the coldest he'd ever seen. "Yeah," she said. "Making it all up. Just don't read the papers for the next few days."

"That's awful," he said.

"That's what I hate about men," she said. "Under the bluster they're so soft. You only go round once in this life, right? Well, this is my chance to get the gold ring."

The man sat staring at her, silenced.

The woman said, "Hey, talking about finally being rid of *her* is making me prickly. You fancy a quickie? We could do it in the toilet at the end of the carriage. You're not HIV positive, are you?"

"No," he said.

"I didn't think so. I can usually tell by looking."

The man said, "Come on, it's a joke, right?"

"You go first. I'll knock twice when I want to come in."

The man rose unsteadily. He left the carriage without looking behind him.

At his fleeing back the woman made a heartfelt V sign. She finished her coffee. She picked up her book.

MICHAEL INNES

The Secret in The Woodpile

CHARLES LENTON WAS THE DEAD MAN'S NAME. He had been a psychiatrist. Inspector John Appleby, viewing what was left of him, unemotionally remarked to Sergeant Aggett that one must expect such chaps to get themselves murdered from time to time.

"Well, yes," Aggett said dubiously. "I suppose you might say, sir, that it's a dangerous job. Constant contact with thoroughly unbalanced types."

"And constant listening to shocking secrets. One might want to rub out somebody in whom one had rashly confided."

"I suppose so." Aggett seemed not particularly impressed. "But that would go for priests as well—the papist ones who hear confessions, that is. And not many priests are murdered."

"Priests don't keep notes. Psychiatrists do. Then one day they give you a fancy name, drape your affairs in a few other perfunctory fictions, and publish your embarrassing past as a case history."

"Not many notes surviving here, sir."

"That's true." Appleby glanced from Lenton's corpse to the wider scene. "And that's our starting point."

One could still see that the spacious consulting room had been handsomely furnished. It was in London's most exclusive medical district. Lenton's practice must have been in a highly lucrative bracket. But the murderer had set the whole place afire in a thoroughly efficient way.

Apart from the body—on which not a stitch remained un-

104

consumed—only ashes, charred wood, and here and there a fragment of curtain or carpet were on view. It was surprising that the building had been saved. But from this floor downward it was as drenched in water as if it had been under the sea.

"It was all antiques, the secretary says," Aggett announced with distaste. "French stuff with fancy names—*armoires*, and the like. A queer way to keep medical records."

"Not much security, certainly. One would expect steel filing cabinets. But I suppose they'd have struck too utilitarian a note."

"That's it, sir. Not that what you might call confidentiality wasn't well guarded in a way. No names, no pack drill. The case histories were all coded, it seems, as far as proper names went, and Lenton carried round a notebook with the key to it always on his own person. But there isn't anything of that left, as you can see. What I'm wondering is why, if there were no names in the files, the killer thought it necessary to burn down the whole works."

"Suppose, Aggett, the criminal is somebody well known. And suppose some state of affairs he had once confided to Lenton had striking or even bizarre features which might point to him—names or no names. That would answer your point."

"Yes, sir. But there's another thing. A setup like this is deserted at night. The whole building consists of surgeries or consulting rooms or the like, and everybody packs up and goes home. It wouldn't have been too difficult simply to break in and remove or destroy the files. Instead of which the fellow marches in in broad daylight and does this. He was frightened not only of what was in the closets but of what was in Dr. Lenton's head as well."

"There isn't much left in it now. Until the fire got them, the brains must have been mostly on the carpet." Inspector Appleby glanced at the dead man again with composure. So did Sergeant Aggett. They were accustomed to what a heavy revolver can accomplish at close range. "But it's only one possibility, you know, that the chap wanted to destroy incriminating material. He may simply have wanted to possess himself of it—say, for purposes of blackmail. Quite speculatively, it may have been. Then Lenton turned up and surprised him, and the rest followed. By the way, have you gathered anything yet about the nature of Lenton's practice? It might be relevant."

"Only what his secretary says and that was not much more than a string of long words. So I told her to write them down in my notebook. And here it is." Aggett, a most competent officer, produced this record from his pocket and read with care. " 'Dr. Lenton's methods were empirical and eclectic. Deep analysis, simple but sustained psychotherapy, prolonged narcosis, medical hypnotism, ECT, insulin shock, psychotropic drugs, abreactive techniques—' "

"All right, Aggett. We'll just say he wouldn't readily acknowledge himself as baffled."

※

APPLEBY DIDN'T FIND OUT MUCH more about Charles Lenton that day, or indeed for many days to come. There was nothing shady about the doctor. High medical authority vouched for that. Not only was he among that minority of murdered persons who prove to be without dubious associations of one sort or another, he was a man distinguished, among other things, for his insistence on the highest standards of professional conduct. That might of course, as Aggett pointed out, be "all in my eye." But somehow Appleby didn't think so.

Any other lead being lacking, it was necessary to inquire about the dead man's current patients. This was a delicate business. The troubles that lead people to seek psychiatric treatment are very often such as few would care to divulge even to the most sympathetic policeman. Not that Appleby was after that exactly. He could do little more than ask these people about Lenton and their impressions of him, rather than about themselves—this while forming his own opinion of them.

And he could be by no means quite certain he had all these sufferers on parade. Lenton's secretary, Miss Nicholson, seemed a capable young woman, and was confident she had produced a complete list out of her head. Her memory, however, went back no more than a couple of years, and this was true of another form of record which turned up in Lenton's home.

The doctor had kept a duplicate engagement book there, scrapping it more or less year by year. But the last two of these diaries were available, and Appleby studied them closely. They confirmed that the secretary's recollection was reliable—except that here and there a name cropped up that meant nothing to

her. These names—there were no more than four or five of
them—were distinguished by a small pencil mark.

Appleby conjectured that they were the names of patients
whom Lenton had seen, for one reason or another, only privately and at home. And Lenton's housekeeper—he had been
an unmarried man—confirmed that this appeared to have happened from time to time.

There was nothing heartening in all this. What can one do
with a few surnames scribbled in a diary? Very little—except
look them up in the London telephone directory, and find each
reproduced by the score or the hundred. But Appleby, having
drawn a complete blank with Lenton's known patients, was
reduced to just that.

Only one name wasn't hopelessly common. It was Woodpile,
and that wasn't common at all. There were only one Woodpile,
and he turned out to be a university professor. Appleby re-
solved to have a go at him.

He found Professor Woodpile at work—an untidy man in
an untidy room with a view of the British Museum through
the window. And Appleby wasted no time.

"Professor Woodpile, you may have read that a certain Dr.
Charles Lenton was recently discovered shot dead in his consulting room. I have called to ask if you were acquainted
with him."

"Lenton? Charles Lenton?" It was evident that Woodpile
was a highly nervous man. "Never set eyes on him."

"I must tell you, Professor, that your name has been found
in his current engagement book—apparently as one with
whom he had an appointment at his home. You would appear
to be the only person in London named Woodpile. I wonder
if I may invite you to comment on the circumstance?"

"My cousin. My Canadian cousin." Woodpile gulped violently. "Turned up out of the blue. Never knew I had one. But
here he was—in London, and down with some nervous trouble. He wanted me to recommend somebody who might help
him. I knew Lenton's name. Had heard he was a very distinguished and well-reputed psychiatrist. So I told my cousin—"

"What's his other name?"

"His other name?" The learned Woodpile appeared completely at sea.

"This cousin's Christian name."

"Oh, that! Arthur. I think it was Arthur."

"Thank you. Please go on."

"But that's all! I gave my cousin Lenton's name, and he went away. Never saw him again. Nor heard from him either."

"Have you any means of tracing this Arthur Woodpile, this wandering Canadian in search of medical aid?"

"Oh, none whatever. Out of the blue, as I said. And back into it again."

"Professor Woodpile, am I right in thinking that your subject is English literature?"

"Perfectly right. Everybody knows that. Or everybody in my field."

"Quite so. And it is a field concerned with the deliverances of the imagination?"

"I don't understand you. I don't understand you at all."

"I rather think you do, sir. And I need hardly emphasize that this is a very serious matter. In the light of that would you care to reconsider your statement?"

"Certainly not."

"There is nothing further you wish to say?"

"Yes, there is. Go away and leave me alone."

❊

THIS HAD BEEN A MOST ENCOURAGING INTERVIEW. Hitherto—at least to Appleby's practiced ear—everybody had told the truth. Even those patients of Lenton's who had been obliged to touch or skirt matters of some embarrassment to themselves, even they had faced up to the gravity of the issue. Woodpile, on the other hand, for reasons still known only to himself, had improvised an absurd fiction. Why had he gone to see the dead man? And why did he want to conceal that he had done so?

There might be some perfectly innocent reason for each of these actions. Woodpile had perhaps consulted Lenton in a normal way—yet abnormally in the sense that he had been in a very unstable state. As a consequence of this he had perhaps quarreled violently with his prospective physician, and even made a nuisance of himself on subsequent occasions. And he might now simply be in a panic because of Lenton's violent end.

The perturbed Woodpile was worth following up. Appleby called on an acquaintance named Howard Collins, also a professor of literature.

"What's Woodpile's chief line?" he asked.

"He has only one. He's one of those single-subject scholars who get their teeth into a chap and keep them there for life."

"I see. Who's his chap?"

"The poet Richard Furey."

"Surely he's still alive?"

"He is indeed—and immensely old and eminent. Woodpile's two main books are called *Furey: The Poet* and *Furey: the Man*. Perhaps he'll end up with *Furey: the Corpse*. Furey's said to be pretty far gone."

"Physically, do you mean, or mentally?"

"Chiefly the latter, I believe. He's said to be enormously irascible and egotistical. A Grand Old Man of Letters, and so forth."

"Have you any notion how he gets on with Woodpile—this pertinacious critic and biographer? I imagine a great writer might be irritated or even infuriated by a learned hanger-on of that sort."

"I rather think it's not like that." Professor Collins had shaken his head decisively. "Woodpile has really done quite a lot for Furey's reputation. He discovered the early poems, you know. You must remember about that, Appleby."

"I'm afraid I don't. But how can one be said to discover the early work of a poet still living? I'd imagine the poet would do that for himself, if he had a mind to."

"You have a point there. And it's more accurate to say that Woodpile discovered in manuscript both some very early poems that had never been published and some well-known poems in early versions. Surprisingly early, indeed, in Furey's career."

"Furey was precocious?"

"That's precisely what Woodpile revealed—that Furey was far more of a prodigy than, say, Chatterton or Rimbaud. If he had been a musician it wouldn't have been that remarkable. The infant Mozart, and all that. But poets don't get powerfully going in their nurseries. Alexander Pope liked to claim that he lisped in numbers. But Pope fudged the evidence. Isn't this a bit far from your murdered psychiatrist, my dear Appleby?"

"It does sound that way. Do you think Furey would ever have had occasion to consult a mad doctor? That's what the early mental specialists were called. It's a finely ambiguous expression."

"No doubt. But how should I know? All poets are dotty, of

course. Possessed by the Muse, or by the divine *furor*, or what have you. But Woodpile's biography records no visits in the neighborhood of Harley Street. But then it wouldn't, would it? It's what they call an official or authorized biography."

Collins paused, then went on, "Would you care to borrow Woodpile's edition of that early stuff? I've got it here in my room somewhere. Very handsomely got up. Facsimilies of manuscripts, portraits of the young genius from the family photograph album, and so forth and so on."

"It scarcely sounds like one of the documents in the case. But I want to tackle the aged Richard Furey, and a spot of homework might be in order. I'd gain merit—don't you think?—if I showed knowledge of the chap's inspired infancy. So I'll accept your very obliging offer."

✿

"WELL, JOHN," Judith Appleby asked her husband at their dinner table several days later, "did you gain admittance to the great man?"

"Yes, I did. And it's all over."

"All over?"

"Decidedly so." Appleby, who would have had to be described as looking mildly shaken, poured claret. "I have to ask myself if I mishandled the thing. The Director of Public Prosecutions may ask me that. Or even the Home Secretary himself."

"Nonsense, John!"

"Well, at least the mystery of Dr. Charles Lenton's death is a mystery no longer. But, you see, I presented myself to the aged poet in the character of an admirer. I'd got a tip that he quite liked that. I'd done my prep, as you know, but my pose was a shade rash, all the same. It made it very difficult to get on to the theme of Lenton, as you can imagine.

"Furey proved to be a powerful man still—physically powerful, I mean—but as crazy as they come. A senile craziness. He went off like a gun about himself and held forth for half an hour by my watch. All about his dazzling precocity. I was prepared for that a little by what Howard Collins had told me. But not for its being an obsessional theme.

"The awful thing is that Furey's poetry *is* poetry, and much of it major poetry at that. His reputation is as secure as a reputation in literature can ever be. But all that he had in his head was this lisping-in-numbers stuff—as discovered and celebrated by the tedious Woodpile."

Appleby paused, poured more claret, then paraphrased an old saying. "But there was a secret in the Woodpile. It's been as simple as that."

"John, I know you're tired. But do talk sense."

"Very well. Have you ever seen a stage hypnotist at work?"

"Yes, I have. But what—"

"Describe some of the things you saw him do."

"He'd hypnotize a man from the audience, lay him out flat on three chairs, and then remove the middle one. The man would stay completely rigid, like a girder or tree trunk, supported only by his head and his heels."

"Yes, I've seen that too. Anything else?"

"He'd stick pins in people, and they wouldn't—"

"Yes, yes. More, please."

"He'd tell somebody he was a duck or a hippopotamus, and then—"

"That as well. Anything with a blackboard?"

"A blackboard? I don't think—but yes—"

"That was it, Judith. That was the whole thing. But, before I come to it, I'll tell you about the end of Furey."

"The *end* of Furey?"

"Just that. He's dead. You see, I got on to Lenton, that skilled medical hypnotist, and I went at Lenton hard. Eventually Furey saw that I *knew*. He sprang up, and I thought he was going to murder me. In fact, he *was* going to murder me. Only he had some frightful seizure instead and dropped dead on the instant. I suppose it gives me my niche in English literary history. But it's uncommonly awkward."

And Appleby smiled rather wanly. "To the best of my recollection, Judith, it's something that never happened to me before."

※

"Years ago"—Appleby had left the table and was composing himself with a cigar—"years ago Furey presented himself to Lenton, professing himself very interested in certain of the phenomena of hypnotism, and proposing a series of experiments—experiments in the composition of poetry. Now, Judith, go back to that blackboard. Your stage hypnotist gets his subject to sign his name. He then tells him he is fifteen years old and gives the same instruction. Up goes the signature in a fifteen-year-old hand. Eventually he gets back to a point at which his subject is struggling with his ABC's.

"Furey suggested his operating, as it were, at about the age of twelve. He provided Lenton simply with a number of titles. Lenton would give the command, 'Compose a poem called 'So-and-So,' and off Furey would go. But since what he had in his head were mature poems—some published and some unpublished—with these same titles, precisely that was what he wrote out in the hypnotic state. Lenton may well have had a notion of what was going on, but saw it merely in terms of psychological curiosity. He hadn't a clue that any fraud was in the course of preparation."

"John, you don't mean—"

"Of course I do. Furey got away with a substantial little collection of his own adult work in a hand absolutely verifiable as that of his twelfth or thirteenth year. There would be plenty of his schoolboy letters and so forth to validate the handwriting. And then, to cut a long story short, he contrived to plant this material where the industriously researching Woodpile would be sure to happen on it. And thus did the celebrated Richard Furey juvenilia come into being. Its publication had the incidental result of making Woodpile's reputation."

"And then?"

"The late Dr. Lenton was no sort of literary character, and it was years before the penny, you may say, dropped in his head. But he did at length hear of Furey's fame as a uniquely precocious poetic genius. He got hold of a copy of the book I borrowed from Collins, embellished in facsimile with the actual writings which had been produced under his hypnotic nose—but with never a word in the book about the circumstances of their production. He wasn't a fool; he thought the thing out; and he realized that he had been an innocent party in a monstrous deception. The celebrated Alexander Pope had never fudged evidence in just that way."

"And he determined to expose the racket?"

"Just that. He'd been badly used, duped, but he was a man of complete integrity, and he wasn't standing for it. He informed Furey that he intended to expose the entire deception. By this time Furey's whole ego was bound up with his spurious reputation as a prodigy. In a panic, I imagine, he sent for Woodpile and owned up.

"Woodpile panicked too, feeling that when the truth became

known his own reputation as a competent and respectable scholar would be in ruins. He went to see Lenton at his home, pleaded with him to keep silent, may have tried to bribe him as well. It was no go. The outraged Lenton was adamant.

"Woodpile reported back to Furey, and Furey acted. He had to destroy Lenton's files. His name wouldn't be in them, but the facts would be plain to read, and could point only to himself. And he had to destroy Lenton too. He was a powerful old maniac, as I said. And he achieved the slaughter."

"John, how do you know all this?"

"I've had it out of the wretched Woodpile. He was in a terrible funk."

"Is he in danger from the law?"

"Probably not. He was no party to the original deception—even if it was a crime, and conceivably it was not. He was simply fooled as Lenton was. Of course, if he did try to buy Lenton's silence, that might be another matter. But it's something which, in the nature of the case, we shall never know."

"But it must all come out at the inquest on Lenton's death?"

"Most certainly. It will be a great literary sensation."

"And Woodpile will be sunk, so far as his reputation goes?"

"Quite possibly not. They're a strange crowd, scholars of that sort. Perhaps he'll write a book called *An Inquiry into Certain Twentieth Century Poetic Forgeries*—something of that kind—and triumphantly rehabilitate himself."

JOSEPH HANSEN

A Woman's Voice

GEORGE STUBBS SAID, "Say, that writer feller died—the one that
hired you that time to find his daughter."

"Charles Herkimer?" Hack Bohannon said.

"That's him. Fell downstairs and cracked his skull."

It was a sunny morning at the stables up Rodd Canyon, on
California's central coast. The breeze through the windows of
the plank-walled kitchen carried the tang of sage and eucalyptus. Bohannon stood at the range fixing flapjacks, eggs, and
bacon. Stubbs, stocky, white-whiskered, once long ago a rodeo
rider, sat at the table drinking coffee, rattling the morning
paper in gnarled hands. "Says here Herkimer was Madrone's
most famous citizen."

Bohannon snorted. "He never thought so." He scooped the
pancakes off the griddle and onto plates. "Worked hard all his
life. Published two dozen novels. The critics praised them. But
other writers got the money, the fame, the prizes." He laid
bacon and fried eggs on the plates and took the plates to the
table. "All he ended up with was bitterness."

"You told me at the time." Stubbs laid aside the newspaper,
took the plate from Bohannon, and set it down. "Some men think
they have to win it all or they've failed." He tucked a napkin in
at the collar of his faded plaid shirt and reached for the butter.
"I read that last book of his a few years back. 'Course, he made
up the people, but he got the measure of this place—the ocean,
the canyons, Madrone, Settlers Cove. Got it down perfect. He
could make pictures with words good as any artist. Like to have
shook his hand, but he never came here."

"No, I went to him." Bohannon set his plate down, drew

114

out a chair, sat himself down. "He was in the hospital when he sent for me. Prostate surgery. It was successful, there was no malignancy, but he was having somber thoughts, and he asked me to find his long-lost daughter. What was her name? Beatrice. Herkimer wanted to reconcile with his only child before he died."

"Only she was having thoughts—" Stubbs tilted the syrup bottle over his pancakes "—of another kind."

"Leave a little for me," Bohannon said. "All that sugar will rot your teeth."

"Not mine." Stubbs passed him the bottle. "Store bought." He grinned to show them off. "Lifetime guarantee."

Bohannon poured the remaining trickle of syrup onto his flapjacks and ate in silence, remembering. Herkimer was a gray, rumpled, homely man of sixty-five, wearing glasses mended at the hinges with paperclips. Nothing you'd call writerly about him. Except for the precise way he spoke, always in complete sentences, never a word misplaced or mispronounced. Propped against pillows in his hospital bed, surrounded by books and magazines, he answered Bohannon's praise of his last book grumpily.

"It didn't sell worth a damn. But then, none of my books ever did. See, Bohannon, I never understood the importance of the fame game—not until too late. I thought a writer's job was to write. I was a fool. A writer's job is to get out there in the spotlight, hobnob with the rich and famous, get booked on all the TV talk shows, pass out from drink and drugs before sixty million viewers, stab your wife at a literary cocktail party. Anything to get your name in the paper. Writing? What's writing got to do with it?"

Bohannon pushed away his empty plate, swallowed some coffee, lit a cigarette. He hadn't answered. He privately thought Herkimer'd had a fair shake. He'd earned enough to retire on. Maybe his books weren't bestsellers, but they were respected, and even though he'd stopped writing, they still seemed to sell. Bohannon didn't think Charles Herkimer had much cause to complain.

Bohannon had turned the conversation to the reason Herkimer had phoned him, the daughter he hadn't seen in twenty-odd years.

Herkimer said, "I want you to find her and tell her I'm truly sorry for whatever I did that sent her packing with never a

word, then or since. I love her. I want her to be my friend
again. Remind her that we were friends once, good friends.
When she was a little girl. Bring her back to me, Bohannon. I
want her to smile at me before I die."

"You're not dying," Bohannon said.

"I'm not getting any younger," Herkimer said.

※

SAN FRANCISCO IS KNOWN for fog and rain, but whenever Bohannon went there, the sun shone. It was that way on the day he
found Herkimer's daughter, who didn't use her father's name.
She called herself Beatrice Spencer.

"It was my mother's maiden name," she said.

She was short, wore no makeup, and had her hair cut to
make her look like a boy. Only she was forty and too broad
in the butt for the illusion to work. She wore jeans and a
pullover sweater, sleeves pushed up to the elbows. She sat at
a drafting table in a loft where sunlight poured down from
skylights to make dazzling the whiteness of desks and cabinets, paint and carpeting. Wong's was a smart store. What it
turned out were greeting cards. Also smart. Most of the sam-
ples on the walls were signed *Beatrice*.

"He lied to you, Mr. Bohannon," she said. "At the cemetery,
after my mother's funeral, I told him in plain English the reason I was leaving. Because I wasn't going to live the way she'd
lived, in his cold shadow, devoted as a nun, scurrying to attend to his every need, when all he cared about was one thing.
His damned books."

"He claims he doesn't understand." She had brought Bohannon coffee in a Styrofoam cup stenciled with chipper stylized
daisies. He drank some of it. "He told me when you were little
you had good times together."

"If I made the mistake of having a good time in his presence," she said sourly, "all it got me was, 'Will you be quiet?
Daddy's trying to write.'" Perched, short-legged on a tall stool
at that shiny white table, Beatrice shook her head and grimly
laughed. "His friends are dying off, aren't they? The few he
ever had time for. That's why he wants me back. Well, I
watched my mother wither and die of loneliness, a bright,
cheerful woman before his total self-absorption drained the life
out of her. That's never going to happen to me. Not with any
man. Certainly not with him."

On a triangular scrap of tagboard Bohannon wrote Herkimer's address and phone number. "If you won't go see him, at least write to him. Give him a call. He loves you."

She didn't give the note a glance. "Loves? He doesn't know the meaning of the word. There's only room in Charles Herkimer for one emotion. Ambition."

Bohannon let the note lie there. "I think he's learned now there's more to living."

She had picked up a brush and dipped it in a very small jar of red paint. She looked at him. "Ah?"

"Whatever he expected from life, he didn't get it," Bohannon said. "I have a hunch he figures sacrificing everything else to writing was a mistake, a waste."

"Feeling sorry for himself?" She bent and touched color into a delicately traced drawing push-pinned to the table. "That kind always do." She dabbled the brush in water, dried it on a paint-stained cloth. "The ones who can't feel sorry for anyone else." She grimaced. "Too bad, Mr. Bohannon. But I'm afraid you've wasted your time."

Bohannon shrugged. "I earned my pay. I found you."

"I didn't want to be found," she said. "Not by him."

Bohannon put on his weathered Stetson. "Is that what you want me to tell him?"

She studied him, tilting her head. "I want you to tell him you couldn't find me. But you won't do that, will you? You're a man who always tells the truth."

"I hope you don't regret this someday," Bohannon said.

"I won't even remember it," she said briskly and smiled. "Tomorrow it will be as if it never happened."

✳

THE SUN WAS ABOUT TO DROP behind the ridge to the west. The shadows of the trees were long on the hardpan and flowerbeds. The kids who'd come for riding lessons had been picked up by their parents in vans and four wheelers and BMW's. Most of the horses were in their stalls. Soon the last of the day's riders would be back from exploring the canyon. Bohannon was filling galvanized bins with oats when Fred May's battered white Volkswagen bug rattled into the yard.

He parked it among customer pickups and cars, heaved his bulk out of it, and came at a waddle to where Bohannon worked under the long roof of the stable. May was Madrone's public defender when one was wanted, a fat man with an almost saintly need to help the helpless—whether furred, finned, feathered, or human. You don't earn big lawyer's fees that way, but neither he nor his wife and kids seemed to mind. In fact, they were as cheerful a tribe as Bohannon had ever met. "You want to do some investigating for me?" May said.

Bohannon grinned. "Who's innocent this time?"

"Kevin Milford." May was sweating. He went to a bucket at a corner of the stable and used a tin dipper that hung from a nail there to get himself a long drink of water. "An instructor at the Community College." He hung up the dipper and came back, wiping his chin with his hand.

Bohannon filled the last of the triangular metal bins and put the sack of oats back where it belonged. He squinted at May in the red glare of the sun. "What's he accused of?"

"Murder," May said. "Of his neighbor. Him you know. Charles Herkimer. The writer."

"I thought he fell downstairs." Bohannon picked one of the bins of oats and carried it to the far end of the stable. Then he set it down outside the first box stall door. Fred May came after him with another bin. This Bohannon took from him and set by the second door. "Cracked his skull."

"The county attorney," May said, "claims it wasn't the fall that cracked it."

"It was Milford?" Bohannon gathered up another bin and went along with it to the third box stall. "Why?"

"It seems Milford was beneficiary of Herkimer's will."

Bohannon, stooping, stopped and stared. "Not his daughter?" He set the bin down and straightened. "He had a daughter—Beatrice. An artist in San Francisco."

"They were estranged, so Archie Fitzmaurice says." Fitzmaurice was a local lawyer. "Didn't you locate her for Herkimer once?"

"And she refused a reconciliation. She was angry at him for mistreating her mother. But Herkimer still loved her. Or so he told me." Bohannon moved along, picking up the bins and installing them, coming out and leaving the top half of each door open. "Well—she didn't lose out on much, surely. Herkimer wasn't rich."

"Far from it." May had sat himself down on a bench against the stable wall. "The house and lot. Car's old. No value. He was using his savings. There's a trickle of income, maybe eight thousand a year in royalties from his books, the odd small check from newspapers for book reviews. And his Social Security checks—around seven hundred each."

Bohannon sat down beside him and lit a cigarette. "What happened to Milford?"

"He's out on bail," May said. "All the prosecution's got is circumstan—"

"No, no. What's supposed to have happened to make him so desperate for money he'd murder his benefactor to get it?"

"Ah, that. Herkimer decided not to be his benefactor, after all. He'd phoned Fitzmaurice, and set up an appointment to change his will the next morning."

Bohannon whistled. "And told Milford so?"

"That evening, after supper, when Milford dropped by his house to see if there was anything he needed."

Bohannon grunted. "Did he give a reason?"

"Not that Milford wants to share with me."

"Wonderful," Bohannon said. "Who's he protecting?"

May sighed and got up off the bench. "That's what I want to find out."

"And how much else?" Bohannon dropped his cigarette, stepped on it, and stood up, too.

"It would help to know who really did the killing." May started off toward the white VW. "I don't have to tell you you'll be generously paid. You know how our county rewards its servants."

"It's made you rich." Bohannon ambled after him in the gathering dusk. When May had got himself into the broken seat of the little car, Bohannon slammed the door for him. You had to slam that door; the latch was almost worn out. He heard the clop of hoofs up the road. His riders were coming in. Fred May started the clattering engine. Bohannon looked down at him. "He was an old man. Why didn't he just have a dizzy spell?" he asked. "Why wasn't it an accident?"

"Because the medical examiner—" May let go the handbrake and ground the gears "—says the body should have been bruised from the fall, and it wasn't. Which means he was dead before he fell. From a blow on the head." May began to back the car. "With a stick of firewood. Discarded afterwards in the lot next door. When they knew what to look for, deputies found it easily. With the bark on. Good for preserving blood and hair." May shifted gears again. "No good for finger-prints." He drove off.

And five shadowy riders came in at the gate.

❊

THOUGH NOT THAT UNUSUAL for Settlers Cove, the site of Mil-ford's small, brown house interested Bohannon. He walked around it, undergrowth crackling beneath his boots. There were two ways in. One sloped downward between pines, ferns, and poison oak to a deck and the front door; the other one started at a road much lower down, which meant an up-ward path and then a long, climbing zigzag of stairs to a rear deck and a back door. It was a deserted road, but a car parked here. Often. Tires had dug ruts, oil had dripped, high-heeled shoes had left footprints. Something glittered on the ground. Bohannon crouched and peered at it. An empty lipstick tube. He left it where it lay and climbed toward the back door of The house. A good-looking man in his mid-thirties, with a neatly clipped beard, came out that door and frowned down at him.

"Who are you? What are you prowling around about?"

"Bohannon." He began to mount the shaky steps. "Working for Fred May. You're Kevin Milford? We have to talk."

"Stop," Milford said. "Show me some identification."

Bohannon stopped, dug his wallet out of the hip pocket of his old Levis, let it flop open to show his license, and held it up. Milford chewed his lip worriedly for a minute before he privately decided he was probably making a fool of himself, nodded, and said, "All right. Come on up. I'm sorry, but TV reporters have been driving me crazy. I've had to unplug my phone."

"I noticed."

Because of the pines, the house was dim even in sunny day-light, but Milford kept it neat. Or someone kept it neat for him: a hint of a woman's perfume hung in the air. In a bare-floored sitting room of bookcases and thriftshop furniture, pic-ture windows framing the woods outside, Milford invited him to sit down. "Coffee?"

"If it's no trouble." Milford went away and came back shortly to set a mug in front of Bohannon and occupy a thread-bare wingchair facing him. The coffee mug had the logo of the college on it, and a faint touch of lipstick. Ignoring this, Bohannon tried the coffee, and said, "Tell me about your relationship with Charles Herkimer."

"They've put me on a sabbatical," Milford said with a brief laugh. "I've asked for sabbaticals before, but something always came up to prevent it. Now I've got it. All it takes is to be arrested for murder." His smile was wry. "If I'd known that, I'd have got around to it sooner."

"You didn't kill him," Bohannon said. "Who did?"

Milford blinked at him. "How would I know?"

"You know something you're not telling me."

"Not that. If I knew that, I'd tell you." Milford went to stand at a window, looking out. "My relationship with Charles Herkimer? It began with my noticing his name on his mailbox when I drove by. A day or two before I took this house. He's really the reason I rented it—I can't afford it. But Charles Herkimer lives—lived just down the road."

"That's right," Bohannon said. "You knew his books?"

"I'd read them all," Milford said. "Brilliant. It's a crime how he's been neglected by the literary snobs, the Ivy League old boy network, the New York estab—"

"And you introduced yourself?" Bohannon said.

"And told Mercer Stoltz—that's my department head—we ought to arrange for Herkimer to be Writer in Residence."

"Is it all right if I smoke?" Bohannon said.

"But we're not that well funded," Milford went on. "The best we could manage was a set of six lectures." He dropped into the wing chair again. "At the glorious fee of five hundred dollars."

Bohannon lit a cigarette. "But he accepted?"

"Gratefully. He wasn't a rich writer. The movies never bought his novels. Television, either. That's where the money is in writing. Not books."

"I guess that's why most writers teach college," Bohannon said. "Like you. Are you a writer?"

Milford's smile was self-mocking. "One novel."

A desk in a corner held a word processor and disorderly heaps of paper. Bohannon glanced that way. "Another one in the making?"

"There has been. I'm a slow worker. But I won't go on now. I wouldn't know how. Not without Charles."

"What do you mean?"

"He helped me through the first," Milford said. "Showed

me where I'd gone wrong, set the book on the rails again. I don't know how many times."

Bohannon squinted through cigarette smoke. "For pay?"

Milford shook his head. "He was generous with his time and talent. People of real attainment usually are."

"He must have thought you had something," Bohannon said. "I only knew him slightly. He seemed bitter to me. Soured on life. Hated kids in particular, they say."

"Maybe he only helped me," Milford said, "out of gratitude for the occasional table scraps I scrounged for him from the English department."

"How did your novel do?" Bohannon said.

"It was published, with a paragraph of praise from Charles Herkimer on the jacket, and vanished without a trace. Not one major review. A notice in an Iowa paper was fulsome—but the book was set in Iowa. It's my home state."

"How did Herkimer feel about that?"

"That his comment had put a curse on it," Milford said with a sorry smile. "He blamed himself for ruining my chances. Of course that was nonsense."

"This was some time ago?" Bohannon asked.

"Some time ago," Milford said wanly.

"But you remained friends?"

"We saw a lot of each other. I made that happen. It was no sacrifice for me. I'm divorced, no one to claim my time. He was alone too much, with nothing to occupy him. He got a few books to review, but not many. That wasn't right. He had an astonishing mind. Marvelous memory. As for novels and novelists—there wasn't anything he didn't know. It was a crime the way he was neglected. Sometimes he'd snarl at me for invading his solitude, but alone, he only brooded on his bad luck, and that's dangerous. I barged in almost every day, if only to wash up the dishes, run errands, market, post office, laundromat. Yes, we remained friends. And it was an honor for me."

"So it didn't surprise you when he made you his heir?"

"Surprise?" Milford frowned over that, and scratched his beard for a second. "Maybe—but what I principally felt was pity. That there wasn't anyone but me, a chance neighbor he'd met only late in life, for this great man to leave his worldly goods to."

Bohannon stubbed out his cigarette. "And when he told you he'd changed his mind? How did you feel about that?"

Milford shrugged. "Disappointed. His books still sell, you know. They bring in a small income. It would have helped me buy time to write in. That's what he'd meant for it to do." He glanced around. "I'm not a big wage-earner."

"Disappointed—that's all?" Bohannon finished his coffee. "Not hurt? Not angry?"

Milford left the chair and stood at the window again. Stood there for a long, silent time. Bohannon didn't know that he was ever going to answer. He opened his mouth to ask again, when Milford said, "No. I understood."

"What do you understand?"

"His reason. The reason why."

Bohannon rose and went to him. "And what was that?"

Milford looked at him. "I'm sorry. I can't tell you."

"When you get into court," Bohannon said, "you'll have to tell a jury. You might as well practice on me. I'm on your side. And it will make my job a hell of a lot easier."

"I didn't kill him," Milford said. "I was here at home when it happened. That's all I can tell you. I don't know what your job is, but you're going to have to do it without my help."

"My job is to clear you of suspicion," Bohannon said.

"Even if you do that," Milford said, "the college won't take me back. I'm finished here." He gestured at the window. "I've loved this place—the woods, the hills, the ocean. I'll miss it."

"And her?" Bohannon said.

Milford scowled. "What are you talking about?"

"The woman who comes to see you by the lower road." Bohannon tilted his head to indicate the rear of the house. "Pretty often. In a European car, from the tire tracks. At night, I expect, so as not to be seen."

Milford made a sound and bunched his fists.

"Whose wife is she?" Bohannon said.

"Get out of here," Milford said through clenched teeth.

"Don't be romantic," Bohannon said. "Putting your neck in a noose for a woman who cheats on her husband? Tell me her name. She was here with you that night. She can alibi you. Use your head."

Milford used his fists. Or tried to. But he knew nothing about fighting. Bohannon jerked his chin back, and the intended blow went past. Bohannon didn't like to do it, but he drove a fist into Milford's midriff, and the teacher bent double and dropped to his knees, gasping for air. Bohannon laid his business card on the coffee table.

"Phone me," he said, "when you come to your senses."

✾

HE FROWNED. A car stood beside Charles Herkimer's mailbox. He parked his pickup on the road edge opposite, climbed out, crossed the trail. It was a new car, recently washed and waxed. Not touching it—cars had a way of yelping for their owners these days—he peered in through curved glass windows. Nothing personal. A rental. Frowning, he climbed the path to the set of eleven wooden steps that mounted to Herkimer's front deck. At their foot, where the writer's body had been found, he stopped and looked around. Something white lay under the steps. He stooped, and stretched an arm to recover it. An empty envelope, addressed to Herkimer, the sender some L.A. bank. Probably junk mail, but he pocketed it.

Up on the deck, firewood was stacked to one side of the house door. The door was locked, and a paper seal was taped door to doorframe—printed with a sheriff's warning not to trespass. The seal was intact, but someone had trespassed. He heard movement inside, stepped to a window, put his face to the glass, and saw a figure dodge out of sight.

"Peace officer," he called. "Hold it right there."

The deck wrapped the house to one side. He went that way, and when she came out the back door, he was within a few strides of her. He guessed she realized that her short legs couldn't outrun his long ones because she stopped.

"Mr. Bohannon," she said.

"How did you get in?" he said. "He didn't move here until after you'd left home. Where did you get a key?"

"He always left the bathroom window open," she said, "wherever we lived. I counted on that, and—" she tried a little smile "—I was right, wasn't I?"

"What did you want?" he said.

"Things of mine I left behind all those years ago," she said. "Photographs. A high school yearbook. Childhood drawings and paintings. Nothing of value—except to me."

"You didn't find them," Bohannon said.

"He must have thrown them away when he moved here. It wouldn't have been hard for him. He wasn't sentimental. And—" she glanced over her shoulder "—there's not much storage space here." She tilted her head. "Why did he buy such a tiny place? It's hardly more than a—a shack."

"Big places run to money in these woods," Bohannon said. "All of a sudden everyone wants to live here."

"But he was world-famous," she protested. "His books are classics. Surely he could have afforded—"

Bohannon shook his head. "When he died, his savings were almost gone. His income from those classic books averaged eight thousand a year. He picked up a little money writing reviews. But he banked his Social Security checks promptly, Ms. Spencer—he needed them to live on."

She peered at him. "You expect me to believe that?"

"Ask the county attorney. He'll confirm it."

"But—" A bench was built against the railings of the deck. She sat down on it. As if her legs wouldn't hold her. "But I thought—all these years I thought—" She was dazed.

"You thought he was wealthy," Bohannon said. "It wasn't old snapshots you were looking for in there just now. It was money, wasn't it? Securities. Shares. Anything of value."

"No." She shot up angrily off the bench. "I'm not like that. You know that's not true. Five years ago you begged me to come back to him. I wouldn't do it. I didn't give a damn how much money he had."

"Principled," Bohannon said. "Cruel, but principled."

"He was the cruel one," she cried.

"There's a question about the status of his last will and testament," Bohannon said. "He'd notified his attorney he planned to change beneficiaries. As things stand, the will could be voided, and then, as next of kin, you'd become the heir. The attorney's name is Archie Fitzmaurice. Talk to him. This house isn't worth much, but the lot is."

Her smile was wry. "Not enough." She read her watch. "Excuse me." She started off. "I have a plane to catch."

"There'll be other planes," Bohannon said. "Right now, you're under arrest."

She laughed disbelief. "Arrest? What for? Breaking and entering my own father's house?"

"That would be the charge, yes," Bohannon said. "But while

you're talking to the sheriff, he'll probably want to ask you where you were the night your father was killed."

She stared. "You don't think I murdered him?"

"Any healthy adult can pick up a piece of firewood and bash a frail old man over the head with it."

"I was at home. In San Francisco."

"Witnesses?" Bohannon said.

"I live alone." Her mouth twitched. "By preference."

"Anybody call you up on the telephone?"

"If they did, I didn't answer. I work a long, hard day. When I get home, I eat a light supper, shower, listen to music or watch a video, and go to bed. But first, I unplug the phone." She looked at her watch again. "I really must go. Jasmine Wong died visiting relatives in Singapore last month. The owner of Wong cards. You remember the studio?"

"White," he said. "Very white."

"Well, her death leaves me in charge. Those two sons of hers are absolutely worthless. They care nothing about the business, nothing. Only the cash they can get out of it as soon as their mother's estate is cleared. Meanwhile, I've got the whole responsibility for keeping it going."

"I understand," Bohannon said, "but you broke the law, and I have to take you in." He recited the Miranda warning and took her arm. "Shall we go?"

"Suppose I run?" she said. "Would you shoot me?"

"With what? No, I'd hog-tie you. You'd hate that."

⁂

LENA BIANCHI STOOD IN DAPPLED SUNSHINE on the trail, shading her eyes with a hand, looking up as Bohannon steered Beatrice Spencer down the steps from Herkimer's. When Lena's husband was alive, he and she had operated a busy little bakery in Madrone. The shop stood empty now, the windows unwashed, the glass display cases thick in dust. The ovens and other equipment were all there, and she paid the rent on the place, but she couldn't operate it alone. Now and then she'd run up a few loaves of her deliciously crusty Italian bread at home and take them around to favored customers—like Bohannon. But not often. Everybody missed the bakery and kept asking when she planned to start it up again.

"When my son comes to live here," she kept telling them. "Vittorio. Then we will open the bakery again. It will not be

much longer. As soon as I can build a house for him and his
wife and my grandchildren. Right here."

She meant on the overgrown lot that lay between her place
and Charles Herkimer's. The trouble was, the owner of that
lot had dreams of building on it himself someday. He lived in
Los Angeles. The years went by, but he stubbornly refused to
sell. And Lena had to content herself with holiday visits by
Vittorio and his noisy brood of kids.

Now Lena said, "Mr. Bohannon. Good morning." She was
a gaunt woman with dark, sunken eyes. These eyes looked
piercingly at Beatrice Spencer. "Is there trouble?"

"Mrs. Bianchi," Bohannon said, "Beatrice Spencer. She's
Charles Herkimer's daughter."

"A fine daughter," Lena said, "not to come and see her poor
old father until he is dead. In my village in Sicily they would
stone such a daughter."

Bohannon still held Beatrice Spencer's arm. He felt a tremor
run through her. He heard her draw breath to make a sharp
retort. "Times change," he told Lena quickly, and hurried his
fuming prisoner across the road to the green pickup. When
he'd got her and himself into it, and started the engine, he
called to Lena, "When do I get to taste some of your wonderful
bread again?"

She laughed with delight. "One day soon," she called. "I
will bring it to you." She waved as the truck rolled off. "I
promise."

❋

BOHANNON WORKED HIS WAY against a heedless, jostling current
of loud-voiced young people, laughing, arguing, pouring along
a corridor of the college. He found at last the door number
he'd been given, and walked into a lecture room whose floor
was strewn with papers, soda cans, plastic cups, burrito wrap-
pers, and where all the tiered seats were empty. At a steel and
Formica table at the front of the room, a bespectacled bald man
was bent over a spread of papers. A pen was in his fingers. He
didn't look up when Bohannon reached the table. Bohannon
stood and waited. When Stoltz had finished reading, he made
a note in red at the top of the paper, graded it B, and laid it
aside. He looked at Bohannon, and was startled. He hadn't
expected a fortyish outsider in Levis, weathered Stetson,
scuffed cowboy boots.

"Can—I—uh—help you?"

"Mercer Stoltz?" Bohannon asked. And when the man nodded, Bohannon gave his name and showed his license. "I'm on special assignment for the public defender. In the matter of Charles Herkimer's death."

"Ah." Stoltz stood up and held out his hand. "You'll be helping Kevin Milford."

Bohannon shook the hand. "He's not making it easy."

"Sit down, sit down." Stoltz pushed at him a bentwood chair with spindly iron legs. Bohannon found it wobbly, but it held him. Stoltz took his own chair again. "I regard Kevin as highly gifted. Madrone was lucky to get him."

"He thinks he's going to be fired," Bohannon said.

Stoltz's egg-shaped face clouded. "Not if I can help it," he said. "This whole thing is ridiculous. Kevin adored Charles Herkimer. The sun rose and set in him. He'd be the last person on earth to kill the man."

"That's how it looks to me," Bohannon said. "But he was over at Herkimer's place the night he was killed. He admits that. And Lena Bianchi confirms it. She's a near neighbor. She heard his voice. Just after sunset."

"He looked after the old man," Stoltz said. "He worried about him. He was in and out of Herkimer's almost daily." He glanced around the large room with its scarred walls and nicked furniture. "If we were more than a poor stepchild of the California university system, the college itself would have had Charles Herkimer as its ward. And rejoiced in the distinction it brought us. That's how these things are done in civilized places." Stoltz frowned. "Sunset? But didn't I read the—the death occurred late that night?"

"Ten thirty, eleven. But Milford has no alibi for that time. Which leaves the county attorney free to argue that he stayed with Herkimer all evening, trying to get him not to change his will. Finally Milford got ugly. Herkimer ordered him out of the house, and on the front deck, Milford picked up a stick of firewood and struck the old man on the head with it, killing him instantly—after which his body fell, or Milford dragged it, down the stairs."

"No." Stoltz shook his head. "Absolutely impossible."

Bohannon said, "Who's the woman Milford's been seeing?"

"Woman?" Stoltz jerked his head back. Behind his thick

glasses, he blinked, bewildered. "He's—he's divorced. His ex-wife lives in—Spokane. She's married again."

"I didn't mean his ex-wife." Bohannon pushed back his hat, tilted back the rickety chair. "I meant somebody else's wife." He explained that. "Milford hasn't confided in you? There's no gossip around the campus? You can't help me?"

Stoltz laughed, and turned a little red. "Well, I can tell you one wife it's not. Mine. Shanna detests Charles Herkimer and all his works. One of the highlights of the year was the alumni barbecue at which she told him so to his poor old astonished face." Stoltz wagged his head. "She's an ardent feminist, and his novels, to her mind, are an insult to women, demeaning, sterotyping, exploitative . . . the whole arsenal of pejoratives. They seem to multiply on their own like amoebas. I don't try to keep up."

"Was Milford there?" Bohannon asked. "Did he hear her?"

"Everyone heard her." Stoltz frowned to himself. "It's odd, now that you mention it. Kevin can be fiery. I've had to caution him a few times for being too outspoken in disputes, with higher-ups. But he didn't rush to Herkimer's side that day. He walked off across the grass, putting as much distance between him and the fracas as he could." Looking puzzled, Stoltz nibbled the top of the ballpoint pen. He turned to Bohannon. "Did he think I'd be offended? Surely he knows me better than that."

"Maybe militant feminists scare him," Bohannon said. "Or maybe he didn't think Herkimer needed help. I've heard the old man had a whiplash tongue."

"Oh, true, true." Stoltz nodded, bald head gleaming in the light from the high windows. Then he laughed. "Did you read his treatment of Ronald Loughlin's latest novel? In the *New York Times Book Review?* Front page. Sunday before last? Devastating."

"I missed that," Bohannon said.

"Much fanfare for the book," Stoltz said. "Loughlin's first in seven years, you know. He had a long struggle with alcohol. Everyone believed he was finished. Not so. Full-page ads, television interviews, a nationwide tour. First printing of a hundred thousand copies. And here comes good, gray Charles Herkimer, whose entire *oeuvre* hasn't sold that many, and simply chops it to pieces. And not big pieces, either. Fragments. Shreds. Brilliant analysis. Savage. Simply deadly."

Bohannon grunted. "Herkimer probably resented his success. Even five years ago, when we talked a little, he was pretty bitter. Figured he was as good as the big names, but he'd never gotten his due."

"He hadn't. But that doesn't signify here. He was right—Loughlin's book is empty and pretentious. And the word is, Loughlin's tour is a failure. No one comes to the bookshops where he appears to sign copies. He was canceled from the *Today* show. And *Good Morning, America*."

"The power of the press," Bohannon said.

❈

CHORES WERE WAITING FOR HIM at the stables, but on his way to Rodd Canyon, he stopped in at the sheriff station where Fred May had his small office. Children's paintings, in bright, sloppy colors, were Scotch-taped to the walls. May's feet in worn tennis shoes were up on his desk. He was eating a pizza. A large pizza. One slice at a time, but steadily, washing the bites down with apple juice from a big jug. Apple juice was his nod to healthy intake. The pizza was the opposite.

"Gerard," he told Bohannon, "let her off with a notice to appear. Next month. The twenty-fifth." He pushed the pizza box toward Bohannon. "Help yourself."

"Not hungry," Bohannon said. "Did he search her?"

"T. Hodges did that," May said. "You shouldn't smoke so much. Heart attack, lung cancer. I can't spare you."

"And you shouldn't eat so much," Bohannon said. "Hypertension, diabetes. And none of us can spare you. Had she taken anything from her father's house?"

"Nothing. How could she? Between the county attorney, Archie Fitzmaurice, and me, we've got every scrap of paper that means anything. Anyway, what would she be hoping for?"

"Money," Bohannon said. "She's in need of money."

May squinted. "Did she say so?"

"Indirectly," Bohannon said. "When I told her there was a chance she'd inherit, and that her father's property would bring a good price, she said, 'Not enough.' "

"For what?" May said.

"Have somebody in San Francisco find out," Bohannon said. "Can you do that?"

May put his feet down, wiped his mouth and fingers on a flimsy little paper napkin, and sat forward to riffle through a

Rolodex. "I think so. There's a deputy D.A. up there who owes me a favor. What's his name? Fensky."

"She works for Wong Greeting Cards," Bohannon said. "On Sutter Street."

"I know that," May said, and picked up his telephone.

※

DEPUTY T. HODGES WORE SUNGLASSES today, against the glare on the water. A trim, dark young woman, her lustrous brown eyes were her most fetching feature—and Bohannon regretted those glasses. They were in a cove along the beach, a place they often came to, where the tide, in restlessly shifting blues and greens, swirled around ragged black rocks. Gulls, cormorants, pelicans perched on the rocks. And below them, sea otters bobbed sleek heads up through floating tangles of brown kelp.

T. Hodges opened the picnic basket Bohannon had brought with him in the green pickup when he stopped by for her at the sheriff's station at noon. She and Bohannon had been seeing each other for years now. There was no more to it than that. Bohannon had a wife. In a mental hospital over Atascadero way, on the far side of the mountains. Bohannon never forgot her, not for a minute. His love for her was tender as ever, his grieving, his regret. It used to be he went to visit her every week, though she never knew him, never spoke a word, rarely even looked at him. But he'd been no good to himself, Stubbs, Rivera, anyone for days afterward. The horses were neglected, and the owners. It was no way to get on with life. He'd made himself stop going. Not stop loving her. Not stop longing to see her. Just going.

T. Hodges held out sandwiches in both hands. "Roast beef or chicken?"

"First I'll pour the wine." The basket sat on a rock between them. He took a bottle from it, rummaged out the corkscrew, popped the cork. Sturdy flat-bottomed glasses were the only kind to set on the rough tables nature provided here. He filled two of these, handed one to her, thumped the cork back into the bottle, pushed it down into a bed of sand at his side, picked up his glass, and lifted it to her.

"To us," she said with a smile.

"Yup," he said, but he suddenly felt glum. "You ought to find yourself some young guy and get married. This is no good. There's no future in me, Teresa."

"What?" She stared. "What brings this on?"

"I don't know." He squinted up at the cloudless blue sky and gave her half a smile. "Maybe the day's too beautiful. Maybe I'm liking these times with you too much. I do, you know."

"I do, too," she said. "Very much. Always."

"But that's not how it should be," Bohannon said. "I don't deserve you. And you deserve better."

"Hack, please stop this." She said it sharply, angrier than he'd bargained for. "I hate it when you start telling me what's best for me. You're not my father."

He barked a brief laugh. "I'm old enough."

She drew a breath to argue, then instead reached for his sandwich. "That's roast beef. You'll want horseradish sauce on it." She found a jar and a knife in the basket, carefully opened the sandwich, spread on the white stuff, closed the sandwich, handed it back. "The wine is lovely."

He was grateful for her common sense. "Thank you," he said. "Did the department get a fax addressed to me?"

"Ah." She had bitten into her sandwich. Now she laid it on its plate, wiped her fingers, and took a folded paper out of her uniform jacket. She handed it to him, nodding instead of speaking because her mouth was full.

"Good. Thank you." He put his sandwich down, too, opened the paper. Something shrieked and whacked the paper in a frantic furry of wings, and a gull flew off with its beak full. "Hey!" Bohannon yelled.

T. Hodges laughed. "He stole your sandwich."

"Half, he did," Bohannon said. The gull was circling above the surf rocks. He had to land to eat, but he was leery of his fellows. Now they saw that he had food and lifted off to try to snatch it away. The gull dropped the sandwich into the surf. "You pirate," Bohannon shouted, shaking a fist. "Serves you right."

"You'd better eat what he left you," T. Hodges said. "Before he comes back."

Bohannon looked around for the fax. It went blowing away toward the sea cliff. "Whoa," he shouted, and took off to catch the paper. He sat down with it, ate the half sandwich the gull had left him, and read the itinerary Ronald Loughlin's publisher had sent from New York. He washed the last bite of sandwich down with wine and handed the page back to T. Hodges. "He was here, all right. Close enough."

She studied the list of towns on Loughlin's book tour and cocked an eyebrow at Bohannon. "Fresno, Santa Maria, and—San Luis Obispo. All on the date when Charles Herkimer was murdered."

"I want to talk to him," Bohannon said. "Where's he gone to now?"

"Let's see." She peered through the dark glasses. "Madison, Minneapolis, Chicago . . . that's all history."

Bohannon dug into the basket and handed her a waxed-paper wrapped wedge of Stubb's special double-chocolate cake with marshmallow frosting. Bohannon unwrapped his piece of cake and, warily eyeing the seagulls, ate it in big bites while she read on.

"Then there was Philadelphia, New York, Boston. Ah, here. Seattle, Portland, and yesterday San Francisco."

Bohannon gulped wine. "And today?"

"San Diego, Los Angeles, and—ta-da!—the last stop on the tour, Santa Barbara." She handed back the paper. "One of those late-night radio call-in shows."

"It would have to be," Bohannon groused, "wouldn't it? Just perfect for a man who has to get up at sunrise."

"Loughlin?" She carefully unwrapped her cake. "What in the world for?"

"Not him," Bohannon finished off his cake and licked his fingers. "Me. For my horses."

"Ah. But you have to talk to him. You said so."

"On the theory that Charles Herkimer's review ruined his book's chance to become a bestseller, or any kind of seller at all. Scuttled his attempt at a comeback after seven years of silence and steady drinking."

T. Hodges frowned and tilted her head. "Do you really believe anybody would commit murder over a bad review?"

Bohannon filled their glasses again. "Not unless they were a little crazy. I think Herkimer was. Maybe Loughlin is, too. It appears to me writers can take themselves pretty seriously."

"I suppose," T. Hodges mused, "after a lifetime of sitting alone all day filling imaginary worlds with imaginary people they might get the idea they're gods."

"It's possible." Bohannon put his glass down so he could shield a match from the sea wind and light a cigarette. "And gods can take life as easily as they bestow it, can't they?" He blew away smoke and gazed glumly at the sparkling sea.

"Yup. Late night or no late night, I have to talk to Ronald Loughlin."

�֍

LOUGHLIN PARTED HIS DYED HAIR in the middle. At sixty he had pouchy eyes, baggy cheeks, sagging jowls. His flashy Western togs featured a lot of hand-wrought silver—hatband, belt buckle, and a bolo set with an enormous hunk of polished turquoise. In a deep-cushioned leather booth in the bar of a Santa Barbara hotel at one-thirty in the morning, Bohannon asked him, "Do you keep horses?"

"I was raised with horses," Loughlin said. "In Nebraska I rode before I was five. It's part of my legend."

"What about the facts?"

"My readers don't care about facts." Loughlin drank from a squat glass filled with Wild Turkey and shaved ice. "No, I don't keep horses." He eyed Bohannon. "But I guess you do."

"I own stables. But I used to be a deputy sheriff, and sometimes I still get asked for help. Right now, it's in the matter of Charles Herkimer."

"Nobody can help him. Not any more."

"The county attorney's arrested a friend of his, a young college instructor. He's the one I'm trying to help."

Loughlin squinted. "What's it got to do with me?"

"On the night it happened, you were in San Luis Obispo. That's only an hour's drive from Madrone."

Loughlin squinted. "You suggesting I killed him?"

Bohannon shrugged. "You had a motive."

Loughlin looked around the dim and empty barroom. Someplace in the shadows, a waiter was counting his tips. The clink of the coins was the only sound. "You're joking."

"He hurt your book with that review he wrote in the *New York Times*. You lost television appearances. Your bookstore signings were a bust."

Loughlin laughed annoyance. "Good God. It happens. Ask any writer. Some books you luck out with, some you don't. It's a gamble."

"Only you'd bet your life on this one," Bohannon said. "After seven years, when the world thought you were through, you were back with a novel that was going to prove you were still the undisputed champ. And then Charles Herkimer knocks you out with a single punch in the first round."

Loughlin sneered. "Charles Herkimer was a pathetic, envious little paper-tapper."

"Can you account for your time after that TV broadcast in San Luis at nine?"

"I sat in my motel room getting drunk," Loughlin said. "The bitch who interviewed me hadn't even read my book. All she wanted to talk about was Herkimer's review."

"Anyone come to the room?"

"Not even a hooker. I got blasted, Bohannon, all alone, by myself, and eventually I passed out."

"You didn't drive over to Madrone?" Bohannon said. "To have a talk with Charles Herkimer?"

"He was nothing to me," Loughlin snorted. "Just another nobody with a typewriter. They're all over." He tilted up his glass, drained the whisky from it, held the glass high. *"Compaaah-draaay!"* he bellowed. *"Por favo-o-ohr!"*

Bohannon said, "Your publisher faxed me your complete itinerary. With the names of all the places where you slept. I checked with the motel in San Luis this afternoon. You didn't arrive back at that room until nearly midnight. To get there, you had to pass the office window. The night clerk saw you. You're not a man easy to forget."

Loughlin started another lie, but stopped while a mustachioed, middle-aged Mexican barkeep in a red vest came with a fresh whisky, glanced at Bohannon's untouched glass of iced coffee, picked up Loughlin's empty glass, and went away. Loughlin leaned across at Bohannon, and said in a soft, whining voice:

"You don't know what these tours are like. The hotel rooms, motel rooms, the bookstores, the shopping malls, the planes, the airports, the TV stations, the radio stations—after awhile they become a blur. You're in a different city every day, sometimes two, even three. How do you expect me to remember one night from another?"

"I'd like you to try," Bohannon said. "It was a very important night for my client. And for Charles Herkimer."

Loughlin gave a dry laugh. "You're right there." He picked up the full glass and drank from it. Deeply. Avoiding Bohannon's gaze. He wiped his mouth with the back of his hand. "Will you stop staring at me. Hell, I don't even know where the son of a bitch lived."

"The sheriff found a letter from you among his papers. Written at what I guess a writer would call white heat. Dated the same Sunday as the review appeared. Addressed to his house in Madrone. You knew where he lived."

Loughlin said, "That doesn't mean I went there."

"Come on," Bohannon said. "You were too near that night to resist the chance to tell him to his face what you thought of him. And you drove to Madrone, the section called Settlers Cove. No, don't lie again. It's too easy to check out the mileage on a rental car."

"So I went there. That doesn't mean I killed him."

"You were steamed about the TV interview. It had you talking, but you ended by smashing his head in."

"No." Loughlin was pale. "Yes, all right, I went. Dark as hell in those woods. I saw lights on in the house, and I crept up on the porch. I was going to knock, when I heard voices inside. He had someone with him. A woman."

Bohannon stared. "A woman? What woman?"

"I couldn't see her. The curtains were closed. I only heard her voice." Loughlin snorted. "But it brought me to my senses. Skulking around out there, ready to kill. I was acting like a damn fool." He wagged his head. "God, am I grateful to that woman."

�֎

WHEN HE SWUNG THE GREEN PICKUP in at the stable gate, gray light was beginning to outline the canyon ridges. He jounced the truck to a stop in its usual place and slid down out of it bone weary. All that had kept him from falling asleep on the long, dark, lonely drive back from Santa Barbara had been that barroom iced coffee he'd finally forced himself to drink. Its effect was gone now. He ached for sleep, but there was no time to sleep. He heard the horses moving in their stalls. He drew a couple of deep breaths, then started for the stables. And like an angel of mercy, a figure stepped out of the shadows. Rivera.

"Go to bed, Hack," he said. "I will look after things."

"What are you doing here?" Bohannon said. "Suppose the monsignor wakes up and misses you?"

"Stubbs phoned me," Rivera said. In the very dim light his teeth shone in one of those gentle smiles of his. "The monsignor is old—he will not waken until I wake him." Buckets clattered. He began to fill them from a tap at the corner of the stable. "Was your errand a successful one?"

"Surprising," Bohannon said, and walked numbly away. "Thanks, Rivera."

"Seashell!" Rivera had rattled open a box stall door, and was talking to a horse. *"Buenos días, querida."*

It seemed to Bohannon no more than minutes before someone opened his door in that same way. He was under a patchwork quilt in his pine poster bed. The quilt was yanked off him, and a hand shook his shoulder. His face was to the knotty pine wall. He opened his eyes, and there was hurtful daylight in the room. He squeezed his eyes shut again and tried to brush the pestering hand away.

"Come on, Hack," Stubbs said. "It's past noon. And you got a visitor."

"If it's the president," Bohannon mumbled, pulling up the quilt, "tell him I'm voting for the other guy."

It wasn't the president. It was Fred May. He had used the time it took Bohannon to shower, shave, and dress to build for himself and wolf down a thick turkey sandwich. Seated at the round pine table, he was polishing off a chunk of Stubb's chocolate cake when Bohannon came into the kitchen. May pushed the plate away and wiped his fingers.

"The news from San Francisco," he said, "is that Wong Greeting Cards will go on the market as soon as the old lady's will clears."

"I knew that already," Bohannon said. He dragged out his chair and slumped into it, still not sure he was ready to start the day. "Is there coffee, George?"

"Pretty strong," Stubbs observed, pouring from the tall, white-speckled blue pot. "Been waiting a while."

"Her sons inherit, right?" Bohannon asked May.

May nodded. "And they'll sell. It seems they're gamblers. It's all they know, it's all they do."

Stubbs hobbled to the table with a mug of steaming coffee, and Bohannon put his mouth to it right away. And burned himself, and set the mug down, and lit a cigarette. "And what's the value of Wong Greeting Cards?"

"Half a million," May nodded. "Best estimate."

Bohannon whistled. "That's what she meant by 'not enough.'"

Noises outside made Stubbs clatter a pan and start limping for the open door. "Damn kids."

"I'll see to it." Bohannon went. Out in the white-fenced oval, three twelve-year-olds were practicing barrel racing. Two on their own horses, one on Buck. The horses had more sense than the kids. But the kids were pushing them. There was a lot of high-pitched yelling, hoof pounding, and dust. Bohannon stepped to the edge of the plank walkway and shouted at them, "Yo! Take it easy." They looked at him, red-faced, resentful, but after a restless minute or two, they settled down, and he went back into the kitchen. The coffee mug was in his hand. He blew at the coffee and tried it again.

"She wants to buy the place herself," he said.

"It will likely go to Hallmark or one of the other big ones," May said. "It's a small line, but profitable."

"When I was there," Bohannon said, "most of the designs seemed to be hers."

"And there's where it gets interesting," May said.

Bohannon blinked at him. "How's so?"

"The copyrights belong to Wong," May said. He had discovered a drizzle of mayonnaise down the bulging front of his faded red "Save the Whales" sweatshirt. He was rubbing at it with a napkin. "Spencer's been there twenty years. If the company's sold, her designs are part of the assets. She loses a lifetime's work."

"No wonder she was shocked to learn her father wasn't rich. She'd counted on him for a six-figure loan."

May cocked a skeptical eyebrow. "And when he wouldn't give it to her, she lost control and bashed his head in?"

"Sounds farfetched, but some woman was with him late that night." Bohannon ambled back to the table and sat down again. "I have a witness who heard them talking."

"You do?" May sat straight. "That's new."

"I never sleep," Bohannon said.

"Heard," May said carefully, "but not saw?"

Bohannon repeated Ronald Loughlin's story. "His tour is finished. He lives in Phoenix. There must be some low lawyer's trick you can use to get him to come here for a day. When he does, the daughter should be here, too, shouldn't she? So he can listen to her. Maybe he'll recognize her voice."

※

IN FRONT OF BUCK'S BOX STALL, Bohannon was wiping sweat off the big gelding with handfuls of straw. He'd tended to the horses that were boarders first. He was seething about how the kids had lathered all three mounts up, planning in his mind the lecture he was going to deliver to their parents when they showed up next time. But he knew he himself was much to blame. Trying to get along here with only Stubbs as help was stupid. Rivera was indispensable. But the monsignor, at eighty-two, was failing fast. More and more, the burden of the seminary rested on Rivera's shoulders. Before long, he'd have to stop coming down here at all. Bohannon was going to have to hire and break in a new, green hand. He sure as hell did not look forward to that.

Now a van rolled into the yard and stopped near him, and a dark, thick-set young man got out. He wore a suit and tie. "Hi, Mr. Bohannon," he called. He sounded cheerful. Bohannon watched him go to the side of the van, open a door there, and bring out white paper sacks holding long, tawny-crusted loaves of bread. And he knew who the young man was—Victor Bianchi, Vittorio as his mother always called him. In the years since Bohannon had last seen him, he'd put on weight. The van door rolled shut, and the baker's son came toward Bohannon, arms loaded.

"My mother says you asked for these," he said.

Bohannon grinned. "Thank you, that's right. Just a minute. Come on, Buck." He led the horse into the stall, fastened the lower half of the door, and turned back to Bianchi. "Let's take them to the kitchen. Here, let me help you." They walked toward the green-trimmed white ranch house. "How is Lena? Pleased to see you, I'll bet." Bohannon opened the screen door and stood aside so Bianchi could go inside. "She talks about you all the time."

"I know." Bianchi made a wry face, and laid his burden on a counter, the crisp white paper of the sacks crackling. "About how I'm coming back and we'll open the bakery again."

"That's it." Bohannon added his loaves to Bianchi's. There were six in all. He laughed and scratched his head. "How does she think I'm going to eat all these?"

Bianchi looked around. "Aren't there three of you?"

"There used to be," Bohannon said, "But—"

"Freeze them," Bianchi said. "They freeze just fine. Keep forever. Taste fresh-baked as soon as they thaw out." His dark face sobered. "Mr. Bohannon, I know you're busy, but if you've got a minute, can we talk?"

"I've got a minute." Bohannon opened the refrigerator. "Sit down. Would you like a beer?"

"No, thank you." Bianchi drew out a chair at the table.

"There's lemonade. Homemade. What about lemonade?"

"Fine." Bianchi's smile was brief. Bohannon dropped ice cubes into a glass, poured lemonade over them from a big, frosty pitcher, set the pitcher back, got himself a bottle of Dos Equis, closed the refrigerator. He set the lemonade in front of Bianchi and sat down across from him with his beer. "Thank you." Bianchi sipped the lemonade. "Mr. Bohannon, I don't know what to do." He looked miserable. Bohannon waited, attentive. Bianchi said, "My mother's plans—they're impossible. I own three trattorias in Los Angeles. They keep me going sixteen hours a day, seven days a week." He waved his hands. "Can I control them from Madrone? That's crazy. I can never move up here."

"I guess not." Bohannon swallowed some beer. "But surely your mother understands that." He cocked his head. "You mean you've never told her?"

"It would only have upset her. And there wasn't any need. Not till now."

Bohannon frowned. "What's happened?"

"You know that lot next door to her place?"

"She plans to build a house there," Bohannon said, "for you and your wife and kids." He nodded. "Yes, she's told me many times. Told everyone. It's her big dream."

"Yeah," Bianchi said gloomily. "But a dream was all it was. The man who owned the lot refused to sell. A doctor. Dr. Steiner. She used to write to him every year, but he always answered, sorry, he was going to build on it himself when he retired, and she finally stopped writing. It got too discouraging. Well, guess what." Bianchi's smile was wry. "All of a sudden, he's dead, and my mother's arranged with his bank to buy the lot. I've never seen her so happy. She plans to start building that house before the year is out. What am I going to do?"

"You could sell your restaurants," Bohannon said. "This is a safer place to raise kids than L.A."

Bianchi snorted. "Maybe you're right, now that old Herkimer's dead. He used to raise hell when I'd bring the kids to see their grandma. Always snarling and snapping at them, threatening to call the sheriff. There's nothing he'd have hated more than for us to move in next door. And he told my mother so."

"See how things work themselves out?" Bohannon said.

"Not everything," Bianchi said.

✳

IT WAS TEN AT NIGHT. Bohannon sat with a sulky Beatrice Spencer in the living room of her dead father's house. Books lined the walls and stood in stacks on tables. The place had likely never been tidy, but now dust had settled everywhere. There was a strong sense that the owner was never coming back. Funny how inanimate things could look forlorn, Bohannon thought. These did.

As on the night Charles Herkimer died, the curtains were drawn across the windows. The lamps were lit. A few photographs leaned against the spines of books along the shelves. Bohannon rose, holding a glass of Herkimer's whisky, and went to look at them. He said, "I guess he liked being reminded of these people." His daughter had a drink, too, but it sat beside her untouched. She'd said nothing once she'd failed after repeated tries to get an answer from him as to why he'd brought her here. He asked, "You know any of them?"

"There's my mother," she said. "And a couple of the men had been friends of his since schooldays. No, I don't know them all. I remember that place by the lake."

There were postcard portraits of dead authors. "Kafka, Joyce, Faulkner," Bohannon said. "This one's Yeats, right?"

"As a young man," she said. "It's from the National Portrait Gallery in London. I forgot the painter's name." She studied him, with her head tilted. "You're an odd man, aren't you? I'd never have taken you for a reader."

"I didn't get a lot of schooling as a kid," Bohannon said. "Later on, it came to me you can't be much help to yourself or anybody else if you don't know anything."

"And you're a man who wants to help people," she said.

"So I took to reading," he said, "when I had time. I still do. I'll never catch up. But I won't finish as ignorant as I started." He gave her a little smile.

"Whom are you helping tonight?" she asked.

"A young man you don't know," Bohannon said. "A friend of your father's. The county attorney claims he killed him. I don't think so."

"I don't see how bringing me here can help save anyone." She looked around her and seemed to shiver. "Certainly not me. It's absurd, I know, but I'm uncomfortable. My father didn't like me in his room. He needed to be alone. To concentrate. On his writing." She gave a short, dry laugh. "To me, this is the room. Just like the ones of my childhood. Filled with his things. And he's still in it. And annoyed that I've intruded. Can't we go now?"

Bohannon, close to a window, heard softly departing footfalls on the deck, a creaking of the steps. "It won't be much longer."

"Good." She took a sip of the whisky and made a face. "He and I will never come to terms."

"Writing's art of a kind," Bohannon said, "isn't it? I guess you don't much appreciate being interrupted painting your designs, either, do you?"

"That doesn't put us on common ground. I don't make life miserable for people who love me, just to get my work done." Now her eyes pleaded with Bohannon. "Why did you bring me here? I have a right to know."

"To check out a witness," Bohannon said, "who claims a woman was in this room with your father the night he was killed. He didn't see her, only heard her voice."

"Her voice?" She stiffened. "You mean my voice."

"Don't know. He's been outside, listening. We're here because we wanted everything the same as that night."

She stood up. "A witness?" She ran for the door and yanked it open. "What witness?" She went out. Her heels knocked the planks of the deck. From the top of the steps, she said, "There's no one." She charged back into the room and glared at him. "And no one heard my voice that night."

"We'll see," Bohannon said, and began to turn out the lamps. He picked up her shoulder bag and handed it to her.

She snatched it. "I wasn't here, Mr. Bohannon. I did not kill my father." She ran across the deck again. "Where is this witness? I want to see him."

"He doesn't want to be seen," Bohannon said.

"But that's not fair." She started down the stairs.

"Watch your step," Bohannon called, and locked the door. He didn't catch up with her until she was standing in the road, looking up and down it. The white Volkswagen bug was gone. The dark woods were quiet. Far away, frogs sang in some creek. "If he says it was you," Bohannon told her, "I guarantee you'll see him. If he doesn't, there'd be no point." He started along the road's edge toward his pickup. "Shall we go find out?"

"I'm not afraid," she said, and followed him.

❋

FRED MAY MET THEM IN THE LIGHTED PARKING LOT of the sheriff station. Along it's margins, old eucalyptus trees loomed up into the dark. The wind off the sea rustled them. Leaves and seed pods pattered down. May waddled toward the green pickup from his white VW, where he'd been leaning, eating a candy bar. He finished it off, tucked the wrapper into the hip pocket of his threadbare jeans, and blinked up at Bohannon in the truck.

"No luck. Wrong voice. Too high. Talked too fast."

Beside Bohannon, Beatrice Spencer breathed relief, and muttered under her breath words he didn't catch. Bohannon asked May, "Where is he now?"

"Balboa Motor Inn," May said. "He's not happy."

"I guess not," Bohannon said. "He needs for us to find that woman or his story isn't worth a dime."

"He's added a lot of credibility to it tonight. I'm ready to believe there was a woman." May yawned. "But who? How the hell do we find her?"

Bohannon shrugged. "Keep looking," he said.

"Am I free to go now, please?" Beatrice Spencer said.

"Absolutely." Bohannon reached across and worked the door handle for her. As she climbed down, May walked around to shake her hand.

"Thank you very much," he said. "We really appre—"

"Mr. May," she snapped, "I realize I have no choice but to see you on the twenty-fifth of next month, but if you bother me one more time before that, I swear I will sue you and your godforsaken county for every penny you and it possess." And digging into her shoulder bag to find the key, she marched off toward her rental car.

"Would that get her the half million?" Bohannon asked.

"I doubt it," May said.

❋

BOHANNON WAITED IN THE GREEN PICKUP on the dark lower road behind Kevin Milford's house. A few yards away a red Italian sports car stood in the place Bohannon had earlier judged she always parked it—the married woman Milford wanted no one to learn about.

Bohannon had radioed the car's license number in, and now knew who owned it. The information made such perfect sense he had to laugh. But it wouldn't seem funny to Mercer Stoltz, the bald and trusting chairman of the English department. *I can tell you one wife it's not. Mine.*

Bohannon wasn't alone. May was with him. So was Ronald Loughlin. Loughlin wore a ferocious cologne. Even with the windows of the pickup rolled down, Bohannon's eyes smarted, and now and then May, who sat between them, gave a small strangled cough.

Bohannon hoped the stink wouldn't warn the woman off as she came down the back steps—if she ever did. He checked his watch. Fifteen minutes past midnight. Up the hillside, a rectangle of light appeared, voices murmured, a door closed, the light was gone. Heels tapped steps.

'She's coming," Bohannon said.

Loughlin groaned. "Jesus, I hate this."

"Take it easy," Bohannon said, "it'll be over soon." He cautiously worked the door handle and slipped down out of the truck. "All you have to do is listen." He let the door stand open, and moved down the road, to station himself in deep tree shadow near the convertible.

It sat in a patch of moonlight, and when she reached it, he stepped into the road, touching his hat. "Excuse me, ma'am," he said. "Peace officer."

"Dear God," she said, "you frightened me."

"Sorry, but I need to ask you a few questions."

"Here? Now?" She was a tall woman, handsome, but years older than Kevin Milford. She stepped backward, put her hand on the car door. "What about?"

"This vehicle," Bohannon said. "It's been reported stolen."

She gave a disbelieving laugh. "Not by me, it hasn't."

"You want to show me the registration, please?"

"No," she said. "I don't think you're a police officer. I think you're a rapist."

"He's not, ma'am." Soft shoes cracked twigs on the roadway. They brought Fred May. He gave his name. "I'm the public defender. This is Hank Bohannon. A private operative. He's doing some investigating for me."

"Of my supposedly stolen automobile?" she scoffed.

"No—of the death of Charles Herkimer." His face a soft moon in the night, he glanced up at the house. "Kevin Milford has been charged with the murder. I'm trying to get evidence for his defense."

"You're trying to destroy my life." She yanked open the car door and dropped inside. She started to thrust a key into the ignition, and Bohannon leaned in and took her keys away from her. "Give me those back," she cried.

"Did you go visit Herkimer the night he was killed?" Bohannon asked. "We have a witness who heard him talking to a woman inside his living room that night. Was it you?"

She hooted. "Why would I talk to Charles Herkimer?"

"Because, Mrs. Stoltz, it was over you he was going to change his will. He'd made Milford his heir. Then he discovered you and Milford were sleeping together. You'd insulted Herkimer and his books in public. His attitude to Milford did a complete turnaround. Milford knew you were the reason. Herkimer had told him early that evening. You felt guilty, and went to the old man to try to change his mind. You love Milford, maybe you think he has a future as a writer. You're not in a position to help him financially, you wanted him to have the money Herkimer could leave him. But Herkimer wouldn't listen to you, and you killed him."

"Ridiculous." She scrambled out of the car. "Kevin, come down here. Now. Please."

Up the hill, the back door banged open. "Shanna?" The rectangle of light was back. Milford was silhouetted in it. Kicking into trousers. Zipping them up, he came at a run down the rickety steps. Barefoot. At the foot of the stairs he stopped and stared. "What the hell is going on? May, Bohannon? Is that you? What are you doing to Mrs. Stoltz?"

"What you wouldn't do for yourself," Bohannon said.

The door of the pickup slammed, and the heels of Ronald Loughlin's fancy tooled cowboy boots knocked the paving. "Forget it," he said. "It's not her. It's the wrong voice—again." He lifted his hat, and in the moonlight his hound dog face looked pained. "I'm sorry, ma'am."

Kevin Milford stared at him. "Are you who I think you are?" He looked around, bewildered. "What kind of craziness is this? Will somebody goddamit explain?"

Somebody explained.

※

A WASHER AND DRYER STOOD in a white-washed shed behind the kitchen. For years the laundry had been Rivera's job. Bohannon had scarcely set foot in here. Now he stood in the doorway of the sunlit place, breathing smells of soap and bleach and blinking around. He peered into the machines, crouched to squint under counters and tables, and at last, beneath sweaty shirts and mismatched socks in a green plastic laundry basket, he located the jeans he'd worn the morning he stopped at Herkimer's house. The envelope he'd found under the stairs there was still in the hip pocket, rubbed and creased, but there. He took it to the kitchen, got himself hot coffee, and carried it to the old pine chest that served as a sideboard. A telephone squatted there. He lit a cigarette, picked up the receiver, and punched buttons.

※

THREE STURDY, DARK-HAIRED BOYS, maybe six, eight, and ten, kicked a soccer ball around on the patchy gray asphalt of the trail. They gave the green pickup only a glance as he parked it. Their shouts and laughter made him even gloomier. The ball soared up among the pines of the vacant lot, and all three of the kids scrambled up the bank and into the woods after it, crashing through dry underbrush. Bohannon climbed down out of the truck and headed for the house. On the front deck, two small girls played with dolls on a rumpled rag rug. When he neared the door to knock, the beeping of an electronic game reached him. Colored lights flickered in the room beyond. He knocked. And in a minute, Lena Bianchi came to the door. It took her a moment to make out who he was in the noon brightness. Then her face lighted up in a smile. She opened the screen.

"Mr. Bohannon. How nice to see you."

"Where's Victor?" Bohannon said, "I don't see his van."

"You're so solemn." She frowned. "Is something wrong?"

"This is important. I—hoped he'd be here."

"He will be back tomorrow. He had to drive down to Los Angeles." She gave a little resigned laugh. "Business, business, always business. When he moves up here, there will not be all this strain on him. Come in, come in." She motioned Bohannon inside, into dimness and the restless racket of the game. A girl of perhaps twelve sat on the floor, with grave and intense concentration working a joy stick while angular figures dodged and burst apart on the tube. Her grandmother gave her a loving glance and led Bohannon to a room at the back of the house, behind the kitchen. It was almost quiet there. "Sit down," she said, eyeing him closely. "You say this is important?"

Bohannon didn't sit. He took a folded paper from his pocket. "I want you to look at this." He held it out.

She took it, looked, and her rawboned body jerked with surprise. She raised her eyes to his. They were filled with dismay. "Where did you get this?" She stared at it again. "How could you? It's some kind of trick. I—" She stopped her words, and thrust the paper stiffly back to him.

He took it, with a sad smile. "You thought you had the only copy anyone would ever see, didn't you?"

"He showed it to me, that wicked, hateful old man," she said. Her voice trembled. "I was out for my walk before bedtime. Always I take a walk. He knew. He was up there on his deck, waiting—and he called to me, 'Signora, I have something you'd better see.'"

"A letter from the late Dr. Steiner's bank in Los Angeles," Bohannon said, "giving Charles Herkimer first option to buy the lot next door, the lot where you'd dreamed of building a house for Victor and your grandchildren. You'd neglected to keep tabs on the status of the lot, but Charles Herkimer hadn't. He was determined to keep you off it."

"A family should be together," she said stoutly. "What did that coldhearted old man know about such things? Whose own daughter never came to him in twenty years? Who hated children, the sound of children playing. He was a devil."

"After you killed him, you made sure to take the letter so the sheriff wouldn't find it. But you dropped the envelope. And I found that. And this morning I phoned the bank to learn what had been inside it. Papers can be sent quickly these days. The bank faxed it to me at the sheriff's office. It was what I thought it would be."

She sank into a wicker chair. "Why did you think that? We are friends." She looked up at him with tears in her eyes. "Wasn't I always nice to you? You asked for bread, I sent you bread. Why would you think I was a murderer?"

"You were always nice to me," Bohannon said, "and I'll

never forget that. But I have my job to do. To keep a young man out of prison for a murder he didn't commit. Lena, a witness heard a woman talking to Herkimer the night he was killed. There were only three women it could have been. The voices of the other two were the wrong voices. I guessed then whose voice it had to be. I didn't like it. But I knew it had to be yours."

She stared out the window at the trees in the lot next door. "I wanted a house for Vittorio and the young ones. Not two hundred miles away. Next door to me. Close to me."

Bohannon slid the paper into his pocket. "You could have had it. You didn't need to kill him."

Her head jerked up. "What?" She rose trembling from the chair. "What are you saying?"

Bohannon smiled bleakly. "He didn't have any money, Lena. The bank's offer was no use to him. He couldn't buy that lot. He was only bluffing you."

A young woman in jeans and a chambray shirt opened the door and looked in. "Mama—is anything wrong?"

Lena Bianchi turned away from her daughter-in-law. "I must go with Mr. Bohannon," she said, and picked up a shawl. "If I am not back by five, will you start supper, please?"

The young woman looked at Bohannon, alarm in her eyes. "What's happened? It's not Victor. Victor's all right, isn't he?"

"It's not Victor," Bohannon said.

CARL MARTIN

Something Ventured

IT WAS A TYPICAL JULY EVENING in Los Angeles. The daytime temperature had been over a hundred and now it wasn't much cooler. A hot, dry breeze was coming from the desert at about five miles per hour, drying the sweat as soon as it popped onto my brow. My sport shirt was sticking to my back. I thought how nice it would be to have a convertible, or at least a car with air conditioning.

The freeway was filled with high-priced foreign cars, and old clunkers like the twenty-year-old Ford I drove. But the new automobiles looked somehow more shiny and sleek than they did in other cities, and the clunkers were far less rusty than they were back East.

Both men and machines were feeling the heat. I passed several vehicles, new and old, that had been pulled to the side of the road to allow their engines to cool.

I was forty-five and had been out of prison about three years. Three dull, boring years. A stretch in federal prison hadn't rehabilitated me, but it had done the next best thing— I'd lost my nerve. I could no longer be the lone-wolf bandit I had been. Since my release, I had eked out a living as a writer.

They say a writer should write about what he knows, so I had become a specialist in big-caper crime stories. Unfortunately, I was two decades too late. The short-story market had dried up for that kind of fiction, and the current TV shows were all either situation comedies or westerns. I might have written a book, but after a life devoted to finding and following shortcuts, I didn't have the staying power it takes to write a novel.

Now I had a feeling my luck was about to change. I had

149

been dragging my feet long enough. As they say, nothing ventured, nothing gained. I had to do something, even if it was wrong. It was time to put a plan I'd been considering into action. All I had to do was toss out the bait, be cautious, reel them in slowly, and let everyone think the final idea was someone else's. Nothing to it.

I pulled off the freeway at Laurel Canyon Boulevard, crossed Ventura, and climbed through the canyon till I reached Mulholland Drive. Then I turned right and snaked along the crest of the mountains until I reached the narrow lane where Rita Penny lived. The structure was a pseudo-Spanish bungalow with white walls and a red tile roof. She had planted flowers along the front of the building.

As usual, I was late for our monthly writers' meeting. There were already a couple of cars filling Rita's carport, so I parked on the street and walked back. The windows were open, telling me Rita's air conditioning hadn't been fixed. The thought of sitting in her sweltering living room made me slow my pace.

Alfie Norton's high-pitched voice drifted out an open window: "He reached for his gun and I shot him, shattering his kneecaps. His legs flew from under him and he crashed, screaming, to the barroom floor like a sack of bloody garbage ..."

Alfie wanted to be a writer. He had even sold a couple of short stories, despite the fact that he'd never had an original thought in his life. Even his style was borrowed. From what little I'd heard, I guessed the last book he had read was either an early Spillane Mike Hammer novel, or something by one of Spillane's imitators. So far he had resisted the temptation to rewrite Hemingway, or perhaps he hadn't discovered him.

I opened the screen door and stepped into the living room. It looked like something out of a western movie—pine paneling, a couple of leather armchairs and a sagging leather couch, a few wicker chairs filling in the gaps against the wall near the open windows. A wagon-wheel coffee table sat in front of the couch, and Frederick Remington prints hung on the walls.

Beside the doorway was a varnished wooden plaque with several pegs sticking out and the inscription: LEAVE YOUR SIDEARMS HERE. I always smiled when I saw it.

Rita's dead husband had decorated the house before marrying her. He had been a writer of westerns, "sagas" he had called them. She didn't particularly like his taste in furnishings, but it would have taken money to change it. Her part-time job at a local hospital didn't earn her any more money than I was making, which wasn't much.

Alfie Norton was sitting on the floor between the two scuffed and worn leather armchairs. He was twenty-seven years old, married, and a new father, but I couldn't help thinking of him as a kid. He seemed to look, think, and act like a teenager. He was wearing tight jeans and a red T-shirt he'd bought from one of the stuntmen's organizations. His mouse-colored hair was far longer than was fashionable. An inscription on the front of the T-shirt read: TO HELL WITH DIALOGUE—LET'S WRECK SOMETHING! He favored clothes that had to be read.

In the armchairs sat Harvey and Mary Farris, the oldest couple in our writing group. Harvey was a fifty-eight-year-old retired auto dealer. Six foot three, slim as an eel, and with thick silver hair, he looked great in the western clothing he always wore. By contrast, Mary was short and squat, had a mop of unkempt, dirty gray hair, and favored wrinkled cotton-print house dresses.

Finding Alfie sitting at their feet wasn't a surprise. He always seemed to be there, even when he wasn't. Harvey Farris had socked away a few millions before he stopped selling cars, and his wife, Mary, was our most successful writer. She cranked out sexy adult westerns under the name Carson Colt, a new one every other month. Most of them found their way into film or onto the TV screen. Harvey and Mary were who Alfie wanted to be when he grew up.

The aroma of fresh-brewed coffee came from the kitchen, followed by Rita Penny, carrying a tray with cups and the coffeepot. She set it on a table next to the liquor bottles and glasses that were already there.

Rita, thirty-seven, was the widow of Ward Penny, a good writer who had a bad heart. She had met him in the hospital shortly after his first heart attack and they had been together three years when he had his second and final one. He left her with the little bungalow where we were meeting and a pile of debts.

She was wearing a starched white nurse's uniform that rustled when she walked, white nylons, and white, rubber-soled shoes. She had the easy stride of a tomboy who has grown up to become a confident and self-assured woman.

Rita was slender, had black, shoulder-length hair and huge blue eyes that always seemed to look through me. She wore no make-up. No one would have called her beautiful, but she was attractive in a basic, no-nonsense way. We had been seeing each other for a couple of months.

I stood, leaning against the wall while Alfie continued to read his terrible, pointless story. Just as he finished, the screen door opened again and Bill McDade and George Greene arrived.

McDade was a fifty-two-year-old retired army officer and police buff. He wrote mediocre police procedural novels, the first of which had been his best. Scripted by an Academy Award-winning screenwriter and directed by another award winner, it had been made into a blockbuster movie almost ten years before. Nothing he had written since had been very good. With his close-cropped hair, stocky build, and aggressive walk, he reminded me of every cop I'd ever known.

He thought like a cop, too. I'd been told he had informed the others it was just a matter of time before I did something criminal and was sent back to prison. He was the only one there I didn't like, the one who could cause me trouble.

George Greene, the other late arrival, was our only black member. A writer of conventional mysteries, he had white hair and skin so black it was nearly blue. He was of medium height and build, except for his heavy shoulders, and I used to kid him that a picture of him looked like a negative of me. He was as dark as I was fair. Like me, he wore running shoes, baggy cotton trousers, and a sport shirt with the sleeves rolled up.

Mary Farris made a few comments about the story Alfie had read. She pointed out a weakness or two and praised a couple of strong points. She was trying to give him a gentle nudge in the right direction without bruising his ego too badly.

While she spoke, McDade and Greene went to the liquor set-up and fixed themselves drinks. I waited until they had seated themselves on the couch beside Rita and everyone was looking around to see who would read next. Then I pushed away from the wall, reached into my hip pocket for the snub-nosed revolver I had there, and hung it by its trigger and guard from one of the pegs on the plaque. After that, I took a seat and casually crossed my legs.

They were all watching me. Alfie had his mouth hanging open in surprise, Greene's eyes seemed unusually round, and

McDade looked like he was about to pull out a pair of hand-cuffs and snap them onto my wrists. Convicted felons aren't allowed to own or carry firearms.

"Joe, have you gone crazy?" Rita asked.

"Now that I have everyone's attention," I said, "I want to tell you a story."

I leaned forward and cleared my throat. "Years ago, there was a robbery at an armored car company in Buffalo, New York. What made it unusual is that one man did it by himself.

"The main garage was a square, one-story cinder-block building. And every evening after the last race at the Fort Erie, Canada, race track, a truck would arrive from the track. It carried American currency collected at the betting windows. Only one man remained on duty to meet the truck.

"The bandit waited until it was a particularly hot summer evening. Then he entered the building by simply stepping through one of the large, low windows the guard inside had raised to cool the place. When the truck arrived, and the crew thought they were safe inside the garage, he took a canvas sack containing $340,000 from them and fled."

George Greene's face was split by an appreciative grin. "How come I never heard about that before?" he asked. "That one deserves to be in the record books."

"It probably would have been, but he didn't get away with it. He ran outside, got into his waiting car, and it refused to start. He was still sitting there, pumping the accelerator and grinding his starter, when the police arrived a few minutes later. The newspaper said the car probably had vapor lock."

"So, what's the point?" McDade asked.

"I'm just giving you a little background. At the time, I thought if that guy could figure out how to get that currency shipment without firing a shot, so could I. So I spent a few weeks studying the armored car garage and the route from the track."

"Did you do it?" Harvey Farris asked. There's nothing like a big caper story to get a man's interest.

"Yes, I did. But it wasn't something I could do by myself. It would have taken three or four people to pull it off."

"It would probably make a great story, though," Alfie Norton enthused.

"Yeah, but I always thought the scheme was too good to waste on fiction. I always thought I'd like to do it someday."

"You 'always thought,' " Mary Farris echoed. She was quick. "What's different now?"

"Now I think my plan would be perfect to build a book around," I said.

"You couldn't write a book," McDade said, unkindly.

"Probably not," I admitted. "But *we* could."

"We?" someone asked.

"Sure, there have been a lot of successful books that were written by committees."

Everyone was quiet for a couple of minutes while they toyed with that thought. Then Mary asked, "What do you have in mind?"

"Well . . ." I said, pretending to talk off the top of my head. "We could . . . ah . . . create a bunch of characters much like ourselves. Have them decide to rob the armored car using my plan, then each of us write a couple of chapters." Then, to set the hook more firmly, I told them my plan.

"Say," George Greene exclaimed. "That *would* work!" He sounded surprised.

"Sure, it would," I said.

"No, it wouldn't," Bill McDade said. He got to his feet and began walking around the room with that cop walk of his. "It would be completely out of character for people like us to commit an armed robbery no matter how good the plan was." He pointed an accusing finger at me. "I wouldn't put anything past Joe Dyson here, but can any of you imagine yourselves running around with loaded guns and maybe using them?"

I didn't give anyone the chance to answer. "There would be no loaded guns," I said.

"Your plan calls for guns," McDade pointed out.

"Sure, it does," I went to the plaque, took down the .38, and handed it to McDade. "This kind—realistic toys. No one can be hurt with one of these, even by accident."

There were more questions, but I had been thinking about this for a long time. I was ready with the answers.

Finally, when I had almost given up hope, Mary began to nod her head. "You know," she said, "that really is an excellent plan."

Alfie and George Greene quickly agreed.

"Let's do it," her husband, Harvey, said.

"You mean you want to write the book?" McDade asked, apparently forgetting that Harvey wasn't a writer.

"No," Harvey said. "I want to do the crime."

Grandmotherly Mary continued to nod. "So do I," she said.

"And so do I," both Alfie and George chimed in.

Rita came over to stand beside me. She put her hand on my shoulder. "I guess I'll have to come along, too," she said. "Someone has to keep Joe out of trouble."

McDade stared at us for a long moment. Then he asked, "How much money did you say the truck carries?" And I knew I had him, too.

"There was $340,000 when it was robbed the first time, but today it's three times as much."

"A million," McDade said softly, and I could see him doing the mental arithmetic to arrive at his share.

We didn't talk about writing the rest of the night. We were too busy working out the details.

When I was a teenager, I had always been described as a bad influence. Parents never wanted their sons to associate with me. I was surprised how little had changed over the years.

❈

THE FOLLOWING AFTERNOON I went to a large toy store on Hollywood Boulevard and bought four more replica revolvers and a replica of the Thompson submachine gun. At the same time, everyone else was out buying one or two pieces of the clothing or equipment we'd need.

By the end of the week we were ready. Rita had managed to get a couple of weeks off from her job at the hospital, and Alfie, George, and McDade, the married men, told their wives they were going hunting in Oregon. The rest of us had no one we had to answer to.

We took three cars. Rita's Volvo was better than my wreck, so I rode with her. George drove by himself because a salt-and-pepper team might be remembered. And everyone else piled into Harvey Farris's big Lincoln.

It took us two days to reach Chicago, sleeping in the cars and stopping for gas at large service stations. We always paid cash so there would be no credit card trail.

In Detroit, we rented two Ford Taurus sedans, a blue one and a grey one, because that was the make and model FBI agents favored, and left two of our cars in long-term parking at the airport. Then, while everyone else took the long way to Buffalo, Rita and I crossed into Canada, drove directly to the

Peace Bridge, and reentered the States, shaving a hundred miles and several hours off the trip.

By the time the others reached Buffalo, Rita and I had rented an empty store, blacked the windows, and set up seven canvas cots inside. There would be no motel or hotel records to show we'd ever been there.

That evening we sat at the rear booth in a Denny's Restaurant and went over what we had to accomplish the next day. Then we returned to the vacant store and went to sleep.

In the morning Alfie and I went to a parking garage three blocks from the Federal Building. While I drove, he sat beside me reading a John LeCarré novel. I imagined his next story would be about spies, but I didn't point out that the Cold War was over and no one wanted spy stories anymore.

I parked on the roof. The third floor had been leased by the government for official vehicles, so we took the stairs down to it. Half a dozen unmarked FBI cars were parked near the stairway. I removed the front license plate from one, and Alfie stooped down and got one from another. In less than a minute we were heading back to our car with the two plates.

I spent the rest of the day making plaster-of-Paris molds of the plates, pouring quick-hardening resin into the molds, and painting the counterfeit plates the proper colors. While they were still wet, I dusted the surface with tiny glass beads to make them reflective.

The next day, Alfie and I returned to the parking garage to return the stolen plates. With luck, no one would have noticed they had been missing. The two FBI cars didn't appear to have moved. They were parked in the same spots.

Then we met the others and took a late bus to the Fort Erie track. We spent the afternoon enjoying the fresh air and sunshine. After the last race, we hung around long enough to watch the track security escort the armored car crew to their truck. They carried a bulging money sack the size of a suitcase.

During the ride back to Buffalo, we were all grinning so broadly the other passengers must have thought we were big winners at the track.

✿

TIME WAS GETTING SHORT. It was the last week of the racing meet and there were only two days remaining.

Mary left the store at 8:00 A.M., carrying her knitting bag. The rest of us spent the next hours getting ready and rehearsing our parts. Then we piled into the two rental cars with counterfeit tags installed. The plates had been mounted in chrome brackets so their extra thickness wasn't obvious. They had other flaws, too, but we figured if anyone looked close enough to see them, the game would be up anyway.

Rita was wearing a severe dark blue suit with a plain white blouse. The rest of us, except George Greene, wore business suits. He had on slacks and a light-weight cotton jacket with the letters FBI across the back in yellow letters six inches high. George and Harvey had colored their hair with a water-based dye to look younger and both wore false mustaches. Neither looked like himself.

We drove directly to the Peace Bridge with three to a car, parking directly in front of the U.S. Customs House in spaces marked OFFICIAL USE ONLY. Then we got out of the cars and stood talking. Customs officers entered and left the building, glanced curiously at us, but didn't challenge our right to be there.

Through the window, I could see several men inside behind a high counter, staring out at us. One sat at a computer console. A heavy-set, grey-haired man said something to him and he began punching keys.

I moved closer to McDade. "They're running our plates right now," I told him.

"Are you sure it'll work?" he asked for the hundredth time.

I shrugged. "We'll soon know," I said, "but I'm willing to bet my share of the loot it'll come back *Confidential*."

He smiled wryly. "If you're wrong, there'll be no loot to share." He'd figured that out all by himself.

A few minutes later, the man inside looked up from his keyboard and said something to the others. They lost interest in us and went back to their work.

"It worked," I announced.

McDade made an elaborate show of looking at his watch. Then he marched inside with the rest of us tagging behind him. For the first time since I'd known him, his cop walk didn't irritate me.

"Who's in charge here?" he demanded as we all hung badge cases from our breast pockets. The badges were actually Philadelphia police lieutenant's shields. I'd bought six of them and had them goldplated at a little shop in East L.A. They could pass for FBI badges even with people familiar with the real thing. If no one looked closely, that is. Always if no one looked closely.

The heavyset man stepped forward.

"What time does the bus from Fort Erie get here?" McDade asked.

The man looked at his watch. "Any time now," he said.

"We're interested in one of the passengers," McDade told him. Then he seemed to notice that one of the clerk's eyes was popping out of his head. He turned to look at us. George Greene was bringing up the rear with the Thompson submachine gun hanging casually from the end of his right arm.

McDade waved in a gesture of dismissal. "Put that thing back in our vehicle," he ordered. "We won't be needing it."

When the bus appeared, the customs agent walked over to it with us and stood there watching. Rita and I followed him when he climbed aboard to walk down the aisle, asking each passenger in turn, "Where were you born?"

When he reached Mary Farris, Rita and I took over. We got her out of her seat and walked her to the rear of the bus. I blocked the aisle while Rita ran her hands over the older woman, simulating a quick body search

She came up with a plastic bag filled with suspicious white powder and snapped a pair of handcuffs onto Mary's wrists. Then we hustled her off the bug, crying, and over to one of our waiting cars. McDade paused to thank the customs agent for his cooperation before we drove off.

※

BACK AT THE VACANT STORE, we sat on a couple of the cots and rehashed the whole operation, trying to find anything that might be improved. We couldn't. At last, Harvey Farris peeled off his false mustache and gave his wife a hug.

"You should get an Academy Award for that performance," he said. "We all should."

McDade was the only specter of gloom. "Taking that money sack from the armored car won't be as easy as it was to get Mary off the bus," he said.

"No," I said, "it'll be easier. That bus could have been a problem. Suppose there had been a real smuggler aboard? He might have panicked when we climbed on to get Mary. There's no telling what might have happened. We can be certain that armored car crew won't try to resist federal agents."

"That's right," Greene seconded. He hefted the Thompson replica. "Or my little toy. Did you see their eyes bug out in the Customs House?"

"It's like we are playing April Fool, only we have the month wrong," I said. Everyone laughed.

The adrenaline was pumping in all of us. It was an hour before any of us wanted to stop celebrating our success. Then we went out to eat in ones and twos to keep from being remembered.

When Rita and I were waiting for our dessert in Denny's, I spotted Alfie in a booth by himself. He was busy scribbling in a thick notebook. I had to marvel at how he could think of his writing with everything that was going on. It made me reevaluate him. Anyone who was that determined to make it as a writer would surely succeed. It was just a matter of time.

There had been one disquieting thing that day. When McDade let his jacket swinging open so the customs agent could see his holstered revolver, I had seen it, too. It'd had ivory grips. None of the replica revolvers I had bought on Hollywood Boulevard had ivory grips. I kept that fact to myself.

Everyone else slept late the next day, but I was out of the store before anyone could ask where I was going. I bought a canvas sack similar to the one used to transport the race track currency, stuffed it with dummy bundles of paper, and put it in the trunk of the blue Taurus. I've never been accused of being too trusting.

❊

THE ROBBERY WENT OFF WITHOUT A HITCH. While the "arrested" armored car crew was being hustled into the back seat of the grey Taurus, I placed the money sack in the blue's luggage compartment beside the dummy satchel. We sped away in minutes with no one the wiser. The customs officers even waved goodbye to us.

We stopped a mile away to handcuff the crew around a telephone pole beside the thruway. Then we raced to the parking lot behind a school on Elmwood Avenue to remove the phony plates and put the Michigan tags back on the cars.

McDade got there ahead of us and finished first. Then he

came over to me and stood menacingly with his hand on the butt of the ivory-handled revolver.

"I want to carry the money in my car," he said past tight lips.

"No problem," I answered. I went to the rear of the blue Taurus, hoisted out the dummy sack, and gave it to him. I'd never seen him look so surprised.

When Rita, Harvey, and I left the parking lot, we headed directly for the store. At the intersection of Sheridan and Elmwood, we saw Alfie and George standing on the corner.

"McDade pushed us out of the car," Alfie complained when I coasted to a stop beside them.

"Don't worry about it," I told him. "Climb in. We have plenty of room."

The plan called for us to spend the night in the store and leave town in the morning after the initial search had passed. That's what we did. McDade never showed up. I figure he drove all the way to Erie, Pennsylvania, before stopping to look at the money. I would have loved to have seen is expression when he discovered the sack was stuffed with cut-up telephone books.

The next day everyone was awake at first light, but we remained inside the store until traffic picked up. George Greene took the guns, badges, and just about everything else that could be incriminating to the foot of Ferry Street and dumped them into the river. The rest of us stopped at the UPS office on our way out of the city to ship the money to Rita's address in Los Angeles.

We drove straight through to Detroit and rejoined Greene there. He turned in the blue Taurus and learned that McDade had already returned the other rental. I half expected McDade to jump out at us when we went to pick up the cars in the long-term parking lot, but he didn't.

We retraced our route across the country the same way we had come. Only this time we were one man short. No one missed him.

The newspapers were filled with stories about the robbery. The FBI was looking for a gang of seasoned professionals, but they admitted they had few clues to go on. That made us feel more confident, but it didn't stop us from looking through our rear windows more often than necessary. None of us would have been surprised to see an army of federal agents in hot pursuit.

I suppose McDade took a bus or plane out of Detroit, but I never did find out for sure how he got back to California. I only know that when I drove to his home in Sherman Oaks to give him his share of the loot, he answered the door. He took the package without a word. He didn't even have the courtesy to be embarrassed.

It took about two weeks for the stories to disappear from the newspapers. It was two months before we stopped looking over our shoulders and resumed our normal lives. We didn't talk about the robbery even among ourselves. It was almost as though doing so might jinx us in some way.

But none of the others hesitated to spend his share. As usually happens with a first big score, the money ran through fingers like water. They all thought of the loot in terms of money, something to spend. Capital was a concept they didn't understand.

Rita paid off all her debts and had her air conditioning repaired. Alfie quit his job at the shoe store where he had worked and devoted all his time to writing. George Greene bought his wife a new car and got another for himself. The Farrises took a first-class cruise to the Orient. When I drove past McDade's house one night I noticed there was a new wing and the old roof had been replaced. They all made dozens of smaller purchases, too.

Like the Farrises, I had been involved for the action, not the money. All I did was trade in my old Ford for a slightly less ancient convertible. I didn't want to set off any alarms in my parole officer's head.

Rita and I were spending more time together despite the fact that she now worked full-time at the hospital. And I began thinking of marriage. She wanted a husband, and I knew a writer could always use a wife with a job. I was almost convinced it was the thing to do.

Then a year after the robbery, I received a postcard from McDade, saying he wanted to hold our next meeting at his house. I was pretty sure I knew what was on his mind. We had gotten away clean, and his share was gone. Full of confidence, but like me, needing the bravery only a group could provide, he wanted us to do it again. If it hadn't been him, it would have been one of the others. I had been expecting it.

The day of the meeting I drove to Encino to kill a little time at a bookstore before driving to McDade's place. I read the dust jackets on a few best sellers and bought myself a couple of new books. Then I took a leisurely drive to McDade's home.

All except Alfie had arrived ahead of me. They were gathered around the pool table in McDade's new game room, waiting.

McDade didn't waste any time. "Let's do it again," he said as I came through the doorway.

His selective memory was amazing. He had forgotten the sneaky trick he had tried to pull in Buffalo, or he hoped I had.

He pressed on: "The robbery went off like magic," he said. "There wasn't one problem. We're a great team. We can pull off another one somewhere. I know it."

"That's right," Green said. "We can do it again."

The Farrises nodded agreement.

Rita remained silent, taking her lead from me.

I shook my head. "No, we can't."

"But we got away with it once. You're not sore about that little misunderstanding we had in Buffalo, are you?"

"There's no misunderstanding," I told him, "and we didn't get away with it. We'll be in jail within a week."

McDade's mouth fell open in consternation. "What the hell are you talking about?" he blustered.

"This!" I tossed a book into the center of the pool table. "Alfie had a book published today. It's called *April Fool in August,* the story of how a group of Los Angeles writers rob an armored car in Buffalo and get away with it. He even uses our real names."

JULIAN SYMONS

In the Bluebell Wood

LANCE COULD NOT REMEMBER a time before he knew about King
Arthur, the Knights of the Round Table, and the fact that he
had been named for the most famous of them. The bluebell
wood too had its place in this. It was his father who told him
the stories, about the coming of Arthur, the beauty of Guinevere, and her love of Lancelot. At first the stories were from
a big book called the *Morte D'Arthur*, but then they came from
poems, poems called the *Idylls of the King* written by a man
named Tennyson, which was his father's surname and, as he
learned, his own.

In adolescence, thinking back, he remembered being in
bed, fingers twitching the sheets, his father's face above him
uttering passionately words he did not quite understand—
honour, chivalry—and phrases that stayed in his mind even
though he did not understand their meaning—"Live pure,
speak true, right wrong, follow the king—else, wherefore
born?" There was nothing in the poems about a bluebell
wood, yet when he closed his eyes after the readings he
quite distinctly saw himself, Lancelot, riding with Guinevere, dismounting at a stile, then walking hand in hand with
her down a grassy path to the dimness of a wood carpeted
with bluebells. . . . And when he opened his eyes the words
flowed round him still:

> Many a bard, without offence,
> Has linked our names together in his lay,
> Lancelot, the flower of bravery, Guinevere
> The pearl of beauty

163

The face of the storyteller loomed large above him, eyes magnified by round spectacles. He knew the rough feel of army cloth on his bare arm, the smell of tobacco. His father was home on leave during the war. What was the war, why did his father wear a uniform and not armor, what did he do when he left home again, did he follow the king?

Nothing like that, his mother said. Anyway, she added laughing, if Lionel did follow the king he'd soon lost sight of him. "Your father's blind as a bat without his glasses. He does hush-hush work."

"What's hush-hush?"

"Secret. Work that keeps him away. Very important."

"For the king?"

"I suppose you could say that. For king and country."

They lived on the fringe of London, in an area that had missed almost all the wartime bombing. They had a little red brick house with a tiny front garden and one at the back that was a little bigger. The house next door was just the same, and the one next door to that, and so on down the road. "Only way to tell 'em apart is by numbers," his mother Esme said. "Know what we are?" she asked neighbors. "Rabbits in hutches, that's what."

"Good job we don't breed like 'em."

"You can take precautions."

They went off into fits of laughter. Esme was small, dark, quick moving. The neighbor, whose husband was fighting somewhere in Italy, was named Louise. They saw a lot of each other. When Lance came home from the school that was just three minutes' walk away, Louise would often be in the kitchen. Esme got his tea and they sat with him while he ate it, both smoking so that the room became blue with it, and talking incomprehensibly. He imagined Lancelot riding through those blue mists, freeing a fair maiden; then meeting Guinevere, they crossed the stile . . . Fragments of phrases came through to him.

". . . Dead and alive hole . . . see more life in a factory . . . you got a kid, you got a millstone around your neck . . ."

His father came home on weekend leave from the hush-hush job quite often and read from the *Idylls* about Gareth and Lynette, Merlin and Vivien, and what he loved most, Lancelot and Guinevere. Lying in bed, waiting for his father to come upstairs, he heard voices raised, his mother's sometimes almost a shriek.

It was when his father was at the hush-hush job that the visitor came. He was there when Lance came back from school, a tall smiling man who wore a much smarter uniform than his father's, and one with stars which the boy knew meant he was an officer, while his father had only the stripes of a sergeant. The officer's name was Pierre, and Esme said he belonged to the Free French. Pierre made pennies and a shilling come out of his ears, and gave them to Lance. Then Esme said she'd arranged for him to have tea and play with Tim Collins, who lived a few doors down the road. The arrangement was unusual, almost unknown.

"I don't want to." He began to cry.

Esme's temper was short. "You'll do as you're told. You're going out to tea, is that a reason to be a crybaby?"

"Look here." Pierre produced another shilling from his ear. "Why don't you and your friend Tim see what you can buy with this?"

When he was home again his mother said: "I was ashamed of you, crying just because you'd been asked out to tea." He made no reply. "Did you like Pierre?"

"Don't know."

"He's just a friend. Of Louise's really. No need to mention him to your father. Did you hear me?" He nodded. "Say yes when you're spoken to."

"Yes."

He said nothing to his father, even though he saw Pierre again more than once—just leaving as he came home from school, in the kitchen where he made jokes when they had tea together, once coming out of the bathroom wearing only shirt and pants. Did Lance understand what was happening? That was a question he never asked himself later on. At the time he was simply puzzled when Tim Collins, who never had been a friend of his, and his mother was having it off with a frog. Having what off? he wondered, and he had only seen pictures of frogs.

But although he said nothing, he did compare the round-shouldered goggle-eyed figure in a uniform that never seemed to fit properly with upright, trim, smiling Pierre, whose trousers had a crease of knife-edged sharpness, and who could make shillings come out of his ears. Then suddenly the war was over, there was a big party in their road with lots of food, including things he had never seen, like bananas, all set out on trestle tables, dancing and drinking. Pierre was seen no more; someone said he had gone back to France, and good riddance. Esme went around red-eyed, and shorter tempered than usual. And Lionel Tennyson, no longer Sergeant Tennyson, was demobbed, came home, went back to his work in the Ministry. Yes, he said to Lance, who was now in primary school, the war was really over.

"And we won. We beat the bad men like Sir Mordred, the good knights won." By this time Lance was reading the *Idylls* himself, knew some of the exciting bits by heart.

"The good knights won," his father echoed. They were in the bow-windowed living room. On the walls were reproductions of Victorian pictures, one showing the passing of Arthur, another Lancelot and Guinevere. He stood, in full armor, looking at his drawn sword, she knelt and gazed at him yearningly, her long fair hair around her face and falling to her waist, feet showing below the pure white of her robe. A silver-plated figure of King Arthur stood on the mahogany sideboard, drawing the magic sword Excalibur from its scabbard.

Yes, his father said, but it was not like King Arthur. "Bombs instead of swords nowadays. More's the pity."

"But the stories are all really true, aren't they?"

"Oh yes, yes, yes." His father became excited, as he had been reading aloud about Lancelot's deeds as an unknown knight at a tournament. "They are all true, and you must never forget them. That's why you were named Lancelot." He still read to his son sometimes at night, until Esme said the boy was too old for that now, it just encouraged him to be childish.

Afterwards Lance remembered these years of adolescence as an idyll in his own life. His father went to work each day to the Ministry and he went to school, got good reports, came back, did his homework, and then read a romantic story like *Kidnapped* or *Under the Red Robe*. Later, in bed, he read the *Idylls*. Afterwards he tried to remember something Esme had said that showed dissatisfaction with this life, which for her was one of keeping house and cooking, but could recall nothing. There was none of the arguments he had heard downstairs when he was a child, she was meticulous as ever in seeing that meals were cooked on time and in cleaning the house so that everything smelt of furniture polish.

Then one day she was gone. He came home one day to find tea on the table, bread and margarine, jam, scones she had made the previous day. He ate, washed up the things, settled down in the kitchen to his homework. When his father came home he said: "Mum's out." Mr. Tennyson nodded, went upstairs, came down again five minutes later looking paler than usual, eyes behind thick glasses vacant as those of a fish. He sat down at the kitchen table, put his head in his hands, and said to his son: "She's taken all her things, everything. Gone."

Lance was aware of his open mouth, closed it, said gone where? His father shook his head. "When will she be coming back?"

"She isn't. You remember a man coming round two or three weeks ago selling vacuum cleaners, or trying to?" Lance nodded. "She's gone off with him. With a vacuum cleaner salesman."

Lance put an arm around his father's shoulder. "We can manage. Until she comes back."

"She hates me, she says so in the letter. She'll never come back." He raised a face wet with tears.

Esme didn't come back. And Mr. Tennyson was quite incapable of managing. He burned meat and undercooked vegetables, and since these were days before frozen foods, they ate mostly out of tins. A woman who came in to do housework stole the few valuable things in the house, including the figure of King Arthur. Within a year, the house had been sold and they moved into a small flat in the same area, but in a main road with lorries rattling by day and night. It was cheaper, less trouble, a cleaner came in from a couple of hours each week, there was nothing to steal. The Victorian prints of Arthur, Lancelot, and Guinevere remained, although they looked out of place in the tiny living room. There was no garden, and Mr. Tennyson loved gardening. One day Lance asked what the secret work was that his father had done in the war.

"Helping to decode German messages. I'm a statistician, you see, good at analyzing sets of numbers and figures. I was one of a team. What we did was really quite important."

He sensed that this was delicate ground. "But no fighting?"

"No fighting. I wouldn't have been much good at it. Like you, I can't see very well." And Lance, looking in the mirror, saw that his glasses were almost as thick as his father's, his face the same moon shape. So what was his father's job now at the Ministry, was it still important work?

Not really. Mostly paperwork. Ordering materials for use in government contracts, then following them through, checking prices, keeping suppliers on their toes about delivery, making sure they don't overcharge. It's secure, you see, that's the great thing. When you're in the civil service you have a job for life. I'm not a doer, you know, but I love the stories, and I wanted you to love them too. And of course there's my name, that made me read the poems first of all. I was called Lionel, and Lionel Tennyson was a great cricketer, captain of England. But I'm a reader, not a doer. It was kind of separate life for me."

A separate life, a secret life. Perhaps that conversation was the beginning for Lance of the secret life in which he was somebody different from the awkward teenager who looked uneasily at the world through round spectacles, was shy with girls and no good at games. In the secret life Judy, who burst into laughter when he asked if she would like to go with him to a rock concert, said wistfully that she thought Lancelot was a beautiful name, and wished she was called Guinevere and not dull Judy. "To me you will always be Guinevere," he said as she leaned towards him, opening her lips for the kiss.

The closest of Lance's few friends at school was Rod Williams, who told all sorts of tales about his father's adventures as a scrap dealer. "What's your father do?" Rod asked. "Office job, isn't it, pen pushing?"

"Not really. It's hush-hush work."

"But what's he *do?*"

"He's an agent."

"What, MI 5?"

"More secret. He's part of a very small group, they have to protect the queen. The other royals too, but the queen especially. I think it's mostly the IRA they're worried about, but he doesn't tell me the details. I'm not supposed to talk about it. Swear you won't tell anyone."

Rod swore, but of course told his father. Later Lance showed Rod a newspaper photograph of an IRA bomb explosion in the Midlands and said one of the figures inspecting the wreckage as his father.

"Thought you said he was protecting the queen. What's this got to do with her?"

Lance realized he had made a mistake. "That isn't all his group does. They've got other duties."

Rod was a large youth with small eyes and a pig's upturned nose. "My dad says you're making it all up. Just fairy stories, he says."

"Your dad doesn't *know*." But after that Lance gave up the stories about his father, who was becoming more and more absent-minded, withdrawn into what Lance supposed were secret thoughts. In the evening, after supper, he switched on the television and sat staring at it with no apparent awareness of what he was watching.

He received a few letters, but one morning a long envelope came, name and address typed. Mr. Tennyson examined the postmark, turned over the envelope, and looked at the back (Lance thought immediately of secret messages), slit it open, read the contents carefully, pushed aside his cereal, took off his glasses and wiped his eyes, spoke.

"Your mother. She's dead. A car accident. She was on her own. Apparently she'd been drinking."

Lance felt nothing. It seemed to him an age ago that they had lived in the red brick house with the front and back garden, that Pierre had made shillings come out of his ears, his father had come home on leave and read the *Idylls* to him. A curtain had been dropped in his mind, concealing that world as if it had never existed. Reality was here and now, the little flat where he lived, the school he would soon be leaving, and the secret world in which Judy/Guinevere entered the arms of Lancelot.

"I loved her, you know. In spite of everything, I loved her. We were never divorced and I always hoped she could come back. I know it was my fault." At that, Lance was indignant. Esme had left her home and her child, how could it have been her husband's fault? Mr. Tennyson shook his head. "You don't understand, how could you? She was a kind of dream to me, and she didn't like dreamers." He gave his son what almost seemed a glare through the pebbled glasses. "What about you? You're leaving at the end of this term, what do you want to do?"

"I don't know. I don't want to go to a university. Something exciting."

His father's laugh was a rusty caw. "No money for a university, I can tell you that. Something exciting, that's stupid."

"What you used to read me, the *Idylls*, that was exciting."

"That was reading, poetry. Very nice, but not real. Perhaps I shouldn't have—you must get started, that's the thing. I might be able to help." For a moment Lance had a vision of his own place in that imaginary world in which his father was an agent, but the next words dispelled it. "Customs and Excise."

"What?"

"A customs officer, a good safe job. I'll make inquiries, might be able to pull some strings."

And the strings were pulled, so that Lance became a member of HM Customs and Excise. There was a training period in which he learned what to look out for, the sort of travellers likely to have watches loaded on both arms, the likely drug stuffers and swallowers, the foolish innocents who thought they could break the rules just this once and showed awareness of it in their faces and gestures.

It sounded exciting, and he imagined scenes in which the secret life became reality. There would be a woman traveler, not exactly beautiful but elegant, stylish, the kind of woman whose very appearance left him tongue-tied. She walked through the "Nothing to Declare" channel at the airport, cool and faintly disdainful. He asked her to open a case, and her raised eyebrows asked, *Can you really mean it?*, but were then replaced by a panic-stricken *I may just have forgotten* . . . And then the opened case revealed—what? Something forgivable, an undeclared item from St. Laurent, a small storehouse of scents, something on which she need not be taken to court.

Afterwards she was grateful, asking his name, was enchanted to know that it was Lancelot, suggested a meeting— but at that point fantasy was checked, for there were strict rules about such matters and he was not sure that he wanted to break them. In any case, the disdainful elegant ladies remained in his imagination. He encountered in his duties instead pathetic Africans or South Americans who carried drugs in stomach or anus, or petty villains who traveled a lot by air on genuine business, and fancied their chances of getting drugs or watches through Customs as a kind of perk. Being a Customs officer at an airport, as he said to his father, was as dull a job as any other.

A few months after Lance began to work, Mr. Tennyson

took early retirement from the Ministry. Was the retirement purely voluntary, or had it been urged on him by his superiors? Either way, he showed unmistakable signs of a mental decline that was more than absentmindedness. He would go out shopping, wander off to a nearby park, sit there for an hour or two, and return having forgotten to do the shopping. In the flat he let milk boil over on the stove, forgot to turn off a gas fire so that it burned all night, and almost caused a fire by leaving an electric iron on while watching television. At times he thought Esme was still alive and was coming back to live with them, so that he cleared a cupboard for her clothes and rearranged all the furniture. When Lance first got the Customs and Excise job he thought of looking for an apartment on his own, but it was borne in on him that this was not possible. He would have to look after his father, who although insisting that he was perfectly well (and seeming healther than when he was at the Ministry) admitted to becoming absent-minded.

Mr. Tennyson's interest in the *Idylls* had lapsed after news of Esme's death, but it revived in retirement. He read biographies of Tennyson, and deluged Lance with quotations from the *Idylls*, most of them designed to dampen what he saw as his son's unhealthy yearning for excitement. Life, he said, was a great teacher, and he quoted: "A young man will be wiser by and by." Not only a great teacher, Life, but it cut you down to size. "The dirty nurse, Experience, in her kind hath foul'd me"—Lance should remember that this had happened to his father in the sad loss of his wife. After he had gained experience, he should look for a nice girl, and inevitably he quoted: "In the spring a young man's fancy—"

Brutality was not in Lance's nature, but he came near to it then. "And what would you do when I found a girl, live with us? My wife might have something to say about that."

Nothing like that, Mr. Tennyson said, adding with insufferable complacency: "No need to worry, I can look after myself." The obvious truth was that he couldn't.

But the problem didn't arise, because Elaine, the fair maid of Astolat who died for love of Lancelot, and Guinevere, whom he loved guiltily, remained as much figures of the secret world as the disdainful woman traveler. Lance found it hard to know what to say to girls. When he looked in the glass a moon face stared back at him with eyes owlish behind the round glasses and a head that wobbled so much on its thin neck that it seemed likely to fall off. What girl would fancy someone who looked like that?

On the other hand, it was true that Rod, who was certainly not handsome, pulled plenty of girls. He chatted them up when they stopped at the stall he had in the local market, where he sold all sorts of odds and ends including stuff bought by his father the scrap merchant. "Nothing to it," Rod said, little pig eyes twinkling. "Couple of drinks, bit of chat, and bang you're in."

That was all right perhaps for Rod, who had his own place, but Lance couldn't possibly have shocked his father by taking a girl back to their flat. Rod immediately said to go back with him, Lance could have the bedroom, he wasn't fussy, he and his girl would manage on the sitting room sofa. Got to get your leg over sometime, Rod said, plenty of nooky about, no need to pay prossies for it. The sly sideways glance he gave when saying that was justified. Lance had been with prostitutes. Such encounters at least involved no chatting up, but although as Rod put it he got his leg over, these brief encounters were not satisfying. After them he felt ashamed, for they seemed a betrayal of the tall, fair, slender girl he met in the secret life, the girl to whom no words had been spoken, no explanations made. They met, crossed the stile, walked hand in hand towards the darkness of the wood and the brightness of the bluebells that made a carpet within it, and then lay down together.

It was through Rod that the secret life and Lance's everyday world became one. Rod played for a pub darts team, and occasionally Lance went along to watch. Two girls were with Rod, one fair, one dark.

"Del, you know Lance," Rod said. "Gwyn, this is Lance I was telling you about, works in Customs. Want to watch out for him, he's a tiger, so they tell me." General laughter. "You should see him in his uniform, he's hot stuff."

"I can imagine," the dark girl said, not joking, as if she meant it.

Lance bought a round. The dark girl spoke to him. "Rod was on about you, said you were dead clever, only you don't talk much. Why's that?"

"Nothing to say, I expect."

"Doesn't stop me, Del, does it? You either." She laughed, showing regular teeth. "Who was it said 'I've got a big head, only there's nothing in it,' Princess Di was it? Anyway, that's me. But you, Lance, I bet you're deep. Is he deep, Rod?"

"Deep as the deep blue sea," Rod said. At this too there was laughter, and Lance did not feel it was directed at him. When the dark girl went on to ask what he was thinking about he said: "All right, I'll tell you. Your name, Gwyn. Why are you called that, what's it short for?"

"Nosy, aren't we? Okay, I don't mind telling, it's Gwyneth. Gwyneth Lewis, there's Welsh for you. What about Lance, what sort of name is that?"

For once, strangely, he did not mind saying his name was Lancelot, even added that he thought Gwyn might have been short for Guinevere.

"That's King Arthur, I know about him, saw the film. She was Arthur's wife. But then she and Lancelot—" She looked at Lance, burst out laughing.

A couple of hours and more than a couple of drinks later, the darts match lost, Rod said to him at the bar: "You're well away there, boy, Gwyn fancies you."

"She does?" Rod closed one little eye. But it still seemed incredible to Lance, and in any case, where could he take Gwyn, who was dark instead of fair but still might really be Guinevere? He was not sure he had enough money for a hotel. But that turned out to be no problem at all. When they left the pub she took his arm and said: "My place, all right?"

What followed was shocking, exciting, and exhausting, quite unlike the brief encounters he had known. Just after midnight he remembered his father, said he must telephone.

"You what?"

"I must tell my father. He'll be worried."

She stared at him, and for a moment he thought she was going to tell him to get out, go home. Instead she put up a hand, stroked his cheek. "You're funny. Okay, there's the phone."

His father's voice was first indignant, then petulant. Did Lance know the time, surely he could have rung earlier, where was he, why couldn't he come home? At the end he said Lance was unkind and thoughtless, and put down the telephone without saying goodbye.

In the morning she made toast and coffee, then went back to bed. He asked if she was out of work.

"I'm on and off, and this week's off. I do jobs for a travel agency, escorting groups, mostly Spain and Portugal. Bloody hard work, don't let anyone tell you different. Next week I'm taking some old dears to Amsterdam, coach tour." She laughed. "Last time I mislaid one, turned out he'd gone to the casino, won a bagful of money, got beaten up, landed in hospital. They blamed me, wouldn't you know?"

When Lance had dressed, he didn't know what he should say. "Can I—" He began again. "I mean, I don't suppose you're free—"

"Thought you'd never ask. Free as air, Lance. Funny name, but I like it, reminds me of something, wonder what it can be?"

"What—oh, I see." He blushed, and she laughed. She did not speak the language of Guinevere, and she was not like the woman who inhabited the secret world, but her face coalesced in the image of the fair-haired Guinevere who knelt at Lancelot's feet.

When he stood in the Customs hall and sat in the canteen, the Gwyn who walked beside him in the secret world, who crossed the stile and went down the path with him to the bluebell wood, was Gwyn who had been transformed into Guinevere.

Each evening after work he met her. Twice they went out with Rod and his Delia, but he liked it best when they were on their own. They saw a movie, went to a concert, ate in cheap restaurants, and talked—or for the most part Lance talked and she listened, for his difference had gone, he had become eloquent, talking of King Arthur and the *Idylls* and Lancelot's love for Guinevere. And they went to bed, about which she was more urgent than he. The physical act offered a kind of fulfillment of his worship of Guinevere, yet something about it seemed to him messy and coarse, unlike love in the secret world. There you kissed and fondled, but there was none of the sticky gluing of mouth to mouth, nor the moans and subdued shrieks that Gwyn uttered, sounds that had no place in a Tennysonian idyll.

After that first night they spent only evenings together. Mr. Tennyson grumbled about his late return to the flat, but accepted Lance's explanation about being short-handed and working extra hours, and one of his colleagues at work said he seemed almost human, instead of going through the motions like a robot. Only Gwyn showed dissatisfaction when he left her. "You don't want to stay, that it?" she asked. Lance said his father, an old man, couldn't be left alone to look after himself. She shook her head.

"You got to look after number one in this world. And have fun. Still, we do that, don't we?" He said yes, although the physical business was something he found increasingly a problem, and having fun was not an adequate description of the joy he had in the secret world which he could create even in the canteen or walking along the street—but most of all in bed alone at night when coarse-speaking Gwyn became sweet Guinevere. He was transported into that life even in her presence now, so that one evening she tapped his forehead and said: "Anyone home? Didn't hear, did you? I said next week I can't see you, taking these old dears to Amsterdam. Not that the red-light district there will do any of 'em much good." Her laugh was loud. "We'll be back Saturday though, I can see you Sunday. Thing is, are you on that weekend?" He said he was.

"I want you to stop me, check my bags." She went on quickly. "Tell you why. My boss is coming on the trip, nosy bastard, one of the other girls has got it in for me, told him I'm bringing in stuff I shouldn't, know what I mean? So my younger brother, Billy, he wants to watch, I'm going to buy one out there, go through the 'Something to Declare' channel, pay the duty, okay?"

"Yes, but I don't see—"

"You look at the rest of my gear, check it, give it the okay, show the little fat bastard that's my boss where he gets off trying to climb into bed with me. Which is all he wants, I may say. I hate fat men, starving lean hungry ones are my meat." She giggled. "Just think what Sunday'll be like when I'm back, I'll have been good for a week."

He hardly missed her physical presence in the week while she was away. She existed in the secret world, transformed into the Guinevere of the *Idylls* by a chaste radiant glow that surrounded her. He imagined her watching him fighting in the tournament, telling him that she loved him even though she knew this love to be a betrayal, but the scene more persistent in his mind was that when they walked along the path to the bluebell wood, and there lay down together in a tree's green shade. It was the world he had so often read about made real, that world

Where falls not hail, or rain, or any snow,
Nor ever wind blows loudly, but it lies
Deep-meadow'd, happy, fair with orchard lawns
And bowery hollows crown'd with summer sea

Mr. Tennyson cheered up no end having his son home every
evening, managed some shopping and cooking successfully,
and said it was just like old times. The Chief Customs Officer
at the airport, on the other hand, said Lance wanted to wake
his ideas up, he looked like a tit in a trance, and it was true
that as he stood with a couple of other officers, smart in their
uniforms, he absented himself from the passengers who
streamed past looking happy, eager, or anxious, pushing and
wheeling bags and cases.

He was absent in the world of Lancelot, or only half present,
when a voice said: "Got the receipt somewhere," and he was
suddenly aware of Gwyn before him, Gwyn pushing a trolley
that held a suitcase and a holdall. She wore a dark blue rain-
coat and a jaunty blue hat with a red feather in it. Behind her
a fellow Customs officer whose carrot-colored hair had
brought him the name Red, mouthed something silently and
grinned. There was no sign of the little fat boss, who had
perhaps gone through the "Nothing to Declare" channel with
the rest of the party.

Lance looked at the watch she showed him in its case, and
at the receipt, got a list to check the duty payable, tapped the
case and holdall, and asked her to open them.

Gwyn looked at Red in mock despair, he shook is head sympathetically. She unlocked the case, zipped open the holdall,
overdramatically gave him her handbag, stood back.

Lance's fingers moved lightly among the jacket and skirts,
underwear, powder, lipstick, scent. He replaced them, and was
about to zip up the holdall when beneath his fingertips he felt
the hint of an obstacle, nothing more than a rucked-up bit of
lining perhaps, except that no lining should have existed there.
He looked up to find Gwyn's large dark eyes staring into his
own challengingly, expectantly. His fingers moved further,
more carefully, over the holdall's surface, and he knew that
obstacle was not a natural one.

There was then a moment of uncertainty for him, a moment
when Gwyn's lips—could they ever have been Guinevere's?—

curved in a confident smile. Then the smile was broken, the whole shape of her face seemed to change and splinter as he picked up her bags and said they would need to examine them more closely. She made for him, claws out and spitting words never used by Guinevere, and Red had to help him restrain her.

The velour-lined false pocket in the holdall contained uncut diamonds, emeralds, and sapphires. As Red said wonderingly, it was hard to see why the little bitch played it the way she did, calling attention to herself over the watch. If she'd gone through the "Nothing to Declare" channel she'd have had a chance of getting through, though they always took a hard look at couriers in charge of groups. As it was, Gwyneth Lewis was duly charged, and released on bail.

✳

"YOU'RE SILENT TONIGHT," Mr. Tennyson said. "Something on your mind?"

"Betrayal."

"What's that? Something from the *Idylls?*"

"Not from the *Idylls*. I'm going out."

He wandered aimlessly about the streets, found himself outside the pub where he met Gwyn, went in. Rod was at the bar, a glass raised. Beer sprayed from his mouth when he saw Lance. "You got a nerve," he said, "coming in here, showing your face."

"I don't understand."

"Gwyn gave it to you straight enough, didn't she? Asked you to check her stuff, what you think she did that for? So you could shop her? All you had to do was charge duty on the watch, pass her through, there was a century in it for you. Woulda been more next time. Whatsa matter, more stupid than you look, are you?" Rod's snout was very close to Lance. "You landed everybody in it, me included for making the intro. And you should look out, she's Corney Barrow's girl."

Corney Barrow was well known locally, a villain reputed to have a hand in everything from acting as a fence to selling dope. "You mean—"

"I said I made the intro, Corney wanted an in at the airport, I said you could be useful getting stuff through. Now you dropped his girl in it. You want to watch yourself, mate. I were you, I'd move out of the area for a while." Lance said that was not possible because of his father. "Suit yourself," Rod said, and turned away.

So he had been betrayed by Gwyn, and betrayed her in his turn, because he had been forced to realize she was Gwyneth Lewis and not Guinevere. But as he went from one pub to another, drinking whisky, to which he was unused, the image of Gwyn faded and was replaced wholly by that of Guinevere, looking as in the picture so lovingly, so yearningly, at Lancelot. The luster of her fair hair was with him as he left the last pub, and three of them came out after him. He saw light flash and steel, heard only faintly the voice say something about a present from Corney. There was a pain in his side, a dull but deepening pain, and he felt himself truly Sir Lancelot, suffering as "a spear prick'd sharply his own cuirass, and the head pierc'd thro' his side, and there snapt, and remain'd." Lancelot then cried out her name: "Guinevere," he cried, "the flower of all the west and all the world," He hardly felt what seemed the hoofbeats trampling and kicking him, and in his last moments was aware only that Guinevere had taken his hand and was leading him down to the peace of the bluebell wood where they would rest forever.

DONALD OLSON

Willie's Last Trip

EXCEPT FOR MY NEIGHBOR ACROSS THE HALL I have no friends here at the Spanish Gates, nor am I likely to have. Unless a miracle occurs I won't be able to stay here much longer; they've just raised the rent and I am already beyond the break-even point.

I rise and shower and shave, the dullness of my razor blade demonstrating to what extent I'm obliged to practice even the most trivial of demeaning economies. Which reminds me, I must get to the stationery store; my agent, the last time I heard from her, suggested tactfully it might be time I invested in a new typewriter ribbon.

Dragging myself to the ancient Royal, I force myself to overcome the paralyzing inertia that set in the same morning my neighbor Willie Van Netten burst into my apartment with a handful of travel folders about Mexico. As he started babbling about the latest trip he was planning, that insidious worm of envy, nourished by too many descriptions of Willie's exotic holidays, began to swell into a monster of hatred.

Above my desk hangs a small reproduction of an eighteenth-century print titled "The Swiss Drummer." In the forefront a figure in gold and scarlet uniform stares straight into my eyes as I lift my gaze from the typewriter, my fingers frozen above the keys as if for all time, like the hands of the drummer gripping his drumsticks. His piercing black eyes seem to mock the impotence of my imagination. I reach blindly for a cigarette I can't afford and which will leave me as unsatisfied as the one before. Finally, I get up and stand at the window watching the swirling eddies of snow dapple the pane, and I dream of Mexico and the sun.

The telephone rings. I know even before answering it that it will be my neighbor across the hall beseeching some favor. I will myself not to answer, but of course I do. Any excuse to escape from the typewriter.

Suddenly I make up my mind: I shall *make* that miracle happen. "Sorry, Willie, I can't possibly. I'm right in the middle of chapter eleven."

Willie brushes this quibble aside. "Rubbish, old boy. You can squeeze your writing in any time. You must come shopping with me. I need your advice."

How I loathe being told I can squeeze my writing in any time, but I hold my tongue and cross the hall. I sit in Willie's living room, my body licking up the heat like a stray dog let in from the cold. I grow even warmer with resentment as he shows me the maps spread over the coffee table. It was I who'd suggested Mexico when he was pondering where to go on his next trip. He'd grinned at me when I said I would gladly pass up any wonder in the world for a chance to see Mexico. "Then why don't you go?" he'd said. "What's it going to matter when you're dead whether you write that book or not?"

"Not all of us," I'd said drily, "have the good fortune to live on an inheritance."

Pink as a baby and nearly as bald, Willie displays an insensitivity that is probably no more than the egotist's indifference to others, and in many ways he is as artless as a child. His apartment is cluttered with a hodgepodge of possessions ordered mostly from catalogues, for he loves to have parcels delivered to his door, as if Christmas came very day. He always invites me in to admire each new purchase and I have to take care not to betray my distaste for their almost universal vulgarity. (His latest stands on the dining room table: a white plastic fountain spouting a miniature cascade of rainbow-tinted water.)

"I want a whole new wardrobe for Mexico," he announces. "So come along. I'll spring for lunch and pay for the gas, of course." Willie doesn't own a car and has a phobia about driving.

As usual, in the stores we shop, Willie insists I model every garment; we're rather alike in build and coloring and he seems to know my taste is more trustworthy than his. Today, before ending the shopping spree, he also buys two expensive pieces of luggage, which he certainly doesn't need, and then takes me to lunch at the Ironstone, where as usual he does most of the talking. I don't mind. His words drift over my head as I try in my mind to unravel the seemingly insoluble problem of chapter eleven. And then I become aware he is talking about Monica.

"Isn't she still in Florida?" I ask.

"Of course, till the middle of April. That's where she called me from." Willie regards me with a faintly suspicious frown. "She hasn't written to you, or called you by any chance, has she?"

"Me? Why on earth should she?"

"Well, you know Monica. She's not to be trusted with a secret."

"Is there a secret?"

He mumbles some vague reply and tries to change the subject. Monica Dearing is one of Willie's oldest friends, with whom he's enjoyed what he jokingly refers to as the world's longest unofficial engagement. I don't think either of them wish to get married, for they are both set in their ways, headstrong and self-centered. I've met Monica several times at Willie's apartment and found her to be a somewhat tiresome but kindly woman with a sense of humor utterly devoid of malice.

Now I say, "You're not getting any younger, Willie. Who's going to look after you when you're old? You really ought to marry Monica. Take her to Mexico with you on a honeymoon."

His startled reaction to this makes me wonder if the idea has already occurred to him. Could this be the secret he mentioned? But then he shakes his head. "Monica hates Mexico. She's been there. Made her sick."

Presently, he says he'll spare me the bother of taking in his mail while he's away this time. I'll have the post office hold it."

"I don't mind doing it." Willie always entrusts me with his key so I can water his plants and feed the fish and take in his paper and mail. In return, I always receive a postcard from wherever he is and on his return a souvenir of astonishing vulgarity.

"No, I must stop taking advantage of you, dear boy. Monica tells me I don't appreciate your kindness. That's not true. I hope you know that."

"Prove it, I feel like saying. Bring me back something you didn't buy in a souvenir clipjoint. Something not made of *plastic.*

Not that he will have the opportunity. Ever again. But that's *my* secret.

❋

ACROSS FROM THE SPANISH GATES a sprawling municipal park borders an area of dense woodland crisscrossed by bikers' trails. Because his doctor had recommended more exercise, Willie had talked me into joining him on twilight walks around the perimeter of the park, but once bad weather set in he'd lost his enthusiasm. I had not. Now, as I cross the road at sunset and wander through the park and into the woods, I know exactly where I am headed. Excitement warms my body as I reach the spot I've chosen, an area enclosed in a fortress of thorn-bearing trees. The ground is still a bit hard for digging a grave but by the end of the month, when I return from Mexico, it should be no great chore.

Who is to know poor Willie hasn't simply vanished somewhere in the wilds south of the border? It happens all the time.

As I resume my walk I review in my mind each point of my plan. Monica Dearing will not be back from Florida before the middle of April. Willie's apartment will be locked, the key in my possession. His handwriting is so deplorable he always types even his postcards while on a trip. Monica will receive several. I'll drop her a card before leaving to say a relative's sudden demise in California has necessitated my absence from the Spanish Gates. Not that there is much of a chance she'll try to get in touch with me.

Impersonating Willie in Mexico should present no difficulties or alarms, and on my return I shall have acquired a nice little grubstake from his traveling draft, credit cards, and two rings he certainly never bought out of a catalogue. But that is inconsequential. What matters is that in San Miguel de Allende I'll be able to write again. I shall be able to laugh at the Swiss Drummer and his mocking dark eyes.

How could anyone not resent Willie's selfish delight in this upcoming Mexican trip? I seemed to detect in his gloating anticipation a deliberate and callous enjoyment in provoking my envy. Is it any wonder my thoughts have turned murderous?

"Wouldn't you love to be in my shoes?" he said yesterday with a seeming clairvoyance that set my heart to thumping. "Or should I say huaraches? How can you expand your horizons without seeing a bit of the world? What can you write about buried in the Spanish Gates?"

Can you blame me for wanting to murder him? Wasn't he *asking* for it?

And the way he stood there, like a bantam rooster, head cocked to one side, as he insisted I again try on the white linen jacket I'd persuaded him was more suitable than the ghastly plaid he'd wanted to buy. "Can't you just see yourself, my boy, sitting on the terrace of the hotel sipping a Margarita?"

Presently, when I asked him if he was quite certain Monica wouldn't decide to return earlier than planned, he gave me a sharply inquisitive glance. "You haven't heard from her, have you? She hasn't said anything, has she?"

"You already asked me that. Of course she hasn't. But you know how unpredictable women can be."

"Not Monica. She wouldn't dream of coming back early unless she had a very pressing reason. My funeral, for instance."

This gave me a jolt. It was an effort to echo his sudden burst of laughter.

I suffer no doubts about my ability to carry out my plan to murder Willie. My consciousness of the ultimate futility of all human endeavor, coupled with a sad awareness that as an artist my vision far surpasses any gift for expressing it, makes me what I am, explains perhaps that coldness of spirit which is capable under the stress of circumstances of freezing the conscience to a state where even murder is possible. More than possible, vital. My survival as an artist is at stake; only Willie can provide the means of refreshing my deadened sensibilities. Otherwise I myself might as well be dead.

❇

I KNOW ON WILLIE'S DOOR LATE Sunday night, finding him in his robe, in the process of finishing packing the new suitcases. I think for an instant he regards me somewhat crossly, as if I've interrupted him in the midst of an activity I wasn't meant to witness.

"There," he says, shoving a pigskin folder into one of the bags and snapping the latch shut. "My tickets and papers are safely stowed. Here, you'd better hold on to the keys till we get to the airport. You know how forgetful I am. Hard luck if we get there in the morning and I've left the key behind."

Perhaps the only time I feel a tiny spasm of remorse is when he hands me the key: he might be delivering his very life into my hands.

"You don't mind driving me to the airport, do you, my boy? I'm quite willing to take a cab, you know."

"Don't be silly," I say with the merest trace of acerbity. "I wouldn't miss my little game of make-believe. Pretending *I'm* the one taking off."

Now he is eager, he says, to take a warm bath and get into bed. I say I will let myself out; instead, I let myself in—into the closet just off the entrance, and there I stay until I hear Willie turn off the water in the tub. Slipping out of the closet, I pick up an ugly teakwood figurine Willie has brought back from the Philippines, steal silently into the bathroom, and with a couple of well-placed blows send poor Willie on his last trip without so much as a bon voyage.

Except for those monsters among us whose blood lust turns them into serial killers, murder is undeniably the most distasteful of acts, and for a chap as fastidious as myself it is something I should not care to do more than once in my life. Nor do I expect anyone without an artistic temperament to understand the extreme provocation that has led me to do it.

But once the blow is struck—the Rubicon crossed, so to speak—the subsequent tidying up is no more than a disagreeable chore. Cleansed in the tub, Willie's body is soon swaddled in airtight plastic and bundled into that same closet where I concealed myself, there to be left until I return from Mexico at the end of the month.

I may have geared my mind to anticipate the unforeseen; still, the ringing of the phone comes as an awful shock to my nerves. For a second I stand motionless with a pounding heart. I know I can't simply ignore it.

It's Monica.

"Sorry," I say. "Willie's in the tub. He's quite exhausted and wants to go straight to bed. We've just been finalizing the plans for tomorrow."

Her hesitation unnerves me. Has she detected something unnatural in my tone? Then: "I shouldn't have rung so late, darling. I won't disturb him. . . . Tell me the truth. Willie didn't say anything, did he?"

"About what?"

"Our little secret?"

My heart drums louder. "What secret?"

"Oh, good. I know what a blabbermouth he is."

Willie had said the same thing about her. I begin to worry. This is no time for secrets. "Well, as a matter of fact, Monica, he did sort of hint . . ."

It's all she needs. "Darling, that man is incorrigible! I knew he'd let the cat out of the bag. Do you think it's frightfully corny of me to want a June wedding?"

My sign of relief must be clearly audible. "I think it's marvelous. My best wishes, Monica. How's the weather in Florida?"

"Intoxicating! Well, I won't bother Willie now, darling. Give him my love."

I hang up smiling. One thing Monica need never fear is an unhappy marriage, at least to Willie. It suddenly occurs to me that she will need a great deal of consoling when Willie never "returns" from Mexico. Monica is not unattractive, really, if you like the type, and God knows she is well-heeled.

I HAD PLANNED TO LEAVE MY CAR AT HOME and take a taxi to the airport, and as I look down the next morning and see it waiting, I feel for the first time a vivid sense of the reality of what I am doing, while at the same time it seems no longer *I* who am doing it, as if mentally I've already assumed the identity of the man in the closet. The new luggage standing by the door is *my* luggage, containing the clothes and travel accessories *I* have shopped for. *I* an Willie Van Netten. I will *be* Willie Van Netten for thirty glorious days.

I take a final look around the apartment, carry my bags into the hall, lock the door, and walk down the three short flights of stairs. It is still not quite light. None of the other tenants is likely to be awake yet. If I encounter any of them, I'll say I have been called to the Coast by the death of a relative, the same story I've already written on the card to Monica I'll post from the airport.

I have an hour's wait before my flight is scheduled to leave, sixty minutes in which to relax without even a breath of impatience and savor the joys of anticipation. I am escaping at last from the black, accusing eyes of that Swiss drummer. Already I can feel the fresh stirring of my writer's imagination as I study the faces of my fellow travelers, my mind already storing up visions to be transmuted into fiction—and what a wealth

of material yet awaits me in Mexico. I think of that tragic poet
Hart Crane and of Katherine Anne Porter and all those other
writers who have found spiritual nourishment under the blue
Mexican skies. Wonderful, wonderful.

Yes, I remain in a kind of euphoric daze—until I look up at
a handful of arriving passengers streaming into the con-
course—and see Monica!

At first I blink, not believing the evidence of my senses. It
can't be Monica. It's impossible. Monica is in Florida. Monica
called from Florida last night.

But now, clearly searching, her eyes discover me and a broad
smile spreads across her face. She comes hurrying toward me
with arms outstretched.

"My *dear*, she cries. "I am so afraid my plane would be late.
Willie and I had the time schedule planned right down to the
minute, but you can never be certain about anything where
planes are involved."

She gives me a hasty kiss as, stunned, I rise to my feet,
aware of no other emotion than blank confusion. Nor does my
reaction seem to surprise her. She utters a laugh of pure delight at my obvious astonishment.

"But where is Willie?" she demands, looking around.

"Er—well . . . as a matter of fact, Monica, Willie felt a bit
under the weather this morning."

Her face falls. "Oh, drat. That spoils everything. We didn't
want you to know until the very last minute." She gives me
an accusing frown. "I'll bet he told you last night, didn't he?
There was something in your tone when I called. Darling, we
were both worried about you, but I take full credit for putting
the idea in Willie's head. He's really the sweetest and kindest
creature alive, you know that, but he simply never *thinks* about
anyone else. Did you think it beastly of us, keeping it all a
secret?"

I am still in a daze, but now the euphoria has turned into a
kind of horrified bewilderment.

"You mean about getting married? I was surprised, yes—"

"No, no, I mean *this*. The trip. Mexico. I told Willie he really
had to do something to show his appreciation. All the help
you've been to him. And I know if it weren't for you he probably never would have got up the nerve to pop the question.
I'm not sure which he enjoyed more, giving you the trip or
keeping you in the dark about it till the last minute—well, it

was *supposed* to be the last minute. We both wanted to see the look on your face when Willie told you to open that bag and look at the tickets and see *your* name on them."

She is still chattering when the first announcement comes for boarding my flight. Monica gives me a quick hug.

"Godspeed, my dear, and happy landings! I shan't wait for the takeoff. I'll dash straight over to Willie's and make sure the poor lamb is all right. Oh, gosh, I almost forgot. Willie sent me a letter and insisted *I* must be the one to give it to you when we saw you off. He *can* be a shy one at times, you know."

※

DURING THE FLIGHT I READ Willie's letter several times. It repeats pretty much what Monica told me and mentions the bank draft awaiting me in Mexico City. Of course, it's the sheerest fantasy to imagine I won't be stopped the minute I step off the plane. Yet if, as seems likely, I am destined for a cold and darker place, I shall be grateful, all things considered, for even a stop-over in paradise.

DOROTHY L. SAYERS

The Learned Adventure of the Dragon's Head

"Uncle Peter!"

"Half a jiff, Gherkins. No, I don't think I'll take the Catullus, Mr. Ffolliott. After all, thirteen guineas is a bit steep without either the title or the last folio, what? But you might send me round the Vitruvius and the Satyricon when they come in; I'd like to have a look at them, anyhow. Well, old man, what is it?"

"Do come and look at these pictures, Uncle Peter. I'm sure it's an awfully old book."

Lord Peter Wimsey sighed as he picked his way out of Mr. Ffolliott's dark back shop, strewn with the flotsam and jetsam of many libraries. An unexpected outbreak of measles at Mr. Bultridge's excellent preparatory school, coinciding with the absence of the Duke and Duchess of Denver on the Continent, had saddled his lordship with his ten-year-old nephew, Viscount St. George, more commonly known as Young Jerry, Jerrykins, or Pickled Gherkins. Lord Peter was not one of those born uncles who delight old nurses by their fascinating "way with" children. He succeeded, however, in learning tolerance on honorable terms by treating the young with the same scrupulous politeness which he extended to their elders. He therefore prepared to receive Gherkins's discovery with respect, though a child's taste was not to be trusted, and the book might quite well be some horror of woolly mezzotints or an inferior modern reprint adorned with leprous electros. Nothing much better was really to be expected from the "cheap shelf" exposed to the dust of the street.

"Uncle! there's such a funny man here, with a great long nose and ears and a tail and dogs' heads all over his body. *Monstrum hoc Cracoviae*—that's a monster, isn't it? I should jolly well think it was. What's *Cracoviae*, Uncle Peter?"

"Oh," said Lord Peter, greatly relieved, "the Cracow monster?" A portrait of that distressing infant certainly argued a respectable antiquity. "Let's have a look. Quite right, it's a very old book—Munster's *Cosmographia Universalis*. I'm glad you know good stuff when you see it, Gherkins. What's the *Cosmographia* doing out here, Mr. Ffolliott, at five bob?"

"Well, my lord," said the bookseller, who had followed his customers to the door, "it's in a very bad state, you see; covers loose and nearly all the double-page maps missing. It came in a few weeks ago—dumped in with a collection we bought from a gentleman in Norfolk—you'll find his name in it—Dr. Conyers of Yelsall Manor. Of course, we might keep it and try to make up a complete copy when we get another example. But it's rather out of our line, as you know, classical authors being our specialty. So we just put it out to go for what it would fetch in the *status quo*, as you might say."

"Oh, look!" broke in Gherkins. "Here's a picture of a man being chopped up in little bits. What does it say about it?"

"I thought you could read Latin."

"Well, but it's all full of sort of pothooks. What do they mean?"

"They're just contractions," said Lord Peter patiently. " '*Solent quoque hujus insulae cultores*'—It is the custom of the dwellers in this island, when they see their parents stricken in years and of no further use, to take them down into the marketplace and sell them to the cannibals, who kill them and eat them for food. This they do also with younger persons when they fall into any desperate sickness."

"Ha, ha!" said Mr. Ffolliott. "Rather sharp practice on the poor cannibals. They never got anything but tough old joints or diseased meat, eh?"

"The inhabitants seem to have had thoroughly advanced notions of business," agreed his lordship.

The viscount was enthralled.

"I *do* like this book," he said; "could I buy it out of my pocket money, please?"

Another problem for uncles, thought Lord Peter, rapidly ransacking his recollections of the *Cosmographia* to determine whether any of its illustrations were indelicate; for he knew the duchess to be straitlaced. On consideration, he could only remember one that was dubious, and there was a sporting chance that the duchess might fail to light upon it.

"Well," he said judicially, "in your place, Gherkins, I should be inclined to buy it. It's in a bad state, as Mr. Ffolliott as honorably told you—otherwise, of course, it would be exceedingly valuable; but, apart from the lost pages, it's a very nice clean copy, and certainly worth five shillings to you, if you think of starting a collection."

Till that moment, the viscount had obviously been more impressed by the cannibals than by the state of the margins, but the idea of figuring next term at Mr. Bultridge's as a collector of rare editions had undeniable charm.

"None of the other fellows collect books," he said; "they collect stamps, mostly. I think stamps are rather ordinary, don't you, Uncle Peter? I was rather thinking of giving up stamps. Mr. Porter, who takes us for history, has got a lot of books like yours, and he is a splendid man at footer."

Rightly interpreting this reference to Mr. Porter, Lord Peter gave it as his opinion that book collecting could be a perfectly manly pursuit. Girls, he said, practically never took it up, because it meant so much learning about dates and typefaces and other technicalities which called for a masculine brain.

"Besides," he added, "it's a very interesting book in itself, you know. Well worth dipping into."

"I'll take it, please," said the Viscount, blushing a little at transacting so important and expensive a piece of business; for the duchess did not encourage lavish spending by little boys, and was strict in the matter of allowances.

Mr. Ffolliott bowed, and took the *Cosmographia* away to wrap it up.

"Are you all right for cash?" inquired Lord Peter discreetly. "Or can I be of temporary assistance?"

"No, thank you, uncle; I've got Aunt Mary's half-crown and four shillings of my pocket money, because, you see, with the measles happening, we didn't have our dormitory spread, and I was saving up for that."

The business being settled in this gentlemanly manner, and

the budding bibliophile taking personal and immediate charge of the stout, square volume, a taxi was chartered which, in due course of traffic delays, brought the *Cosmographia* to 110A Piccadilly.

✳

"AND WHO, BUNTER, is Mr. Wilberforce Pope?"

"I do not think we know the gentleman, my lord. He is asking to see your lordship for a few minutes on business."

"He probably wants me to find a lost dog for his maiden aunt. What it is to have acquired a reputation as a sleuth! Show him in. Gherkins, if this good gentleman's business turns out to be private, you'd better retire into the dining room."

"Yes, Uncle Peter," said the viscount dutifully. He was extended on his stomach on the library hearthrug, laboriously picking his way through the more exciting-looking bits of the *Cosmographia*, with the aid of Messrs. Lewis & Short, whose monumental compilation he had hitherto looked upon as a barbarous invention for the annoyance of upper forms.

Mr. Wilberforce Pope turned out to be a rather plump, fair gentleman in the late thirties, with a prematurely bald forehead, horn-rimmed spectacles, and an engaging manner.

"You will excuse my intrusion, won't you?" he began. "I'm sure you must think me a terrible nuisance. But I wormed your name and address out of Mr. Ffolliott. Not his fault, really. You won't blame him, will you? I positively badgered the poor man. Sat down on his doorstep and refused to go, though the boy was putting up the shutters. I'm afraid you will think me very silly when you know what it's all about. But you really mustn't hold poor Mr. Ffolliott responsible, now, will you?"

"Not at all," said his lordship. "I mean, I'm charmed and all that sort of thing. Something I can do for you about books? You're a collector, perhaps? Will you have a drink or anything?"

"Well, no," said Mr. Pope, with a faint giggle. "No, not exactly a collector. Thank you very much, just a spot—no, no literally a spot. Thank you; no—" he glanced round the bookshelves, with their rows of rich old leather bindings "—certainly not a collector. But I happen to be, er, interested—sentimentally interested—in a purchase you made yesterday.

Really, such a very small matter. You will think it foolish. But I am told you are the present owner of a copy of Munster's *Cosmographia*, which used to belong to my uncle, Dr. Conyers."

Gherkins looked up suddenly, seeing that the conversation had a personal interest for him.

"Well, that's not quite correct," said Wimsey. "I was there at the time, but the actual purchaser is my nephew. Gerald, Mr. Pope is interested in your *Cosmographia*. My nephew, Lord St. George."

"How do you do, young man," said Mr. Pope affably. "I see that the collecting spirit runs in the family. A great Latin scholar, too, I expect, eh? Ready to decline *jusjurandum* with the best of us? Ha, ha! And what are you going to do when you grow up? Be lord chancellor, eh? Now, I bet you think you'd rather be an engine driver, what, what?"

"No, thank you," said the viscount, with aloofness.

"What, not an engine driver? Well, now I want you to be a real businessman this time. Put through a book deal, you know. Your uncle will see I offer you a fair price, what? Ha, ha! Now, you see, that picture book of yours has a great value for me that it wouldn't have for anybody else. Whan *I* was a little boy of your age it was one of my very greatest joys. I used to have it to look at on Sundays. Ah, dear! the happy hours I used to spend with those quaint old engravings, and the funny old maps with the ships and salamanders and '*Hic dracones*'—you know what that means, I dare say. What does it mean?"

"Here are dragons," said the viscount, unwillingly but still politely.

"Quite right. I *knew* you were a scholar."

"It's a very attractive book," said Lord Peter. "My nephew was quite entranced by the famous Cracow monster."

"Ah yes—a glorious monster, isn't it?" agreed Mr. Pope, with enthusiasm. "Many's the time I've fancied myself as Sir Lancelot or somebody on a white war horse, charging that monster, lance in rest, with the captive princess cheering me on. Ah! childhood! You're living in the happiest days of your life, young man. You won't believe me, but you are."

"Now what is it exactly you want my nephew to do?" inquired Lord Peter a little sharply.

"Quite right, quite right. Well now, you know, my uncle, Dr. Conyers, sold his library a few months ago. I was abroad at the time, and it was only yesterday, when I went down to

Yelsall on a visit, that I learnt the dear old book had gone with the rest. I can't tell you how distressed I was. I know it's not valuable—a great many pages missing and all that—but I can't bear to think of its being gone. So, purely from sentimental reasons, as I said, I hurried off to Ffolliott's to see if I could get it back. I was quite upset to find I was too late, and gave poor Mr. Ffolliott no peace till he told me the name of the purchaser. Now, you see, Lord St. George, I'm here to make you an offer for the book. Come, now, double what you gave for it. That's a good offer, isn't it, Lord Peter? Ha, ha! And you will be doing me a very great kindness as well."

Viscount St. George looked rather distressed, and turned appealingly to his uncle.

"Well, Gerald," said Lord Peter, "it's your affair, you know. What do you say?"

The viscount stood first on one leg and then on the other. The career of a book collector evidently had its problems, like other careers.

"If you please, Uncle Peter," he said, with embarrassment, "may I whisper?"

"It's not usually considered the thing to whisper, Gherkins, but you could ask Mr. Pope for time to consider his offer. Or you could say you would prefer to consult me first. That would be quite in order."

"Then, if you don't mind, Mr. Pope, I should like to consult my uncle first."

"Certainly, certainly; ha, ha!" said Mr. Pope. "Very prudent to consult a collector of greater experience, what? Ah! the younger generation, eh, Lord Peter? Regular little businessmen already."

"Excuse us, then, for one moment," said Lord Peter, and drew his nephew into the dining room.

"I say, Uncle Peter," said the collector breathlessly, when the door was shut, "*need* I give him my book? I don't think he's a very nice man. I *hate* people who ask you to decline nouns for them."

"Certainly you needn't, Gherkins, if you don't want to. The book is yours, and you've a right to it."

"What would *you* do, uncle?"

Before replying, Lord Peter, in the most surprising manner, tiptoed gently to the door which communicated with the library and flung it suddenly open, in time to catch Mr. Pope kneeling on the hearthrug intently turning over the pages of the coveted volume, which lay as the owner had left it. He started to his feet in a flurried manner as the door opened.

"Do help yourself, Mr. Pope, won't you?" cried Lord Peter hospitably, and closed the door again.

"What is it, Uncle Peter?"

"If you want my advice, Gherkins, I should be rather careful how you had any dealings with Mr. Pope. I don't think he's telling the truth. He called those woodcuts engravings— though, of course, that may be just his ignorance. But I can't believe that he spent all his childhood's Sunday afternoons studying those maps and picking out the dragons in them, because, as you may have noticed for yourself, old Munster put very few dragons into his maps. They're mostly just plain maps—a bit queer to our ideas of geography, but perfectly straightforward. That was why I brought in the Cracow monster, and, you see, he thought it was some sort of dragon."

"Oh, I say, uncle! So you said that on purpose!"

"If Mr. Pope wants the *Cosmographia*, it's for some reason he doesn't want to tell us about. And, that being so, I wouldn't be in too big a hurry to sell, if the book were mine. See?"

"Do you mean there's something frightfully valuable about the book, which we don't know?"

"Possibly."

"How exciting! it's just like a story in the *Boys' Friend Library*. What am I to say to him, uncle?"

"Well, in your place I wouldn't be dramatic or anything. I'd just say you've considered the matter, and you've taken a fancy to the book and have decided not to sell. You thank him for his offer, of course."

"Yes—er, won't you say it for me, uncle?"

"I think it would look better if you did it yourself."

"Yes, perhaps it would. Will he be very cross?"

"Possibly," said Lord Peter, "but if he is, he won't let on. Ready?"

The consulting committee accordingly turned to the library. Mr. Pope had prudently retired from the hearthrug and was examining a distant bookcase.

"Thank you very much for your offer, Mr. Pope," said the viscount, striding stoutly up to him, "but I have considered it, and I have taken a—a—a fancy for the book and decided not to sell."

"Sorry and all that," put in Lord Peter, "but my nephew's

adamant about it. No, it isn't the price; he wants the book. Wish I could oblige you, but it isn't in my hands. Won't you take something else before you go? Really? Ring the bell, Gherkins. My man will see you to the lift. *Good* evening."

When the visitor had gone, Lord Peter returned and thoughtfully picked up the book.

"We were awful idiots to leave him with it, Gherkins, even for a moment. Luckily, there's no harm done."

"You don't think he found out anything while we were away, do you, uncle?" gasped Gherkins, open-eyed.

"I'm sure he didn't."

"Why?"

"He offered me fifty pounds for it on the way to the door. Gave the game away. H'm! Bunter."

"My lord?"

"Put this book in the safe and bring me back the keys. And you'd better set all the burglar alarms when you lock up."

"Oo—er!" said Viscount St. George.

ON THE THIRD MORNING AFTER THE VISIT of Mr. Wilberforce Pope, the viscount was seated at a very late breakfast in his uncle's flat, after the most glorious and soul-satisfying night that ever a boy experienced. He was almost too excited to eat the kidneys and bacon placed before him by Bunter, whose usual impeccable manner was not in the least impaired by a rapidly swelling and blackening eye.

It was about two in the morning that Gherkins—who had not slept very well, owing to too lavish and grown-up a dinner and theater the evening before—became aware of a stealthy sound somewhere in the direction of the fire escape. He had got out of bed and crept very softly into Lord Peter's room and woke him up. He had said: "Uncle Peter, I'm sure there's burglars on the fire escape." And Uncle Peter, instead of saying, "Nonsense, Gherkins, hurry up and get back to bed," had sat up and listened and said: "By Jove, Gherkins, I believe you're right." And had sent Gherkins to call Bunter. And on his return, Gherkins, who had always regarded his uncle as a very top-hatted sort of person, actually saw him take from his handkerchief drawer an undeniable automatic pistol.

It was at this point that Lord Peter was apotheosed from the state of Quite Decent Uncle to that of Glorified Uncle. He said:

"Look here, Gherkins, we don't know how many of these blighters there'll be, so you must be jolly smart and do anything I say sharp, on the word of command—even if I have to say 'Scoot.' Promise?"

Gherkins promised, with his heart thumping, and they sat waiting in the dark, till suddenly a little electric bell rang sharply just over the head of Lord Peter's bed and a green light shone out.

"The library window," said his lordship, promptly silencing the bell by turning a switch. "If they heard, they may think better of it. We'll give them a few minutes."

They gave them five minutes, and then crept very quietly down the passage.

"Go round by the dining room, Bunter," said his lordship; "they may bolt that way."

With infinite precaution, he unlocked and opened the library door, and Gherkins noticed how silently the locks moved.

A circle of light from an electric torch was moving slowly along the bookshelves. The burglars had obviously heard nothing of the counter-attack. Indeed, they seemed to have troubles enough of their own to keep their attention occupied. As his eyes grew accustomed to the dim light, Gherkins made out that one man was standing holding the torch, while the other took down and examined the books. It was fascinating to watch his apparently disembodied hands move along the shelves in the torchlight.

The men muttered discontentedly. Obviously the job was proving a harder one than they had bargained for. The habit of ancient authors of abbreviating the titles on the backs of their volumes, or leaving them completely untitled, made things extremely awkward. From time to time the man with the torch extended his hand into the light. It held a piece of paper, which they anxiously compared with the title page of a book. Then the volume was replaced and the tedious search went on.

Suddenly some slight noise—Gherkins was sure *he* did not make it; it may have been Bunter in the dining room—seemed to catch the ear of the kneeling man.

"Wot's that?" he gasped, and his startled face swung round into view.

"Hands up!" said Lord Peter, and switched the light on.

The second man made one leap for the dining room door,

where a smash and an oath proclaimed that he had encountered Bunter. The kneeling man shot his hands up like a marionette.

"Gherkins," said Lord Peter, "do you think you can go across to the gentlemen by the bookcase and relieve him of the article which is so inelegantly distending the right-hand pocket of his coat? Wait a minute. Don't on any account get between him and my pistol, and mind you take the thing out *very* carefully. There's no hurry. That's splendid. Just point it at the floor while you bring it across, would you? Thanks. Bunter has managed for himself, I see. Now run into my bedroom, and in the bottom of my wardrobe you will find a bundle of stout cord. Oh! I beg your pardon; yes, put your hands down by all means. It must be a very tiring exercise."

The arms of the intruders being secured behind their backs with a neatness which Gherkins felt to be worthy of the best traditions of Sexton Blake, Lord Peter motioned his captives to sit down and dispatched Bunter for whisky and soda.

"Before we send for the police," said Lord Peter, "you would do me a great personal favor by telling me what you were looking for, and who sent you. Ah! thanks, Bunter. As our guests are not at liberty to use their hands, perhaps you would be kind enough to assist them to a drink. Now then, say when."

"Well, you're a gentleman, guv'nor, said the First Burglar, wiping his mouth politely on his shoulder, the back of his hand not being available. "If we'd a known wot a job this wos goin' ter be, blow me if we'd a touched it. The bloke said, ses'e, 'It's takin' candy from a baby,' 'e ses. 'The gentleman's a reg'lar softie,' 'e ses, 'one o' these 'ere sersiety toffs wiv a maggot fer old books,' that's wo 'e ses, 'an' ef yer can find this 'ere old book fer me,' 'e ses, 'there's a pony fer yer.' Well! Sech a job! 'E didn't mention as 'ow there'd be five 'undred fousand bleedin' old books all as alike as a regiment o' bleedin' dragoons. Nor as 'ow yer kept a nice little machine-gun like that 'andy by the bedside, *nor* yet as 'ow yer was so bleedin' good at tyin' knots in a bit o' string. No—'e didn't think ter mention them things."

"Deuced unsporting of him," said his lordship. "Do you happen to know the gentleman's name?"

"No—that was another o' them things wot 'e didn't mention. 'E's a stout, fair party, wiv 'orn rims to 'is goggles and a bald 'ead. One o' these 'ere philanthropists, I reckon. A friend o' mine, wot got inter trouble onct, got work froo 'im, and the gentleman comes round and ses to 'im, 'e ses, 'Could yer find me a couple o' lads ter do a little job?' 'e ses, an' my friend finkin' no 'arm, you see, guv'nor, but wot it might be a bit of a joke like, 'e gets 'old of my pal an' me, an' we meets the gentleman in a pub dahn Whitechapel way. W'ich we was ter meet 'im there again Friday night, us 'avin' allowed that time fer ter git 'old of the book.''

"The book being, if I may hazard a guess, the *Cosmographia Universalis?*"

"Sumfink like that, guv'nor. I got its jaw-breakin' name wrote down on a bit o' paper, wot my pal 'ad in 'is 'and. Wot did yer do wiv that 'ere bit o' paper, Bill?"

"Well, look here," said Lord Peter, "I'm afraid I must send for the police, but I think it likely, if you give us your assistance to get hold of your gentleman, whose name I strongly suspect to be Wilberforce Pope, that you will get off pretty easily. Telephone the police, Bunter, and then go and put something on that eye of yours. Gherkins, we'll give these gentlemen another drink, and then I think perhaps you'd better hop back to bed; the fun's over. No! Well, put a good thick coat on, there's a good fellow, because what your mother will say to me if you catch a cold I don't like to think."

So the police had come and taken the burglars away, and now Detective-Inspector Parker, of Scotland Yard, a great personal friend of Lord Peter's, sat toying with a cup of coffee and listening to the story.

"But what's the matter with the jolly old book, anyhow, to make it so popular?" he demanded.

"I don't know," replied Wimsey; "but after Mr. Pope's little visit the other day I got kind of intrigued about it and had a look through it. I've got a hunch it may turn out rather valuable, after all. Unsuspected beauties and all that sort of thing. If only Mr. Pope had been a trifle more accurate in his facts, he might have got away with something to which I feel pretty sure he isn't entitled. Anyway, when I'd seen—what I saw, I wrote off to Dr. Conyers of Yelsall Manor, the late owner—"

"Conyers, the cancer man?"

"Yes. He's done some pretty important research in his time, I fancy. Getting on now, though; about seventy-eight, I fancy. I hope he's more honest than his nephew, with one foot in the grave like that. Anyway, I wrote (with Gherkins's permission, naturally) to say we had the book and had been specially interested by something we found there, and would be so obliging as to tell us something of its history. I also—"

"But what did you find in it?"

"I don't think we'll tell him yet, Gherkins, shall we? I like to keep policemen guessing. As I was saying, when you so rudely interrupted me, I also asked him whether he knew anything about his good nephew's offer to buy it back. His answer has just arrived. He says he knows of nothing specially interesting about the book. It has been in the library untold years, and the tearing out of the maps must have been done a long time ago by some family vandal. He can't think why his nephew should be so keen on it, as he certainly never pored over it as a boy. In fact, the old man declares the engaging Wilberforce has never even set foot in Yelsall Manor to his knowledge. So much for the fire-breathing monsters and the pleasant Sunday afternoons."

"Naughty Wilberforce!"

"M'm. Yes. So, after last night's little dust-up, I wired the old boy we were tooling down to Yelsall to have a heart-to-heart talk with him about his picture book and his nephew."

"Are you taking the book down with you?" asked Parker. "I can give you a police escort for it if you like."

"That's not a bad idea," said Wimsey. "We don't know where the insinuating Mr. Pope may be hanging out, and I wouldn't put it past him to make another attempt."

"Better be on the safe side," said Parker. "I can't come myself, but I'll send down a couple of men with you."

"Good egg," said Lord Peter. "Call up your myrmidons. We'll get a car round at once. You're coming, Gherkins, I suppose? God knows what your mother would say. Don't ever be an uncle, Charles; it's frightfully difficult to be fair to all parties."

❋

YELSALL MANOR WAS ONE OF THOSE LARGE, decaying country mansions which speak eloquently of times more spacious than our own. The original late Tudor construction had been masked by the addition of a whole frontage in the Italian manner, with a kind of classical portico surmounted by a pediment and approached by a semicircular flight of steps. The grounds had originally been laid out in that formal manner in which grove nods to grove and each half duly reflects the other. A late owner, however, had burst out into the more eccentric sort of landscape gardening which is associated with the name of Capability Brown. A Chinese pagoda, somewhat resembling Sir William Chambers's erection in Kew Gardens, but smaller, rose out of a grove of laurustinus towards the eastern extremity of the house, while at the rear appeared a large artificial lake, dotted with numerous islands, on which odd little temples, grottos, teahouses, and bridges peeped out from among clumps of shrubs, once ornamental, but now sadly overgrown. A boathouse, with wide eaves like the designs on a willow-pattern plate, stood at one corner, its landing-stage fallen into decay and wreathed with melancholy weeds.

"My disreputable old ancestor, Cuthbert Conyers, settled down here when he retired from the sea in 1732," said Dr. Conyers, smiling faintly. "His elder brother died childless, so the black sheep returned to the fold with the determination to become respectable and found a family. I fear he did not succeed altogether. There were very queer tales as to where his money came from. He is said to have been a pirate, and to have sailed with the notorious Captain Blackbeard. In the village, to this day, he is remembered and spoken of as Cut-throat Conyers. It used to make the old man very angry, and there is an unpleasant story of his slicing the ears off a groom who had been heard to call him 'Old Cut-throat.' He was not an uncultivated person, though. It was he who did the landscape gardening round at the back, and he built the pagoda for his telescope. He was reputed to study the Black Art, and there were certainly a number of astrological works in the library with his name on the fly-leaf, but probably the telescope was only a remembrance of his seafaring days.

"Anyhow, towards the end of his life he became more and more odd and morose. He quarrelled with his family, and turned his younger son out of doors with his wife and children. An unpleasant old fellow.

"On his deathbed he was attended by the parson—a good, earnest, God-fearing sort of man, who must have put up with a deal of insult in carrying out what he firmly believed to be the sacred duty of reconciling the old man to this shamefully treated son. Eventually, 'Old-Cut-throat' relented so far as to make a will, leaving to the younger son 'My treasure which I have buried in Munster.' The parson represented to him that it was useless to bequeath a treasure unless he also bequeathed the information where to find it, but the horrid old pirate only chuckled spitefully, and said that, as he had been at the pains to collect the treasure, his son might well be at the pains of looking for it. Further than that he would not go, and so he died, and I dare say went to a very bad place.

"Since then the family has died out, and I am the sole representative of the Conyerses, and heir to the treasure, whatever and wherever it is, for it was never discovered. I do not suppose it was very honestly come by, but since it would be useless now to try and find the original owners, I imagine I have a better right to it than anybody living.

"You may think it very unseemly, Lord Peter, that an old, lonely man like myself should be greedy for a hoard of pirate's gold. But my whole life has been devoted to studying the disease of cancer, and I believe myself to be very close to a solution of one part at least of the terrible problem. Research costs money, and my limited means are very nearly exhausted. The property is mortgaged up to the hilt, and I do most urgently desire to complete my experiments before I die, and to leave a sufficient sum to found a clinic where the work can be carried on.

"During the last year I have made very great efforts to solve the mystery of 'Old Cut-throat's' treasure. I have been able to leave much of my experimental work in the most capable hands of my assistant, Dr. Forbes, while I pursued my researches with the very slender clue I had to go upon. It was all the more expensive and difficult that Cuthbert had left no indication in his will whether Münster in Germany or Munster in Ireland was the hiding-place of the treasure. My journeys and my search in both places cost money and brought me no further on my quest. I returned, disheartened, in August, and found myself obliged to sell my library, in order to defray my expenses and obtain a little money with which to struggle on with my sadly delayed experiments."

"Ah!" said Lord Peter. "I begin to see light."

The old physician looked at him inquiringly. They had finished tea, and were seated around the great fireplace in the study. Lord Peter's interested questions about the beautiful, dilapidated old house and estate had led the conversation naturally to Dr. Conyers's family, shelving for the time the problem of the *Cosmographia*, which lay on a table beside them.

"Everything you say fits into the puzzle," went on Wimsey, "and I think there's not the smallest doubt that Mr. Wilberforce Pope was after, though how he knew that you had the *Cosmographia* here I couldn't say."

"When I disposed of the library, I sent him a catalogue," said Dr. Conyers. "As a relative, I thought he ought to have the right to buy anything he fancied. I can't think why he didn't secure the book then, instead of behaving in this most shocking fashion."

Lord Peter hooted with laughter.

"Why, because he never tumbled to it till afterwards," he said. "And oh dear, how wild he must have been! I forgive him everything. Although," he added, "I don't want to raise your hopes too high, sir, for, even when we've solved old Cuthbert's riddle, I don't know that we're very much nearer to the treasure."

"To the *treasure?*"

"Well, now, sir. I want you first to look at this page, where there's a name scrawled in the margin. Our ancestors had an untidy way of signing their possessions higgledy-piggledy in margins instead of in a decent, Christian way in the fly-leaf. This is a handwriting of somewhere about Charles I's reign: 'Jac: Coniers.' I take it that goes to prove that the book was in the possession of your family at any rate as early as the first half of the seventeenth century, and has remained there ever since. Right, now we turn to page 1099, where we find a description of the discoveries of Christopher Columbus. It's headed, you see, by a kind of map, with some of Mr. Pope's monsters swimming about in it, and apparently representing the Canaries, or, as they used to be called, the Fortunate Isles. It doesn't look much more accurate than old maps usually are, but I take it the big island on the right is meant for Lanzarote, and the two nearest to it may be Tenerife and Gran Canaria."

"But what's that writing in the middle?"

"That's just the point. The writing is later than 'Jac: Coniers' signature; I should put it about 1700—but, of course, it may have been written a good deal later still. I mean, a man who was elderly in 1730 would still use the style of writing he adopted as a young man, especially if, like your ancestor the pirate, he had spent the early part of his life in outdoor pursuits and hadn't done much writing."

"Do you mean to say, Uncle Peter," broke in the viscount excitedly, "that that's 'Old Cut-throat's' writing?"

"I'd be ready to lay a sporting bet it is. Look here, sir, you've been scouring round Münster in Germany and Munster in Ireland—but how about good old Sebastian Munster here in the library at home?"

"God bless my soul! It's pretty nearly certain, sir. Here's what he says, written, you see, round the head of that sort of sea-dragon:

Hic in capite draconis ardet perpetuo Sol.
Here the sun shines perpetually upon the Dragon's Head. Rather doggy Latin—sea-dog Latin, you might say, in fact."

"I'm afraid," said Dr. Conyers, "I must be very stupid, but I can't see where that leads us."

"No: 'Old Cut-throat' was rather clever. No doubt he thought that, if anybody read it, they'd think it was just an allusion to where it says, further down, that 'the islands were called *Fortunatae* because of the wonderful temperature of the air and the clemency of the skies.' But the cunning old astrologer up in his pagoda had a meaning of his own. Here's a little book published in 1678—Middleton's *Practical Astrology*—just the sort of popular handbook an amateur like 'Old Cut-throat' would use. Here you are: 'If in your figure you find Jupiter or Venus or *Dragon's head,* you may be confident there is Treasure in the place supposed.... If you find *Sol* to be the significator of the hidden Treasure, you may conclude there is Gold, or some jewels.' You know, sir, I think we may conclude it."

"Dear me!" said Dr. Conyers. "I believe, indeed, you must be right. And I am ashamed to think that if anybody had suggested to me that it could ever be profitable to me to learn the terms of astrology, I should have replied in my vanity that my time was too valuable to waste on such foolishness. I am deeply indebted to you."

"Yes," said Gherkins, "but where *is* the treasure, uncle?"

"That's just it," said Lord Peter. "The map is very vague; there is no latitude or longitude given; and the directions, such as they are, seem not even to refer to any spot on the islands, but to some place in the middle of the sea. Besides, it is nearly two hundred years since the treasure was hidden, and it may already have been found by somebody or other."

Dr. Conyers stood up.

"I am an old man," he said, "but I still have some strength. If I can by any means get together the money for an expedition, I will not rest till I have made every possible effort to find the treasure and to endow my clinic."

"Then, sir, I hope you'll let me give a hand to the good work," said Lord Peter.

�֍

DR. CONYERS HAD INVITED HIS GUESTS TO STAY the night, and, after the excited viscount had been packed off to bed, Wimsey and the old man sat late, consulting maps and diligently reading Munster's chapter "De Novis Insulis," in the hope of discovering some further clue. At length, however, they separated, and Lord Peter went upstairs, the book under his arm. He was restless, however, and, instead of going to bed, sat for a long time at his window, which looked out upon the lake. The moon, a few days past the full, was riding high among small, windy clouds, and picked out the sharp eaves of the Chinese teahouses and the straggling tops of the unpruned shrubs. "Old Cut-Throat" and his landscape gardening! Wimsey could have fancied that the old pirate was sitting now beside his telescope in the preposterous pagoda, chuckling over his riddling testament and counting the craters of the moon. "If *Luna*, there is silver." The water of the lake was silver enough; there was a great smooth path across it, broken by the sinister wedge of the boathouse, the black shadows of the islands, and, almost in the middle of the lake, a decayed fountain, a writhing Celestial dragon-shape, spiny-backed and ridiculous.

Wimsey rubbed his eyes. There was something strangely familiar about the lake; from moment to moment it assumed the queer unreality of a place which one recognizes without having ever known it. It was like one's first sight of the Leaning Tower of Pisa—too like its picture to be quite believable. Surely, thought Whimsey, he knew that elongated island on the right, shaped rather like a winged monster, with its two little clumps of buildings. And the island to the left of it, like the British Isles, but warped out of shape. And the third island, between the others, and nearer. The three formed a triangle, with the Chinese fountain in the center, the moon shining steadily up on its dragon head. *Hic in capite draconis ardet perpetuo—*

Lord Peter sprang up with a loud exclamation, and flung open the door into the dressing from. A small figure wrapped in an eiderdown hurriedly uncoiled itself from the window seat.

"I'm sorry, Uncle Peter," said Gherkins. "I was so *dreadfully* wide awake, it wasn't any good staying in bed."

"Come here," said Lord Peter, "and tell me if I'm mad or dreaming. Look out of the window and compare it with the map—Old Cut-throat's 'New Islands.' He made 'em, Gherkins; he put 'em here. Aren't they laid out just like the Canaries? Those three islands in a triangle, and the fourth down here in the corner? And the boathouse where the big ship is in the picture? And the dragon fountain where the dragon's head is? Well, my son, that's where your hidden treasure's gone to. Get your things on, Gherkins, and damn the time when all good little boys should be in bed! We're going for a row on the lake, if there's a tub in that boathouse that'll float."

"Oh, Uncle Peter! This is a *real* adventure!"

"All right," said Wimsey. "Fifteen men on the dead man's chest, and all that! Yo-ho-yo, and a bottle of Johnny Walker! Pirate expedition fitted out in dead of night to seek hidden treasure and explore the Fortunate Isles! Come on, crew!"

✳

LORD PETER HITCHED THE LEAKY DINGHY to the dragon's knobbly tail and climbed out carefully, for the base of the fountain was green and weedy.

"I'm afraid it's your job to sit there and bail, Gherkins," he said. "All the best captains bag the really interesting jobs for themselves. We'd better start with the head. If the old blighter said head, he probably meant it." He passed an arm affectionately round the creature's neck for support, while he methodically pressed and pulled the various knobs and bumps of its anatomy. "It seems beastly solid, but I'm sure there's a spring somewhere. You won't forget to bail, will you? I'd simply hate to turn round and find the boat gone. Pirate chief marooned on island and all that. Well, it isn't its back hair, anyhow. We'll try its eyes. I say, Gherkins, I'm sure I felt something move, only it's frightfully stiff. We might have thought to bring some oil. Never mind; it's dogged as does it. It's coming. It's coming. Booh! Pah!"

A fierce effort thrust the rusted knob inwards, releasing a huge spout of water into his face from the dragon's gaping throat. The fountain, dry for many years, soared rejoicingly heavenwards, drenching the treasure-hunters, and making rainbows in the moonlight.

"I suppose this is 'Old Cut-Throat's' idea of humor," grumbled Wimsey, retreating cautiously round the dragon's neck. "And now I can't turn it off again. Well, dash it all, let's try the other eye."

He pressed for a few moments in vain. Then, with a grinding clang, the bronze wings of the monster clapped down to its sides, revealing a deep square hole, and the fountain ceased to play.

"Gherkins!" said Lord Peter, "we've done it. (But don't neglect bailing on that account!) There's a box here. And it's beastly heavy. No; all right, I can manage. Gimme the boathook. Now I do hope the old sinner really did have a treasure. What a bore if it's only one of his little jokes. Never mind—hold the boat steady. There. Always remember, Gherkins, that you can make quite an effective crane with a boat-hook and a stout pair of braces. Got it? That's right. Now for home and beauty.... Hullo! what's all that?"

As he paddled the boat round, it was evident that something was happening down by the boathouse. Lights were moving about, and a sound of voices came across the lake.

"They think we're burglars, Gherkins. Always misunderstood. Give way, my hearties—

"A-roving, a-roving, since roving's been my ru-i-in,
I'll go no more a-roving with you, fair maid."

"Is that you, my lord?" said a man's voice as they drew in to the boathouse.

"Why, it's our faithful sleuths!" cried his lordship. "What's the excitement?"

"We found this fellow sneaking round the boathouse," said the man from Scotland Yard. "He says he's the old gentleman's nephew. Do you know him, my lord?"

"I rather fancy I do," said Wimsey. "Mr. Pope, I think. Good evening. Were you looking for anything? Not a treasure, by any chance? Because we've just found one. Oh! don't say that. *Maxima reverentia,* you know. Lord St. George is of tender years. And, by the way, thank you so much for sending your delightful friends to call on me last night. Oh, yes, Thompson, I'll charge him all right. You there, doctor? Splendid. Now, if anybody's got a spanner or anything handy, we'll have a look at Great-grandpapa Cuthbert. And if he turns out to be old iron, Mr. Pope, you'll have had an uncommonly good joke for your money."

An iron bar was produced from the boathouse and thrust under the hasp of the chest. It creaked and burst. Dr. Conyers knelt down tremulously and threw open the lid.

There was a little pause.

"The drinks are on you, Mr. Pope," said Lord Peter. "I think, doctor, it ought to be a jolly good hospital when it's finished."

WILLIAM BRITTAIN

The Man Who Read Dashiell Hammett

"PRICHARD? I know you're in here somewhere. Probably with your nose stuck in another of those mystery thrillers. Well, come out at once. I need you."

Mr. Deacon's nasal whisper was strangely muffled amid the closely set shelves of books that made up the fiction room of the Caldwell Public Library. Clarence Prichard, his aged joints creaking almost audibly, rose stiffly from the little stool on which he had been sitting. With a sigh of regret he closed the book he had been reading and slipped it into its place. The urbane conversations between Nick and Nora Charles would have to remain frozen in print till he could get back to them.

"Oh, there you are, Prichard." Mr. Deacon, the head librarian, rounded the corner of a passageway between the shelves and caught sight of the old man. "I wish you'd keep the front desk informed of your whereabouts. We aren't the size of the big city libraries, but it's sometimes devilishly hard to find a stack boy when we need one."

Boy? Prichard snorted audibly. His sixty-fifth birthday and enforced retirement from his bookkeeping job had both occurred five years before. The long illness that preceded his wife's death had wiped out his savings, and the government check he received each month was insufficient for his needs. The offer of a job replacing library books in their proper places had seemed like a godsend, and boring as it was, it did allow

208

him time to read his beloved mystery stories. So if Mr. Deacon insisted on the term "stack boy," that was all right. Besides, what other term was there? Stack septuagenarian?

He did envy Deacon's well-tailored clothes and his position of responsibility, of course. To deal with the public, to be of real assistance to the library's patrons, to be addressed as "Mister Prichard"—that would be really something. But that was only a dream. Mr. Deacon was trained in every facet of the library's operation, while Prichard's familiarity with mystery stories, encyclopedic as it was, was not in demand.

"Prichard, I've heard rumors that you're uncommonly knowledgeable about mystery stories. Is that true?"

Prichard could hardly believe his ears. It was almost as if Mr. Deacon had been reading his mind.

"Yes, sir," he answered. "I've read all of 'em in the library here and I've got a lot of them in my room. But I don't let it interfere with my job, Mr. Deacon, and that's a fact."

Deacon shook his head and honored Prichard with a rare smile. "I'm not concerned with your work in the stacks right now," he said.

"Then what—"

"Prichard, I—"—the words came out reluctantly—"I need you. It's not part of your regular work, but you seem to be the only one on our staff who reads detective fiction regularly, and I hope you won't consider it an imposition if—"

"You're not imposing, Mr. Deacon. I'd be glad to help in any way I can."

"Very well. There are two men waiting out in the research room. One of them—the short one in the black suit—is a Mr. Farragut. I've never seen him before. But the other is Andrew King. Do you recognize that name, Prichard?"

"Oh, sure. He's the president of the library board, isn't he?"

Deacon nodded ominously. "They insist on talking with a mystery reader. I could hardly admit to Mr. King that nobody on the staff qualifies. So willy-nilly, it's up to you, Prichard. Go. And make the Caldwell Public Library proud of you."

Deacon's gesture of dismissal would have been worthy of King Henry sending his troops into battle at Agincourt.

On reaching the research room Prichard immediately recognized Mr. Farragut from Deacon's description. He was a little balding man with wire-rimmed spectacles, wearing a wrinkled black suit that gave him the appearance of a seedy undertaker.

The other, heavy-set and sporting a checked jacket of blinding red and green, had to be Mr. King.

There was a round of handshaking as Prichard introduced himself. "Sit down, Mr. Prichard!"

Mr. Prichard! The title sounded strange when attached to his own name. The old man fairly glowed with satisfaction.

"Deacon said you knew your mysteries," King went on. "Are you familiar with the works of Dashiell Hammett?"

"Yes, sir. Read everything he ever wrote. *Red Harvest. The Dain Curse*. All of 'em."

"I was thinking in particular of *The Maltese Falcon*."

"Sure. One of the greatest. But if you want it you'd have to apply through our county loan service. This library don't have a copy."

"It does now," wheezed Farragut with a nasty chuckle.

"I don't get you."

"No reason why you should." Farragut's smile threatened to split his face in two. "Get to the point, Andrew."

"All right, Edmund," said King with a sigh. He turned to Prichard. "Mr. Farragut and I have been friends for a good many years. During his lifetime he has amassed a collection of detective-story first editions, many of them quite rare and valuable. And he has expressed a willingness to give the collection—well over five hundred volumes—to our library."

"Maybe so and maybe no," chuckled Farragut. "First, Andrew, you and your library have to prove yourselves worthy."

Prichard shook his head uncomprehendingly.

"The test," added Farragut. "Tell him about the test, Andrew."

"Oh, of course." King leaned toward Prichard. "Both Edmund and I are mystery fans. Like yourself. But we've tended to specialize. I prefer the tough thriller—the so-called Black Mask type of story. Sam Spade, Philip Marlowe, Lew Archer. Yes, even Mike Hammer. The rugged, lone-wolf types who live just barely within the law and sometimes outside it. They're really the only truly interesting characters in mystery fiction. And the greatest of these, of course, is Hammett's Sam Spade."

"Rubbish!" snapped Farragut. "Give me your English country house with rich old Aunt Matilda garroted by her own scarf and skewered to the divan with the antique sword from over the mantel. Enter the great detective—Holmes, Poirot, Fell, or whoever. A sifting of clues, a questioning of suspects, a bit of logical analysis interrupted only by a bountiful meal and perhaps another killing or two, and the murderer is brought to justice. That is, if he doesn't have the decency to commit suicide to protect the family's good name. All nice and civilized. Why, Andrew, those ham-fisted, trenchcoated thugs you read about couldn't detect their way out of a phone booth."

"Not so, Edmund! They deal with real people, not the clay figurines who populate the stories you're so fond of. Furthermore—"

"Gentlemen," whispered Prichard, a finger to his lips. "I'm afraid you're getting a bit loud."

"Quite so," said Farragut softly. "At any rate I've decided on a little test for Mr. Andrew King. I want to see if his idiotic stories have taught him anything about the deductive process. So I've set him a little problem. If he solves it, my collection goes to the library. If not, I'll take it to some other place where fine detective stories are really appreciated."

"But where do I fit in?" asked Prichard.

"Sherlock Holmes had his Watson, Poirot his Hastings, and so on. Even in those shocking Hammett stories the private eyes have friends on the police force who gain access to official reports and open otherwise closed doors. Therefore I agreed that Andrew could have one member of the library staff to assist him in his search."

"Search?" asked Prichard. "What search?"

"That is the test we've been talking about," answered Farragut. "Basically it amounts to this. I have concealed somewhere in this library one of the first editions from my collection. In deference to Andrew's abominable taste in mysteries the volume I selected was Hammett's *The Maltese Falcon.*" He drew a large watch from a coat pocket. "It's now three o'clock. Find the book in one hour and I'll give all my first editions to the library. Otherwise—" Farragut shrugged and spread his hands wide.

For a long moment Prichard and King stared at one another. "But this is hardly fair, Edmund," said King finally. "I mean you can't expect us to start rummaging through all the shelves and cabinets and packing boxes in a single hour. It's impossible."

"A point well taken," murmured Farragut. "But the book is on a shelf—where books would be expected to be."

"Umm." King rubbed at his nose with a fist. "The criminal-hiding-in-the-crowd ploy, eh? The old leaf-in-the-forest ploy? He turned to Prichard. "Well, what about it? Do we have time to scan all the shelves in a single hour?"

"Mebbe, just barely," replied Prichard. "You're sure the book is in plain sight, Mr. Farragut?"

"I didn't say that. I merely said it's on one of the shelves."

"Well, you can't expect us to pull every book down to see if there's something behind it. I mean it would take days just to put everything back."

"That won't be necessary. It's at the front of its shelf. Besides, you're not allowed to grasp books at random. You may look at the spines all you wish, but the very first book you pull from its place will be considered your final selection. Right or wrong, you get only one chance."

There was a long silence. King gnawed at his knuckles. Prichard suspected, quite correctly, that the man was not so worried over the prospect of losing the collection of books as he was annoyed at the possibility of being bested by Farragut.

"See here," King said finally. "This really isn't fair, Edmund. I mean, all detectives have some time to gather clues. That's what this test of yours is lacking—clues. We're expected to go rummaging around the building without having any opportunity to discover when you might have come in here to conceal the book or"—his voice trailed off lamely—"or anything."

"I was wondering when you'd get to that," answered Farragut. "Clues." He reached into his coat pocket and pulled out a white envelope. "Here are your clues. All neatly wrapped."

He threw onto the table a letter-size white envelope. Scrawled on its back was a series of numbers: 3.14.

Prichard glanced hurriedly at the numbers. "Excuse me," he said, getting to his feet. He walked quickly to a corner of the research room. There he paused for a moment, then went out through the door.

A little over ten minutes later he returned, shaking his head morosely.

"Where in blazes have you been?" asked King. "Now we have only about forty-five minutes."

"I figured that number might represent the Dewey system of book cataloguing," said Prichard, catching his breath. "But it didn't. We got no books numbered 3.14. The nearest I could come in the file cards was a pamphlet listing governmental agencies. But then I thought the decimal might have been a red herring, so I tried 314."

"And—" said King expectantly.

"Nothing. Just one book on educational statistics."

"Ten minutes for that?"

Prichard shook his head. "I had another thought. That number—3.14—is what they call pi in mathematics."

"Pi?"

"Yes, sir. It has something to do with circles. So I checked the sections in the catalogue on pure and applied sciences, mathematics in particular. Quite a few cards to look through. Then, thinking it might be another kind of pie, I looked through all our cards on cookbooks."

"You didn't take any book off the shelves, did you?" asked Farragut sharply.

"No, sir."

"Good, tries, all of them, though," said King. "I'm impressed—Deacon didn't make a mistake assigning you to me. That pi business would have escaped me completely. Well, we still have nearly three-quarters of an hour—till four o'clock sharp. And two other clues."

He reached into the envelope, removed a small white card, and flipped it to Prichard. One side was blank. The other had two words neatly printed in pencil:

double dozen

While Prichard examined the card, King handed him the second one. It was similar to the first, except that its message read:

Maltese falcon

Prichard tried to recall every book he'd ever heard of with either "double" or "dozen" in its title. King went to the card catalogue to check each of them. In the meantime Prichard ran down all references to either Malta or falconry. Thirty minutes later, with nothing to show for their labors, they returned to the table where Farragut was waiting—and grinning.

"You're perspiring, Andrew," he said with a chuckle. "Is it the physical exertion or just nervousness at the idea of losing to me?"

"Edmund, you've been smirking at me like that for nearly fifty years. But this time I'll win. I swear it."

"Only fifteen minutes to go."

"Yes, well—" King turned to Prichard, his face drooping.

"What about it?" he asked. "Can you make anything out of those so-called clues?"

"I—I think the mistake we've been making is to take the three clues one at a time," said Prichard. "They must all hang together some way. Two false clues and only one real one would be downright unfair."

"All right." King arranged the cards and envelopes in front of him. "Pi," he said. "Then double dozen. And finally Maltese falcon. I don't know what to make of them."

"Give up, Andrew?" asked Farragut.

"Oh, I suppose we might as well—"

"Wait a minute. Please." Prichard reached across the table and slid the clue cards in front of him. "These don't have to be in the same order, you know." He arranged the cards and envelopes in various ways, each time shaking his head.

"You know, I like Mr. Prichard's style better than yours, Andrew," said Farragut. "He keeps going. What would your hardboiled detectives think if they saw you giving up this way? Just remember, Mr. Prichard, things aren't always what they seem."

Prichard, who had only been half listening, suddenly looked up and stared at Farragut. Something Farragut had said was beginning to penetrate. He swiveled toward King. "How much more time?" he asked.

"About seven minutes. Why?"

Prichard pointed at the envelope. "3.14," he said. "That's pi. Now what's a double dozen?"

"Twenty-four," replied King. "So what?"

"I think I see a little light at the end of the tunnel," said Prichard. "Mr. Farragut just said that things aren't always what they seem. He thought he was being clever and sneaking something past us, but it was a new clue. Isn't that right, Mr. Farragut?"

For the first time the little man in black didn't seem so sure of himself.

"Here we got three clues," Prichard went on, "each saying a thing one way that could be said another. 31.4 is pi. And a double dozen is 24. Now who's to say the second card doesn't do the same thing?"

"Maltese falcon," muttered King. "It's a book, that's all."

"No, Mr. King," said Prichard, his voice rising in excitement. "Look, the word 'falcon' doesn't start with a capital letter. So either Mr. Farragut made a mistake—which I doubt—or he wasn't thinking about the book but the bird itself."

"That sounds reasonable," said King. "Keep talking."

"It seems to me that Mr. Farragut must have read *The Maltese Falcon* at some time, even if he didn't like it too well. I mean, he had it in his collection, didn't he?"

"I've read it," Farragut admitted grudgingly.

"Yeah. So the 'Maltese falcon' card must be connected with the story in some way. Now, I've been giving a little thought to the falcon—small 'f'—in Hammett's book. That falcon was supposed to be a gold statue covered with jewels that Casper Gutman and Joel Cairo wanted Sam Spade to help them find. According to Gutman, the fat man, the Knights of Rhodes had the statue made and sent to the Spanish king as a kind of reward for allowing them to live on Malta some time in the fifteen hundreds. But while it was being taken to the king, the bird was captured by pirates. It got passed from one person to another for a couple of hundred years, and during that time it was dunked in black paint to disguise what it was really worth."

"The man's uncanny," said Farragut to King.

"Because of the black covering," Prichard went on, "Spade and several other characters gave the statue a kind of nickname."

"Sure," said King. " 'The black bird.' "

Again Prichard shuffled the cards and envelope about. Finally satisfied, he took a pencil from his pocket and scribbled on the envelope and on each of the cards in turn. Then he rose from his chair.

"C'mon, you two," he said. "I know where to find that book."

Two minutes later they came to the bottom of the stairs which led to the basement of the building. "But this is the children's section," said King. "Farragut wouldn't try to hide one of Hammett's books here. It would stand out like a sore thumb."

"No?" Prichard nodded toward Farragut. "Take a gander at his face, and then tell me I'm wrong. He looks as worried as a basset hound with fallen arches."

Prichard moved along the shelves, peering intently at the books. "*The Maltese Falcon* on a shelf, according to him," he said to King. "But he wouldn't admit that it's in plain sight.

Therefore there must be a wrapper or dust jacket on it—from another book."

He ran his finger along a line of books, all but one of which had no jackets, and finally pointed to a book with a blue-paper covering. The spine of the jacket had a picture of Humpty-Dumpty. Carefully he leaned over to examine the top of the book.

"It seems a little small for its jacket," said Prichard. "You'd almost think the two weren't made to fit together." He reached out, grasped the book, and jerked it free of the shelf.

"There, Mr. Farragut," he said. "That's the book you hid."

On the wall the clock chugged loudly, and the minute hand pointed straight up. Four o'clock.

King took the book and with trembling hands slid it out of the ill-fitting paper jacket covered with nursery-rhyme characters. He leafed through the pages and then looked wide-eyed at Prichard. "That's it!" he whispered in awed tones. "A first edition of *The Maltese Falcon*." He turned to Farragut.

"I've won, Edmund." King's voice trembled with excitement. "Your collection belongs to the library. At last I've gotten the best of you."

"Oh, I suppose so," replied Farragut testily. "But I still stick to my opinion of your choice of detective stories. After all, it was Mr. Prichard here who did all the detective work."

"I really wasn't—" Prichard began.

"No, it's true, Mr. Prichard," said King. "And I'm eternally grateful. But would you mind telling me how you figured it out? Why here in the children's section, of all places?"

"It was in the three clues," smiled Prichard. "3.14 equals pi. And Maltese falcon is black bird. And double dozen is twenty-four."

He took the cards and envelopes from his pocket and arranged them on a table. King read them aloud, as Prichard had written them.

"Four-and-twenty—black bird—pi."

"Not quite," said Prichard. "Remember, 'pi' was written on the envelope. And the cards were in the envelope."

"All right them, four-and-twenty—black bird—in pi. Of course! The old nursery rhyme. 'Sing a song of sixpence, a pocket full of rye. Four-and-twenty blackbirds baked in a pie.'"

Prichard pantomimed withdrawing the book from the false jacket and took up the chant: " 'When the pie was opened, the birds began to sing.' " He pointed to the book in Andrew King's hand and concluded the poem.

" 'Now wasn't that a dainty dish to set before the *king?*' "

Andrew King applauded heartily. Farragut remained stolidly silent.

"Naturally when I spotted this book jacket I figured I'd found what we were looking for," added Prichard. "Especially when I saw the book didn't fit the jacket."

"*Sing a Song of Sixpence and Other Childhood Poems,*" read King from the paper jacket. "Of course, this had to be it—the only nursery-rhyme book with a jacket. A superb bit of deduction, Mr. Prichard."

"Andrew," said Farragut drily, "I'm attaching another condition to your acquisition of my mystery collection."

"No fair, Edmund," King waved an admonishing finger.

"No, I think you'll like this one. A collection as valuable as mine needs someone to take care of it. And I insist that you appoint Mr. Prichard here. At a whacking good increase in salary, of course. A man of his talents ought to be put to better use than just shoving books onto shelves. And who knows? Maybe he can even get you interested in the truly great detective-story writers. Doyle, Christie, Sayers—"

"Hammett, Chandler, Macdonald," countered King.

As the litany of names droned on, Prichard silently backed out of the room. Hardboiled stories or the classical "great detective" variety—which were better? He didn't care to argue the point.

He liked 'em all.

ROBERT BARR

Lord Chizelrigg's Missing Fortune

THE NAME OF THE LATE Lord Chizelrigg never comes to my mind without instantly suggesting that of Mr. T. A. Edison. I never saw the late Lord Chizelrigg, and I have met Mr. Edison only twice in my life, yet the two men are linked in my memory, and it was a remark the latter once made that in great measure enabled me to solve the mystery which the former had wrapped round his actions.

There is no memorandum at hand to tell me the year in which those two meetings with Edison took place. I received a note from the Italian ambassador in Paris requesting me to wait upon him at the embassy. I learned that on the next day a deputation was to set out from the embassy to one of the chief hotels, there to make a call in state upon the great American inventor, and formally present to him various insignia accompanying certain honors which the king of Italy had conferred upon him. As many Italian nobles of high rank had been invited, and as these dignitaries would not only be robed in the costumes pertaining to their orders, but in many cases would wear jewels of almost inestimable value, my presence was desired in the belief that I might perhaps be able to ward off any attempt on the part of the deft-handed gentry who might possibly make an effort to gain these treasures, and I may add, with perhaps some little self-gratification, no *contretemps* occurred.

Mr. Edison, of course, had long before received notification of the hour at which the deputation would wait upon him, but when we entered the large parlor assigned to the inventor, it was evident to me at a glance that the celebrated man had forgotten all about the function. He stood by a bare table, from which the cloth had been jerked and flung into a corner, and upon that table were placed several bits of black and greasy machinery—cog wheels, pulleys, bolts, etc. These seemingly belonged to a French workman who stood on the other side of the table, with one of the parts in his grimy hand. Edison's own hands were not too clean, for he had palpably been examining the material, and conversing with the workman, who wore the ordinary long blouse of an iron craftsman in a small way. I judged him to be a man with a little shop of his own in some back street, who did odd jobs of engineering, assisted perhaps by a skilled helper or two, and a few apprentices. Edison looked sternly towards the door as the solemn procession filed in, and there was a trace of annoyance on his face at the interruption, mixed with a shade of perplexity as to what this gorgeous display all meant. The Italian is as ceremonious as the Spaniard where a function is concerned, and the official who held the ornate box which contained the jewelry resting on a velvet cushion, stepped slowly forward, and came to a stand in front of the bewildered American. Then the ambassador, in sonorous voice, spoke some gracious words regarding the friendship existing between the United States and Italy, expressed a wish that their rivalry should ever take the form of benefits conferred upon the human race, and instanced the honored recipient as the most notable example the world had yet produced of a man bestowing blessings upon all nations in the arts of peace. The eloquent ambassador concluded by saying that, at the command of his royal master, it was both his duty and his pleasure to present, and so forth and so forth.

Mr. Edison, visibly ill at ease, nevertheless made a suitable reply in the fewest possible words, and the *étalage* being thus at an end, the noblemen, headed by their ambassador, slowly retired, myself forming the tail of the procession. Inwardly I deeply sympathized with the French workman who thus unexpectedly found himself confronted by so much magnificence. He cast one wild look about him, but saw that his retreat was cut off unless he displaced some of these gorgeous grandees. He tried then to shrink into himself and finally stood helpless like one paralyzed. In spite of republican institutions, there is deep down in every Frenchman's heart a respect and awe for official pageants, sumptuously staged and costumed as this one was. But he likes to view it from afar, and supported by his fellows, not thrust incongruously into the midst of things, as was the case with this panic-stricken engineer. As I passed out, I cast a glance over my shoulder at the humble artisan content with a profit of a few francs a day, and at the million-aire inventor opposite him. Edison's face, which during the address had been cold and impassive, reminding me vividly of a bust of Napoleon, was now all aglow with enthusiasm as he turned to his humble visitor. He cried joyfully to the workman:

"A minute's demonstration is worth an hour's explanation. I'll call round tomorrow at your shop, about ten o'clock, and show you how to make the thing work."

I lingered in the hall until the Frenchman came out, then, introducing myself to him, asked the privilege of visiting his shop next day at ten. This was accorded with that courtesy which you will always find among the industrial classes of France, and next day I had the pleasure of meeting Mr. Edison. During our conversation. I complimented him on his invention of the incandescent electric light, and this was the reply that has ever remained in my memory:

"It was not an invention, but a discovery. We have what we wanted; a carbonized tissue, which would withstand the elec-tric current in a vacuum for, say, a thousand hours. If no such tissue existed, then the incandescent light, as we know it, was not possible. My assistants started out to find this tissue, and we simply carbonized everything we could lay our hands on, and ran the current through it in a vacuum. At last we struck the right thing, as we were bound to do if we kept on long enough, and if the thing existed. Patience and hard work will overcome any obstacle."

This belief has been of great assistance to me in my profes-sion. I know the idea is prevalent that a detective arrives at his solutions in a dramatic way through following clues invisi-ble to the ordinary man. This doubtless frequently happens, but, as a general thing, the patience and hard work which Mr. Edison commends is a much safer guide. Very often the follow-ing of excellent clues had led me to disaster, as was the case with my unfortunate attempt to solve the mystery of the five hundred diamonds.

As I was saying, I never think of the late Lord Chizelrigg without remembering Mr. Edison at the same time, and yet the two were very dissimilar. I suppose Lord Chizelrigg was the most useless man that ever lived, while Edison is the opposite.

One day my servant brought into me a card on which was engraved "Lord Chizelrigg."

"Show his lordship in," I said, and there appeared a young man of perhaps twenty-four or twenty-five, well dressed, and of most charming manners, who, nevertheless, began his interview by asking a question such as had never before been addressed to me, and which, if put to a solicitor, or other professional man, would have been answered with some indignation. Indeed, I believe it is a written or unwritten law of the legal profession that the acceptance of such a proposal as Lord Chizelrigg made to me, would if proved, result in the disgrace and ruin of the lawyer.

"Monsieur Valmont," began Lord Chizelrigg, "do you ever take up cases on speculation?"

"On speculation, sir? I do not think I understand you."

His lordwhip blushed like a girl, and stammered slightly as he attempted an explanation.

"What I mean is, do you accept a case on a contingent fee? That is to say, monsieur—er—well, not to put too fine a point upon it, no results, no pay."

I replied somewhat severely:

"Such an offer has never been made to me, and I may say at once that I should be compelled to decline it were I favored with the opportunity. In the cases submitted to me, I devote my time and attention to their solution. I try to deserve success, but I cannot command it, and as in the interim I must live, I am reluctantly compelled to make a charge for my time, at least. I believe the doctor sends in his bill, though the patient dies."

The young man laughed uneasily, and seemed almost too embarrassed to proceed, but finally he said:

"Your illustration strikes home with greater accuracy than probably you imagined when you uttered it. I have just paid my last penny to the physician who attended my late uncle,

Lord Chizelrigg, who died six months ago. I am fully aware that the suggestion I made may seem like a reflection upon your skill, or rather, as implying a doubt regarding it. But I should be grieved, monsieur, if you fell into such an error. I could have come here and commissioned you to undertake some elucidation of the strange situation in which I find myself, and I make no doubt you would have accepted the task if your numerous engagements had permitted. Then, if you failed, I should have been unable to pay you, for I am practically bankrupt. My whole desire, therefore, was to make an honest beginning, and to let you know exactly how I stand. If you succeed, I shall be a rich man; if you do not succeed, I shall be what I am now, penniless. Have I made it plain now why I began with a question which you had every right to resent?"

"Perfectly plain, my lord, and your candor does you credit."

I was very much taken with the unassuming manners of the young man, and his evident desire to accept no service under false pretenses. When I had finished my sentence the pauper nobleman rose to his feet, and bowed.

"I am very much your debtor, monsieur, for your courtesy in receiving me, and can only beg pardon for occupying your time on a futile quest. I wish you good morning, monsieur."

"One moment, my lord," I rejoined, waving him to his chair again.

"Although I am unprepared to accept a commission on the terms you suggest, I may, nevertheless, be able to offer a hint or two that will prove of service to you. I think I remember the announcement of Lord Chizelrigg's death. He was somewhat eccentric, was he not?"

"Eccentric?" said the young man, with a slight laugh, seating himself again—"well, *rather!*"

"I vaguely remember that he was accredited with the possession of something like twenty thousand acres of land?"

"Twenty-seven thousand, as a matter of fact," replied my visitor.

"Have you fallen heir to the lands as well as to the title?"

"Oh, yes; the estate was entailed. The old gentleman could not divert it from me if he would, and I rather suspect that fact must have been the cause of some worry to him."

"But surely, my lord, a man who owns, as one might say, a principality in this wealthy realm of England cannot be penniless?"

Again the young man laughed.

"Well, no," he replied, thrusting his hand in his pocket and bringing to light a few brown coppers, and a white silver piece. "I possess enough money to buy some food tonight, but not enough to dine at the Hotel Cecil. You see, it is like this. I belong to a somewhat ancient family, various members of whom went the pace, and mortgaged their acres up the hilt. I could not raise a further penny on my estates were I to try my hardest, because at the time the money was lent, land was much more valuable than it is today. Agricultural depression, and all that sort of thing, have, if I may put it so, left me a good many thousands worse off than if I had no land at all. Besides this, during my late uncle's life, Parliament, on his behalf, intervened once or twice, allowing him in the first place to cut valuable timber, and in the second place to sell the pictures of Chizelrigg Chase at Christie's for figures which made one's mouth water."

"And what became of the money?" I asked, whereupon once more this genial nobleman laughed.

"That is exactly what I came up in the lift to learn if Monsieur Valmont could discover."

"My lord, you interest me," I said, quite truly, with an uneasy apprehension that I should take up his case after all, for I liked the young man already. His lack of pretense appealed to me, and that sympathy which is so universal among my countrymen enveloped him, as I may say, quite independent of my own will.

"My uncle," went on Lord Chizelrigg, "was somewhat of an anomaly in our family. He must have been a reversal to a very, very ancient type; a type of which we have no record. He was as miserly as his forefathers were prodigal. When he came into the title and estate some twenty years ago, he dismissed the whole retinue of servants, and, indeed, was defendant in several cases at law where retainers of our family brought suit against him for wrongful dismissal, or dismissal without a penny compensation in lieu of notice. I am pleased to say he lost all his cases, and when he pleaded poverty, got permission to sell a certain number of heirlooms, enabling him to make compensation, and giving him something on which to live. These heirlooms at auction sold so unexpectedly well that my uncle acquired a taste, as it were, of what might be done. He could always prove that the rents went to the mortgagees, and that he had nothing on which to exist, so on several occasions he obtained permission from the courts to cut timber and sell pictures, until he denuded the estate and made an empty barn of the old manor house. He lived like any laborer, occupying himself sometimes as a carpenter, sometimes as a blacksmith; indeed, he made a blacksmith's shop of the library, one of the most noble rooms in Britain, containing thousands of valuable books which again and again he applied for permission to sell, but this privilege was never granted to him. I find on coming into the property that my uncle quite persistently evaded the law, and depleted this superb collection, book by book, surreptitiously through dealers in London. This, of course, would have got him into deep trouble if it had been discovered before his death, but now the valuable volumes are gone, and there is no redress. Many of them are doubtless in America, or in museums and collections of Europe."

"You wish me to trace them, perhaps?" I interpolated.

"Oh, no; they are past praying for. The old man made tens of thousands by the sale of the timber, and other tens of thousands by disposing of the pictures. The house is denuded of its fine old furniture, which was immensely valuable, and then the books, as I have said, must have brought in the revenue of a prince, if he got anything like their value, and you may be sure he was shrewd enough to know their worth. Since the last refusal of the courts to allow him further relief, as he termed it, which was some seven years ago, he had quite evidently been disposing of books and furniture by a private sale, in defiance of the law. At that time I was under age, but my guardians opposed his application to the courts, and demanded an account of the moneys already in his hands. The judges upheld the opposition of my guardians, and refused to allow a further spoliation of the estate, but they did not grant the accounting my guardians asked, because the proceeds of the former sales were entirely at the disposal of my uncle, and were sanctioned by the law to permit him to live as befitted his station. If he lived meagerly instead of lavishly, as my guardians contended, that, the judges said, was his affair, and there the matter ended.

"My uncle took a violent dislike to me on account of this opposition to his last application, although, of course, I had nothing whatever to do with the matter. He lived like a hermit, mostly in the library, and was waited upon by an old man and his wife, and these three were the only inhabitants of a mansion that could comfortably house a hundred. He visited nobody, and would allow no one to approach Chizelrigg Chase. In order that all who had the misfortune to have dealings with him should continue to endure trouble after his death, he left what might be called a will, but which rather may be termed a letter to me. Here is a copy of it.

" 'My dear Tom,—You will find your fortune between a couple of sheets of paper in the library.
" 'Your affectionate uncle,
" 'Reginald Moran, Earl of Chizelrigg.' "

"I should doubt if that were a legal will," said I.

"It doesn't need to be," replied the young man with a smile. "I am next-of-kin, and heir to everything he possessed, although, of course, he might have given his money elsewhere if he had chosen to do so. Why he did not bequeath it to some institution, I do not know. He knew no man personally except his own servants, whom he misused and starved, but, as he told them, he misused and starved himself, so they had no cause to grumble. He said he was treating them like one of the family. I suppose he thought it would cause me more worry and anxiety if he concealed the money and put me on the wrong scent, which I am convinced he has done, than to leave it openly to any person or charity."

"I need not ask if you have searched the library?"

"Searched it? Why, there never was such a search since the world began!"

"Possibly you put the task into incompetent hands?"

"You are hinting, Monsieur Valmont, that I engaged others until my money was gone, then came to you with a speculative proposal. Let me assure you such is not the case. Incompetent hands, I grant you, but the hands were my own. For the past six months I have lived practically as my uncle lived. I have rummaged that library from floor to ceiling. It was left in a frightful state, littered with old newspapers, accounts, and what-not. Then, of course, there were the books remaining in the library, still a formidable collection."

"Was your uncle a religious man?"

"I could not say. I surmise not. You see, I was unacquainted with him, and never saw him until after his death. I fancy he was not religious, otherwise he could not have acted as he did. Still, he proved himself a man of such twisted mentality that anything is possible."

"I knew a case once where an heir who expected a large sum of money was bequeathed a family Bible, which he threw into the fire, learning afterwards, to his dismay, that it contained many thousands of pounds in Bank of England notes, the object of the devisor being to induce the legatee to read the good Book or suffer through the neglect of it."

"I have searched the Scriptures," said the youthful earl with a laugh, "but the benefit has been moral rather than material."

"Is there any chance that your uncle has deposited his wealth in a bank, and has written a check for the amount, leaving it between two leaves of a book?"

"Anything is possible, monsieur, but I think that highly improbable. I have gone through every tome, page by page, and I suspect very few of the volumes have been opened for the last twenty years."

"How much money do you estimate he accumulated?"

"He must have cleared more than a hundred thousand pounds, but speaking of banking it, I would like to say that my uncle evinced a deep distrust of banks, and never drew a check in his life so far as I am aware. All accounts were paid in gold by this old steward, who first brought the receipted bill in to my uncle, and then received the exact amount, after having left the room and waited until he was rung for, so that he might not learn the repository from which my uncle drew his store. I believe if the money is ever found it will be in gold, and I am very sure that this will was written, if we may call it a will, to put us on the wrong scent."

"Have you had the library cleared out?"

"Oh, no, it is practically as my uncle left it. I realized that if I were to call in help, it would be well that the newcomer found it undisturbed."

"You were quite right, my lord. You say you examined all the papers?"

"Yes; so far as that is concerned, the room has been very fairly gone over, but nothing that was in it the day my uncle died has been removed, not even his anvil."

"His anvil?"

"Yes; I told you he made a blacksmith's shop, as well as

bedroom, of the library. It is a huge room, with a great fire-place at one end which formed an excellent forge. He and the steward built the forge in the eastern fireplace, of brick and clay, with their own hands, and erected there a secondhand blacksmith's bellows."

"What work did he do at his forge?"

"Oh, anything that was required about the place. He seems to have been a very expert ironworker. He would never buy a new implement for the garden or the house so long as he could get one secondhand, and he never bought anything sec-ondhand while at his forge he might repair what was already in use. He kept an old cob, on which he used to ride through the park, and he always put the shoes on this cob himself, the steward informs me, so he must have understood the use of blacksmith's tools. He made a carpeners's shop of the chief drawing room and erected a bench there. I think a very useful mechanic was spoiled when my uncle became an earl."

"You have been living at the Chase since your uncle died?"

"If you call it living, yes. The old steward and his wife have been looking after me, as they looked after my uncle, and, seeing me day after day, coatless and covered with dust, I imagine they think me a second edition of the old man."

"Does the steward know the money is missing?"

"No; no one knows it but myself. This will was left on the anvil, in an envelope addressed to me."

"Your statement is exceedingly clear, Lord Chizelrigg, but I confess I don't see much daylight through it. Is there a pleasant country around Chizelrigg Chase?"

"Very; especially at this season of the year. In autumn and winter the house is a little drafty. It needs several thousand pounds to put it in repair."

"Drafts do not matter in the summer. I have been long enough in England not to share the fear of my countrymen for a *courant d'air*. Is there a spare bed in the manor house, or shall I take down a cot with me, or let us say a hammock?"

"Really," stammered the earl, blushing again, "you must not think I detailed all these circumstances in order to influence you to take up what may be a hopeless case. I, of course, am deeply interested, and, therefore, somewhat prone to be carried away when I begin a recital of my uncle's eccentricities. If I receive your permission, I will call on you again in a month or two. To tell you the truth, I borrowed a little money from the old steward, and visited London to see my legal advisers, hoping that in the circumstances I may get permission to sell something that will keep me from starvation. When I spoke of the house being denuded I meant relatively, of course. There are still a good many antiquities which would doubtless bring me in a comfortable sum of money. I have been borne up by the belief that I should find my uncle's gold. Lately, I have been beset by a suspicion that the old gentleman thought the library the only valuable asset left, and for this reason wrote his note, thinking I would be afraid to sell anything from that room. The old rascal must have made a pot of money out of those shelves. The catalogue shows that there was a copy of the first book printed in England by Caxton, and several priceless Shakespeares, as well as many other volumes that a collector would give a small fortune for. All these are gone. I think when I show this to be the case, the authorities cannot refuse me the right to sell something, and, if I get this permission, I shall at once call upon you."

"Nonsense, Lord Chizelrigg. Put your application in motion, if you like. Meanwhile I beg of you to look upon me as a more substantial banker than your old steward. Let us enjoy a good dinner together at the Cecil tonight, if you will do me the honor to be my guest. Tomorrow we can leave for Chizelrigg Chase. How far is it?"

"About three hours," replied the young man, becoming as red as a new Queen Anne villa. "Really, Monsieur Valmont, you overwhelm me with your kindness, but nevertheless I accept your generous offer."

"Then that's settled. What's the name of the old steward?"

"Higgins."

"You are certain he has no knowledge of the hiding place of this treasure?"

"Oh, quite sure. My uncle was not a man to make a confidant of any one, least of all an old babbler like Higgins."

"Well, I should like to be introduced to Higgins as a benighted foreigner. That will make him despise me and treat me like a child."

"Oh, I say," protested the earl, "I should have thought you'd lived long enough in England to have got out of the notion that we do not appreciate the foreigner. Indeed, we are the only nation in the world that extends a cordial welcome to him, rich or poor."

"*Certainement*, my lord, I should be deeply disappointed did you not take me at my proper valuation, but I cherish no delusions regarding the contempt with which Higgins will regard me. He will look upon me as a sort of simpleton to whom the Lord had been unkind by not making England my native land. Now, Higgins must be led to believe that I am in his own class; that is, a servant of yours. Higgins and I will gossip over the fire together, should these spring evenings prove chilly, and before two or three weeks are past, I shall have learned a great deal about your uncle that you never dreamed of. Higgins will talk more freely with a fellow servant than with his master, however much he may respect that master, and then, as I am a foreigner, he will babble down to my comprehension, and I shall get details that he never would think of giving to a fellow countryman."

※

THE YOUNG EARL'S MODESTY in such description of his home as he had given me, left me totally unprepared for the grandeur of the mansion, one corner of which he inhabited. It is such a place as you read of in romances of the Middle Ages; not a pinnacled or turreted Franch château of that period, but a beautiful and substantial stone manor house of a ruddy color, whose warm hue seemed to add a softness to the severity of its architecture. It is built round an outer and an inner courtyard and could house a thousand, rather than the hundred with which its owner had accredited it. There are many stone-mullioned windows, and one at the end of the library might well have graced a cathedral. This superb residence occupies the center of a heavily timbered park, and from the lodge at the gates we drove at least a mile and a half under the grandest avenue of old oaks I have ever seen. It seemed incredible that the owner of all this should actually lack the ready money to pay his fare to town!

Old Higgins met us at the station with a somewhat rickety cart, to which was attached the ancient cob that the late earl used to shoe. We entered a noble hall, which probably looked the larger because of the entire absence of any kind of furniture, unless two complete suits of venerable armor which stood on either hand might be considered as furnishing. I laughed aloud when the door was shut, and the sound echoed like the merriment of ghosts from the dim timbered roof above me.

"What are you laughing at?" asked the earl.

"I am laughing to see you put your modern tall hat on that mediæval helmet."

"Oh, that's it! Well, put yours on the other. I mean no disrespect to the ancestor who wore this suit, but we are short of the harmless, necessary hat rack, so I put my topper on the antique helmet, and thrust the umbrella (if I have one) in behind here, and down one of his legs. Since I came in possession, a very crafty-looking dealer from London visited me, and attempted to sound me regarding the sale of these suits of armor. I gathered he would give enough money to keep me in new suits, London made, for the rest of my life, but when I endeavored to find out if he had had commercial dealings with my prophetic uncle, he became frightened and bolted. I imagine that if I had possessed presence of mind enough to have lured him into one of our most uncomfortable dungeons, I might have learned where some of the family treasures went to. Come up these stairs, Monsieur Valmont, and I shall show you your room."

We had lunched on the train coming down, so after a wash in my own room I proceeded at once to inspect the library. It proved, indeed, a most noble apartment, and it had been scandalously used by the old reprobate, its late tenant. There were two huge fireplaces, one in the middle of the north wall and the other at the eastern end. In the latter had been erected a rude brick forge, and beside the forge hung a great black bellows, smoky with usage. On a wooden block lay the anvil, and around it rested and rusted several hammers, large and small. At the western end was a glorious window filled with ancient stained glass, which, as I have said, might have adorned a cathedral. Extensive as the collection of books was, the great size of this chamber made it necessary that only the outside wall should be covered with bookcases, and even these were divided by tall windows. The opposite wall was blank, with the exception of a picture here and there, and these pictures offered a further insult to the room, for they were cheap prints, mostly colored lithographs that had appeared in Christmas numbers of London weekly journals, encased in poverty-stricken frames, hanging from nails ruthlessly driven in above them. The floor was covered with a litter of papers, in some places knee deep, and in the corner farthest from the forge still stood the bed on which the ancient miser had died.

"Looks like a stable, doesn't it?" commented the earl, when I had finished my inspection. "I am sure the old boy simply filled it up with this rubbish to give me the trouble of examining it. Higgins tells me that up to within a month before he died the room was reasonably clear of all this muck. Of course, it had to be, or the place would have caught fire from the sparks of the forge. The old man made Higgins gather all the papers he could find anywhere about the place, ancient accounts, newspapers, and whatnot, even to the brown wrapping paper you see, in which parcels came, and commanded him to strew the floor with this litter, because as he complained, Higgins' boots on the boards made too much noise, and Higgins, who is not in the least of an inquiring mind, accepted this explanation as entirely meeting the case."

Higgins proved to be a garrulous old fellow, who needed no urging to talk about the late earl; indeed, it was almost impossible to deflect his conversation into any other channel. Twenty years' intimacy with the eccentric nobleman had largely obliterated that sense of deference with which an English servant usually approaches his master. An English underling's idea of nobility is the man who never by any possibility works with his hands. The fact that Lord Chizelrigg had toiled at the carpenter's bench; had mixed cement in the drawing room; had caused the anvil to ring out till midnight, aroused no admiration in Higgins' mind. In addition to this, the ancient nobleman had been penuriously strict in his examination of accounts, exacting the uttermost farthing, so the humble servitor regarded his memory with supreme contempt. I realized before the drive was finished from the station to Chizelrigg Chase that there was little use of introducing me to Higgins as a foreigner and a fellow servant. I found myself completely unable to understand what the old fellow said. His dialect was as unknown to me as the Choctaw language would have been, and the young earl was compelled to act as interpreter on the occasions when we set this garrulous talking-machine going.

The new Earl of Chizelrigg, with the enthusiasm of a boy, proclaimed himself my pupil and assistant, and said he would do whatever he was told. His thorough and fruitless search of the library had convinced him that the old man was merely chaffing him, as he put it, by leaving such a letter as he had written. His lordship was certain that the money had been hidden somewhere else; probably buried under one of the trees in the park. Of course this was possible, and represented the usual method by which a stupid person conceals treasure, yet I did not think it probable. All conversations with Higgins showed the earl to have been an extremely suspicious man; suspicious of banks, suspicious even of Bank of England notes, suspicious of every person on earth, not omitting Higgins himself. Therefore, as I told his nephew, the miser would never allow the fortune out of his sight and immediate reach.

From the first the oddity of the forge and anvil being placed in his bedroom struck me as peculiar, and I said to the young man:

"I'll stake my reputation that forge or anvil, or both, contain the secret. You see, the old gentleman worked sometimes till midnight, for Higgins could hear his hammering. If he used hard coal on the forge the fire would last through the night, and being in continual terror of thieves, as Higgins says, barricading the castle every evening before dark as if it were a fortress, he was bound to place the treasure in the most unlikely spot for a thief to get at it. Now, the coal fire smoldered all night long, and if the gold was in the forge underneath the embers, it would be extremely difficult to get at. A robber rummaging in the dark would burn his fingers in more senses than one. Then, as his lordship kept no less than four loaded revolvers under his pillow, all he had to do, if a thief entered his room, was to allow the search to go on until the thief started at the forge, then doubtless, as he had the range with reasonable accuracy night or day, he might sit up in bed and blaze away with revolver after revolver. There were twenty-eight shots that could be fired in about double as many seconds, so you see the robber stood little chance in the face of such a fusillade. I propose that we dismantle the forge."

Lord Chizelrigg was much taken by my reasoning, and one morning early we cut down the big bellows, tore it open, found it empty, then took brick after brick from the forge with a crowbar, for the old man had built it better than he knew with Portland cement. In fact, when we cleared away the rubbish between the bricks and the core of the furnace we came upon one cube of cement which was as hard as granite. With the aid of Higgins, and a set of rollers and levers, we managed to get this block out into the park, and attempted to crush it with the sledge hammers belonging to the forge, in which we were entirely unsuccessful. The more it resisted our efforts, the more certain we became that the coins would be found within it. As this would not be treasure-trove in the sense that the government might make a claim upon it, there was no particular necessity for secrecy, so we had up a man from the mines nearby with drills and dynamite, who speedily shattered the block into a million pieces, more or less. Alas! there was no trace in its debris of "pay dirt," as the western miner puts it. While the dynamite expert was on the spot, we induced him to shatter the anvil as well as the block of cement, and then the workman, doubtless thinking the new earl was as insane as the old one had been, shouldered his tools, and went back to his mine.

The earl reverted to his former opinion that the gold was concealed in the park, while I held even more firmly to my own belief that the fortune rested in the library.

"It is obvious," I said to him, "that if the treasure is buried outside, someone must have dug the hole. A man so timorous and so reticent as your uncle would allow no one to do this but himself. Higgins maintained the other evening that all picks and spades were safely locked up by himself each night in the toolhouse. The mansion itself was barricaded with such exceeding care that it would have been difficult for your uncle to get outside even if he wished to do so. Then such a man as your uncle is described to have been would continually desire ocular demonstration that his savings were intact, which would be practically impossible if the gold had found a grave in the park. I propose now that we abandon violence and dynamite, and proceed to an intellectual search of the library."

"Very well," replied the young earl, "but as I have already searched the library very thoroughly, your use of the word 'intellectual,' Monsieur Valmont, is not in accord with your customary politeness. However, I am with you. 'Tis for you to command, and me to obey."

"Pardon me, my lord!" I said, "I used the word 'intellectual' in contradistinction to the word 'dynamite.' It had no reference to your former search. I merely propose that we now abandon the use of chemical reaction, and employ the much greater force of mental activity. Did you notice any writing on the margins of the newspapers you examined?"

"No, I did not."

"Is it possible that there may have been some communication on the white border of a newspaper?"

"It is, of course, possible."

"Then will you set yourself to the task of glancing over the margin of every newspaper, piling them away in another room when your scrutiny of each is complete? Do not destroy anything, but we must clear out the library completely. I am interested in the accounts, and will examine them."

It was exasperatingly tedious work, but after several days my assistant reported every margin scanned without result, while I had collected each bill and memorandum, classifying them according to date. I could not get rid of a suspicion that the contrary old beast had written instructions for the finding of the treasure on the back of some account, or on the flyleaf of a book, and as I looked at the thousands of volumes still left in the library, the prospect of such a patient and minute search appalled me. But I remembered Edison's words to the effect that if a thing exists, search, exhaustive enough, will find it. From the mass of accounts I selected several; the rest I placed in another room, alongside the heap of the earl's newspapers.

"Now," said I to my helper, "if it please you, we will have Higgins in, as I wish some explanation of these accounts."

"Perhaps I can assist you," suggested his lordship, drawing up a chair opposite the table on which I had spread the statements. "I have lived here for six months, and know as much about things as Higgins does. He is so difficult to stop when once he begins to talk. What is the first account you wish further to light upon?"

"To go back thirteen years I find that your uncle bought a secondhand safe in Sheffield. Here is the bill. I consider it necessary to find that safe."

"Pray forgive me, Monsieur Valmont," cried the young man, springing to his feet and laughing; "so heavy an article as a safe should not slip readily from a man's memory, but it did from mine. The safe is empty, and I gave no more thought to it."

Saying this the earl went to one of the bookcases that stood against the wall, pulled it round as if it were a door, books and all, and displayed the front of an iron safe, the door of which he also drew open, exhibiting the usual empty interior of such a receptacle.

"I came on this," he said, "when I took down all these volumes. It appears that there was once a secret door leading from the library into an outside room, which has long since disappeared; the walls are very thick. My uncle doubtless caused this door to be taken off its hinges, and the safe placed in the aperture, the rest of which he then bricked up."

"Quite so," said I, endeavoring to conceal my disappointment. "As this strongbox was bought secondhand and not made to order, I suppose there can be no secret crannies in it?"

"It looks like a common or garden safe," reported my assistant, "but we'll have it out if you say so."

"Not just now," I replied. "We've had enough of dynamiting to make us feel like housebreakers already."

"I agree with you. What's the next item on the program?"

"Your uncle's mania for buying things at secondhand was broken in three instances so far as I have been able to learn from a scrutiny of these accounts. About four years ago he purchased a new book from Denny and Co., the well known booksellers of the Strand. Denny and Co. deal only in new books. Is there any comparatively new volume in the library?"

"Not one."

"Are you sure of that?"

"Oh, quite; I searched all the literature in the house. What is the name of the volume he bought?"

"That I cannot decipher. The initial letter looks like 'M,' but the rest is a mere wavy line. I see, however, that it cost twelve and sixpence, while the cost of carriage by parcel post was sixpence, which shows it weighed something under four pounds. This, with the price of the book, induces me to think that it was a scientific work, printed on heavy paper and illustrated."

"I know nothing of it," said the earl.

"The third account is for wallpaper; twenty-seven rolls of an expensive wallpaper, and twenty-seven rolls of a cheap paper, the latter being just half the price of the former. This wallpaper seems to have been supplied by a tradesman in the station road in the village of Chizelrigg."

"There's your wallpaper," cried the youth, waving his hand; "he was going to paper the whole house, Higgins told me, but got tired after he had finished the library, which took him nearly a year to accomplish, for he worked at it very intermittently, mixing the paste in the boudoir, a pailful at a time as he needed it. It was a scandalous thing to do, for underneath the paper is the most exquisite oak panelling, very plain, but very rich in color."

I rose and examined the paper on the wall. It was dark brown, and answered the description of the expensive paper on the bill.

"What became of the cheap paper?" I asked.

"I don't know."

"I think," said I, "we are on the track of the mystery. I believe that paper covers a sliding panel or concealed door."

"It is very likely," replied the earl. "I intended to have the paper off, but I had no money to pay a workman, and I am not so industrious as was my uncle. What is your remaining account?"

"The last also pertains to paper, but comes from a firm in Budge Row, London, E.C. He has had, it seems, a thousand sheets of it, and it appears to have been frightfully expensive. This bill is also illegible, but I take it a thousand sheets were supplied, although of course it may have been a thousand quires, which would be a little more reasonable for the price charged, or a thousand reams, which would be exceedingly cheap."

"I don't know anything about that. Let's turn on Higgins."

Higgins knew nothing of this last order of paper, either. The wallpaper mystery he at once cleared up. Apparently the old earl had discovered by experiment that the heavy, expensive wallpaper would not stick to the glossy panelling, so he had purchased a cheaper paper, and had pasted that on first. Higgins said he had gone all over the panelling with a yellowish-white paper, and after that was dry, he pasted over it the more expensive rolls.

"But," I objected, "the two papers were bought and delivered at the same time; therefore, he could not have found by experiment that the heavy paper would not stick."

"I don't think there is much in that," commented the earl; "the heavy paper may have been bought first, and found to be unsuitable, and then the coarse, cheap paper bought afterwards. The bill merely shows that the account was sent in on that date. Indeed, as the village of Chizelrigg is but a few miles away, it would have been quite possible for my uncle to have bought the heavy paper in the morning, tried it, and in the afternoon sent for the commoner lot; but in any case, the bill would not have been presented until months after the order, and the two purchases were thus lumped together."

I was forced to confess that this seemed reasonable.

Now, about the book ordered from Denny's. Did Higgins remember anything regarding it? It came four years ago.

Ah, yes, Higgins did; he remembered it very well indeed. He had come in one morning with the earl's tea, and the old man was sitting up in bed reading this volume with such interest that he was unaware of Higgins' knock, and Higgins himself, being a little hard of hearing, took for granted the command to enter. The earl hastily thrust the book under the pillow, alongside the revolvers, and berated Higgins in a most cruel way for entering the room before getting permission to do so. He had never seen the earl so angry before, and he laid it all to this book. It was after the book had come that the forge had been erected and the anvil bought. Higgins never saw the book again, but one morning, six months before the earl died, Higgins, in raking out the cinders of the forge, found what he supposed was a portion of the book's cover. He believed his master had burnt the volume.

Having dismissed Higgins, I said to the earl:

"The first thing to be done is to enclose this bill to Denny and Co., booksellers, Strand. Tell them you have lost the volume, and ask them to send another. There is likely someone in the shop who can decipher the illegible writing. I am certain the book will give us a clue. Now, I shall write to Braun and Sons, Budge Row. This is evidently a French company; in fact, the name as connected with paper-making runs in my mind, although I cannot at this moment place it. I shall ask them the use of this paper that they furnished to the late earl."

This was done accordingly, and now, as we thought, until the answers came, we were two men out of work. Yet the next morning, I am pleased to say, and I have always rather plumed myself on the fact, I solved the mystery before replies were received from London. Of course, both the book and the answer of the paper agents, by putting two and two together, would have given us the key.

After breakfast, I strolled somewhat aimlessly into the library, whose floor was now strewn merely with brown wrapping paper, bits of string and all that. As I shuffled among this with my feet, as if tossing aside dead autumn leaves in a forest path, my attention was suddenly drawn to several squares of paper, unwrinkled, and never used for wrapping. These sheets seemed to me strangely familiar. I picked one of them up, and at once the significance of the name Braun and Sons occurred to me. They are paper makers in France, who produce a smooth, very tough sheet, which, dear as it is, proves infinitely cheap compared with the fine vellum it deposed in a certain branch of industry. In Paris, years before, these sheets had given me the knowledge of how a gang of thieves disposed of their gold without melting it. The paper was used instead of vellum in the rougher processes of manufacturning gold leaf. It stood the constant beating of the hammer nearly as well as the vellum, and here at once there flashed on me the secret of the old man's midnight anvil work. He was transforming his sovereigns into gold leaf, which must have been of a rude, thick kind, because to produce the gold leaf of commerce he still needed the vellum as well as a "crutch" and other machinery, of which we had found no trace.

"My lord," I called to my assistant; he was at the other end of the room; "I wish to test a theory on the anvil of your own fresh common sense."

"Hammer away," replied the earl, approaching me with his usual good-natured, jocular expression.

"I eliminate the safe from our investigations because it was purchased thirteen years ago, but the buying of the book, of wall covering, of this tough paper from France, all group themselves into a set of incidents occurring within the same month as the purchase of the anvil and the building of the forge; therefore, I think they are related to one another. Here are some sheets of paper he got from Budge Row. Have you ever seen anything like it? Try to tear this sample."

"It's reasonably tough," admitted his lordship, fruitlessly endeavoring to rip it apart.

"Yes. It was made in France, and is used in gold beating. Your uncle beat his sovereigns into gold leaf. You will find that the book from Denny's is a volume on gold beating, and now as I remember that scribbled word which I could not make out, I think the title of the volume is *Metallurgy*. It contains, no doubt, a chapter on the manufacture of gold leaf."

"I believe you," said the earl; "but I don't see that the discovery sets us any further forward. We're now looking for gold leaf instead of sovereigns."

"Let's examine this wallpaper," said I.

I placed my knife under a corner of it at the floor, and quite easily ripped off a large section. As Higgins had said, the brown paper was on top, and the coarse, light-colored paper underneath. But even that came away from the oak panelling as easily as though it hung there from habit, and not because of paste.

"Feel the weight of that," I cried, handing him the sheet I had torn from the wall.

"By jove!" said the earl, in a voice almost of awe.

I took it from him, and laid it, face downwards, on the wooden table, threw a little water on the back, and with a knife scraped away the porous white paper. Instantly there gleamed up at us the baleful yellow of the gold. I shrugged my shoulders and spread out my hands. The Earl of Chizelrigg laughed aloud and very heartily.

"You see how it is," I cried. "The old man first covered the entire wall with this whitish paper. He heated his sovereigns at the forge and beat them out on the anvil, then completed the process rudely between the sheets of this paper from France. Probably he pasted the gold to the wall as soon as he shut himself in for the night, and covered it over with the more expensive paper before Higgins entered in the morning."

We found afterwards, however, that he had actually fastened the thick sheets of gold to the wall with carpet tacks.

His lordship netted a trifle over a hundred and twenty-three thousand pounds through my discovery, and I am pleased to pay tribute to the young man's generosity by saying that his voluntary settlement made my bank account swell stout as a City alderman.

RUTH RENDELL

The Copper Peacock

PETER SEEBURG LIVED IN A FLAT without a kitchen.

"Kitchens make you fat," he said.

Bernard asked if that was one of the principles of the Seeburg Diet which Peter was going to the United States to promote. Peter smiled.

"All one needs," he said, "is an electric kettle in the bathroom and a fridge somewhere else." He added rather obscurely, "Eating out keeps you thin because it is so expensive."

He was lending the flat to Bernard while he was in America.
They walked around it and Peter explained how things
worked. The place was very clean. "A woman comes in three
times a week. Her name's Judy. She won't get in your way."

"Do I have to have her?"

"Oh, dear, yes, you do. If I get rid of her for three months,
I'll never get her back again and I can't do with that."

He would have to put up with it, Bernard supposed. Peter's
kindness in lending him the flat, rent-free, to write his new
biography in was something he still found overwhelming. It
was quiet here—was this the only street in west London not
being renovated, not a noisy jumble of scaffolding and skips?
No sounds of music penetrated the ceilings. The other tenants
in the block did not, apparently, spend their mornings doing
homework for their carpentry courses. The windows gave on
to plane trees and Regency facades.

"She's very efficient. She'll probably wash your clothes if
you leave them lying about. But you won't be sleeping here,
will you?"

"Absolutely not," said Bernard.

As it was, he felt guilty about leaving Ann alone all day with the children. But it was useless to attempt working at home with a two-year-old and a three-year-old under the same roof with him. Memories were vivid of Jonathan climbing on his shoulders and Jeremy trying out felt-tipped pens on his notes while he was last correcting page proofs. Still, he would be back with them in the evenings. He would have to make up for everything to Ann in the evenings.

"There's no question of my sleeping here," he said to Peter as if he hadn't heard him the first time.

Peter gave him the keys. On Monday morning he was flying to Los Angeles, the first leg of his tour. Bernard arrived in a taxi two hours after he left, bringing with him two very large bags full of books. The biography he was embarking on was the life of a rather obscure Edwardian poet. His last book had been the life of a rather obscure Victorian diarist, and some critic had said of it that the excellence of the writing and the pace of the narrative transcended the fact that few had heard of its subject. Bernard had a gift for writing with elegance and panache about fairly undistinguished literary figures and for writing books that sold surprisingly well.

It was his habit to spread his works of reference out on the floor. He would create little islands of books and notebooks, a group here that dealt with his subject's childhood, a cluster there of criticism of his works, an archipelago of the views of his peers. Two or three rooms ideally should be reserved for this purpose. Some of the books lay open, others with slips of paper inserted between their pages. The notes were in piles that might seem haphazard to others but to Bernard were arranged in a complex but precise order.

As soon as he was inside Peter's flat and the front door closed behind him, Bernard began spreading his books out after this fashion. Already he felt a deep contentment that one particular notebook, containing new material he had assembled on his subject's ancestry, would lie undisturbed, surrounded by its minor islets, instead of being seized upon by Jonathan, as had happened to one of its predecessors, and given a new function as a kneading board for play dough. Bernard created a further island in the bedroom. He wouldn't otherwise be using the bedroom and the books could just lie there for weeks, gathering dust. This was another image which afforded him an intense intellectual pleasure. His typewriter set up on the dining table in the absence of a desk, he found himself making an enthusiastic start, something by no means usual with him.

✳

ON THE FOLLOWING MORNING, though, he recalled that the books couldn't just lie there. No dust would gather because Judy would be coming in to see it did not. Resenting her presence in advance of her arrival, he picked up all the books. slipping in bits of paper at significant pages and sealing the bedroom pile by laying on top of it, open and face-downward, the earliest published biography of his poet. Beginning as he meant to go on, he was at the typewriter, busily working away, rather more busily and noisily in fact than the prose he was committing to paper warranted, when just after ten-thirty he heard the front door open and close.

Some few minutes had passed before she came into the dining room. She knocked first. Bernard was surprised by her youth. She looked no more than twenty-seven. He had expected a stout, aproned, motherly creature in her fifties. What clichés we make of life! She was slim, pretty, dark-haired, wearing jeans and a blouse. But the prettiness was worn and the hair was rough and dry. She was too thin for the tight jeans to be tight on her and her hip bones stuck out like the sharp, curved frame of a lyre.

"Could you do with a coffee?" she said. No introduction, no greeting. Her smile was friendly and cheerful. "I get Peter his coffee about now."

Bernard castigated himself for a snob. Why on earth should she call Peter Mr. Seeburg, anyway? "Thank you. That's very kind of you." He put out his hand. "I'm Bernard Hope."

"Pleased to meet you, Bernard. Peter's told me all about you." For all the readily used christian names, her manner was a little shy, her handshake tentative. "Do you mind if I come in here for the milk?" she said. "I have to make the coffee in the bathroom, but he keeps his fridge in here."

"No, please, go ahead."

"Peter said you'd want all your books left just as they were, but you're very tidy, aren't you?" She didn't wait for an answer but said confidingly, with a slight giggle, "I'll never get over him not having a kitchen. You have to laugh. I get a laugh out of it every time I come here."

All this seemed ominous to Bernard. Fearing a prolonged disturbance of his peace, he set himself to typing furiously when she returned with the coffee. Perhaps this was effective as a deterrent or else she genuinely wanted to get on with her work, for she spoke no further word to him until the time came for her departure at half past twelve. Appearing at the dining-room door in a padded jacket, she mimed—to his astonishment—the action of pounding a keyboard.

"Keep on with the good work. See you Wednesday."

Bernard couldn't resist getting up to review the flat after she had gone. He was pleasantly surprised. Surfaces had been polished and there was a fresh flowery scent in the air. His books lay as he had left them, the slips of paper in place, the important notebook still face-downward and guarding the stack beneath it. He recreated his islands. The coffee cups had disappeared, been washed and restored to their home in a china cabinet. On one of the tables in the living room was a tray covered with a cloth and on the tray was a plate of the kind of sandwiches that are called "dainty," with a glass of orange juice, a polished red apple, and a piece of cheese. His lunch.

Bernard felt quite touched, although he quickly realized that she must do this for Peter and no doubt regarded it as part of the duties for which she was paid. Since Jeremy was born, Ann had never got lunch for him, he had always got his own. Not that he expected his wife to wait on him, of course not, she had the children and the house, more than enough to do. Two of the sandwiches were smoked salmon and two egg and cress. Judy must have brought their ingredients with her and assembled them in the bathroom.

※

NEXT DAY HE WAS PREPARING to say something gracious, but he took a look at her and there was only one thing anyone could say.

"What have you done to yourself?"

She put her hand up to her face. She had a black eye. The cheekbone was dark-red and shiny with bruising and the corner of her lip was cut. Her finger touched the bruise. "Fell against the door, didn't I?" she said. It was a curious usage of language, that interrogatory. He wasn't sure if he had ever heard it before. "Kitchen door with a handle sticking out." She giggled. "That's what comes of having kitchens. Maybe Peter's got the right idea."

He asked her if she had seen a doctor. And when she said she hadn't—she hadn't the patience to sit waiting about for an hour or more just to get a prescription she'd have to pay for, anyway—he thanked her for getting his lunch. "You're welcome, love," she said, and "It's all in the day's work." He watched her test the tenderness of her cut lip with a questing tongue. "Ready for your coffee, are you, or d'you want to wait a bit?"

He had it later in the living room, perusing his notebook while she cleaned the dining room. Things were just as he had left them when he went back except that she had closed the work of reference he had left open by the typewriter and had marked his place with a sheet torn from a scribbling block.

Lunch that day was pâté sandwiches and there was a pear on the tray and a piece of walnut cake. Next time he got Gruyère cheese, mandarin yogurt, and a bunch of red grapes. It was something of a chore going out to buy pizza on the intervening days. The awful things that had happened to Judy's face made him think she might be accident-prone and at first he waited to hear her drop things, but she moved almost soundlessly about the flat, putting her head round the door to tell him when she was going to use the vacuum cleaner, apologizing in advance, and in the event getting it over as fast as possible. She made less noise about the place than Ann did, Ann who was exasperated by sweeping and dusting and who loudly cursed both tools and furniture. As soon as this thought came to him he felt guilty, so that night he took home a bottle of champagne and a begonia in a pot.

❊

PETER PHONED ONE AFTERNOON during Bernard's third week there. It was early morning in Denver, Colorado, where he had arrived to spread the gospel of the Seeburg Diet. He wanted a book sent out to him. It was a book on calories and food combining that Bernard would find on one of the shelves in the bedroom up on the righthand side.

"Everything okay?" he said. "How's the poet? How are you getting on with Judy?"

Bernard said the biography was progressing quite satisfactorily, thank you very much, and Judy was fine, marvelous, very efficient. There seemed no point in adding that this morning, though her face had healed and the discoloration around her eye faded, he had noticed bruises on her left arm and a strip of plaster on her left hand. That was hardly the kind of thing to talk about with Peter.

"She's what my poet's contemporaries would have called a treasure." His poet had in fact been attracted by servants, had a long-standing clandestine affair with his sister's nursery maid.

"Mind you say hello to her from me next time she comes . . ."

Her hand was still plastered and her face looked as if bruised anew. Only it couldn't be, he must be imagining this, or she was tired or one of those people whose skin marks at a touch. It couldn't really be that the damaged eye had been injured again.

"Peter said to say hello."

The handy Americanism was evidently new to her but she worked it out.

"Sent his love, did he? You pass mine on next time he gives you a phone. I've got caviar for your sandwiches today—that lumpfish, really, but I reckon it tastes the same."

She showed him the jar. "Lovely color, isn't it? More like strawberry jam."

"You're good to me, Judy," he said.

"Get off. Good to you! You appreciate it, that's what I like. Not like Peter—cottage cheese and beansprouts day after day for him. Still, what can you expect if you don't have a kitchen?"

He remade his book islands once the front door had closed after her. The fate of his books, or rather the preciousness of the position of his bookmarks, no longer worried him. They were safe with Judy. Even if he failed to stack them before she came, they remained inviolate. And a strange thing had happened. He no longer wanted total silence and unobtrusiveness from her. He had arranged with her to bring his coffee at eleven, when he would break off for ten or even fifteen minutes for a chat. Mostly he talked to her and she listened while he spoke about his biography and his aims and his past career, necessarily simplifying things for this untutored audience. A look of wonder, or simple lack of comprehension, came into her thin, hungry face. She admired him, he was sure of it, and he was curiously touched by her admiration. He told himself it made him feel humble.

And he had hardly realized before how much he liked gracious living. The turmoil of home, the chaos, he had accepted as in inevitable corollary of modern life. Peter's flat was as he remembered his mother's home—clean, orderly, the woodwork shining, the upholstery not stained with spilt milk and chocolate smears. In the bathroom it wasn't necessary to pick one's way between the hazards of potty, disposable napkin packets, drying dungarees, and a menagerie of plastic amphibians in order to reach the lavatory. It was peaceful and silent and it smelt, not of urine, milk, and disinfectant, but of floor wax and the civilized dry bitter-sweetness of the chrysanthemums Judy had bought at the same time as the caviar . . .

"You're quite in love with her," said Ann.

"Get off," said Bernard before he realized who he was quoting. "I only said she was a good housewife." She would hardly understand if he said he looked forward to ten-thirty, then to coffee time, to his conversation with this naive listener. It was more than he could understand himself how an interruption had become a pleasure.

❋

PETER PHONED FROM CHICAGO. It was just before seven in the morning there, so not yet one in London and Judy was still in the flat. Bernard thought Peter must be phoning so early to wish him a happy birthday and he felt quite touched. Ann hadn't exactly forgotten what this day was, she had only forgotten to get him a present. But the reason for Peter's call was to say the food-combining book had arrived and would Bernard send him the file of homeophathic pills from the bathroom cabinet.

"I'm halfway through my life today," said Bernard.

"Many happy returns. If I'd known, I'd have sent you a card. Say hello to Judy for me."

"You don't look forty," she said to him, standing in the doorway in her padded jacket.

For a moment he didn't know what she meant. When he did, he was mildly affronted, then amused. "Thirty-five," he said. "Halfway through man's allotted span. You think I'll make it to eighty, do you?"

"I didn't ought to have listened," she said. "Sorry. It was a bit of a cheek."

He had a curious impulse to put his arm round her thin shoulders and press her quickly close to him. But of course he couldn't do that. "Get off," he said. "Why shouldn't you listen? It wasn't private."

She said goodbye and left and he put his books back on the floor. Rather reluctantly he returned to work. His subject had been acquainted with the great literary figures of the day and Bernard was about to write of his first meeting, while at university in Dublin, with James Joyce. Joyce, he reflected, had lived with and later married a servant—a chambermaid, wasn't she? It had been a happy partnership between the giant of letters and his Nora, the nearly illiterate woman.

Ham sandwiches and thinly sliced avocado, sesame-seed biscuits, a glass of apple juice. For once he wasn't hungry for it. What he would have liked—he suddenly saw the rightness of it—was to have taken Judy out for lunch. Why hadn't he thought of it while she was still there? Why hadn't he thought of it as a way of celebrating his birthday? Although she had been gone twenty minutes, he went to the window and looked out to see if, by remote chance, she might still be waiting at the bus stop. There was no one in the bus shelter but an old man reading the timetable.

They could have gone to the Italian restaurant round the corner. She was so thin, he wondered if she ever got a decent meal. He would have enjoyed choosing the dishes for her and selecting the wine. A light sparkling Lambrusco would have been just the thing to please her, and he would have put up with it even though it might be rather showy and obvious for him. But she had gone and it was too late. In her absence he felt restless, unable to concentrate. He had no phone number for her, no address—he didn't even know her surname. If she didn't come on Tuesday, if she never came again, he wouldn't know how to find her, he would have lost her forever.

❋

THIS ANXIETY WAS ABSURD, for of course she did come. His weekend had been unpleasant, with Jonathan developing a virus infection and Ann announcing that she meant to go back to work in the spring. He had to stay at home on Monday to look after the sick child while Ann took Jeremy for a dental appointment. The quietness and order of Peter's flat received him, seemed to welcome him with a beckoning and a smile. Only another month and Peter would be home, but he didn't want to think of that.

At ten-thirty, Judy let herself in. She was always punctual. The bruises faded, the scars healed, she looked very pretty. He thought what an exceedingly good-looking woman she was with that flush on her cheeks and her eyes bright. Instead of going to his work table and his typewriter, he had waited for her in the living room, and when she came in he did something he normally did for women but had never done for her. He laid his book aside and stood up. It seemed almost to alarm her.

"Are you okay, Bernard?"

He smiled, nodded. He had never actually witnessed her arrival before and now he watched her remove her jacket, take indoor shoes out of her bag and put them on, remarking as she did so, reverting to the aspect of the place that endlessly amused her, that if Peter had had a kitchen she would have been able to change there. The scuffed boots she wore outdoors tucked inside the bag, she took from it a small package, a box it looked like, wrapped in silver-spotted pink paper. Her manner becoming awkward, she said to Bernard, thrusting the package into his hands, "Here, this is for you. Happy birthday."

She was blushing. She had gone a fiery red. Bernard untied the ribbon and took off the paper. Inside the box, on a piece of cotton wool, lay a metal object about six inches long and an inch wide. Its shaft was flat like the blade of a knife and attached to a hook on the top, which curved backward in a U-shape, was a facsimile of a peacock with tail spread fanwise, the whole executed in beaten copper and a mosaic of blue, green, and purple glass chips. To Bernard it looked at first like some piece of cheap jewelry, a woman's hair ornament or clip. He registered its tawdry ugliness, felt at a loss for words. What was it? He looked up at her.

"It's a bookmark, isn't it?" She spoke with intense earnestness. "You put it in your book to show where you've got to."

He was still mystified.

"Look, I'll show you." She picked up the book he had been reading, a memoir of the Stephen family, who had also been acquainted with his poet. At the place he had reached, she inserted the copper knife blade and, closing the book on it, hooked the peacock over the top of the spine. "See how it works?"

"Yes—thanks. Thank you very much."

Confidingly, she said, "I couldn't help seeing, while I've been working about, the way you'd always leave one of your books open and face-down. Well, you don't like to turn down the corner of the page, do you, not when it's a library book? It doesn't seem right. So I thought, it's his birthday, I know what I'll do, I'll get him one of these. I'd seen them in this shop, hadn't I? One of those'd be just the thing for him and his books, I thought."

It was a curious kind of shock. The thing was hideous. It seemed more of an affront because it was books it must inevitably be associated with, books which he had such a special, dedicated feeling about. If it didn't sound too silly and pretentious, he could almost have said books were sacred. The peacock's tail, curved breast, and stupid face glittered against the dull brown of the binding. The manufacturer had even managed to get red into it. The bird's eyes were twin points of ruby red. Bernard took the book and his new bookmark into the dining room. He found himself closing the door for the first time in weeks. Of course he would have to use the bloody thing. She would look for it, expect to see it every time she came. If he left one of his books face-downward she would want to know why he wasn't using his new bookmark.

"You do like it, don't you, Bernard?" she said when she brought his coffee.

"Of course I like it." What else could he say?

"I thought you'd like it. When I saw it I thought, that's just the thing for Bernard."

Why did they always have to say everything twice, these people? She had seated herself as usual opposite him to wait for him to begin their conversation. But this morning he didn't want to talk, he had nothing to say. It even seemed to him that she had somehow betrayed him. She had shown him how little his words meant to her, if in spite of everything he had said and shown himself to be she could still have brought him this tasteless, vulgar object. He knew he was being ridiculous but he couldn't help feeling it. He took the coffee from her, feigning an absent manner, and returned to his typewriter.

Honest with himself—he tried to be that—he admitted what had been in his mind. He had meant to make love to her. To what end? Was she to have been his Nora? He had never progressed so far, even in his thoughts. Simply he had thought of love and pleasure, of taking her about and giving her a good time. Was he mad? They were poles apart—a great gulf fixed between them, as she had proved by her gross misunderstanding of everything he was and stood for. Serve him right for having such aims and intents. It must be his subject who was taking him over, his poet, who at sixteen boasted to Frank Harris of getting his mother's kitchenmaid pregnant.

He nodded absently to her when, ready to leave, she put her head round the door. Peter phoned from Philadelphia not long after she had gone, and after he had talked to him Bernard felt better about things. He was able to make quite an amusing story out of the presenting of the peacock bookmark. And Peter commiserated with him, agreeing that there was no doubt about it, he would have to use the thing, and prominently, for the duration of his stay. Naturally, Bernard said nothing about his now vanished desire for Judy, any more than he did when he repeated the tale to Ann that night. Ann had the advantage over Peter in that she could actually be shown the object.

"It's copper," she said. "And it doesn't look mass-produced. It was probably quite expensive. But you can't actually use it, it's dreadful."

"I don't want to hurt her feelings."

"What about your feelings? Aren't they important? If you don't want to say straight out you can't bear the thing, tell her you've left it at home or you've lost it. Let me have it and I'll lose it for you . . ."

Next day he followed her advice and left the bookmark at home. Judy didn't say anything about it, though it was her day for dusting the bedroom and he had left his notebook in the bedroom, lying face-downward on the stack of other books. She watered Peter's plants and cleaned the windows.

He didn't take a break from work when she brought his coffee, only looked up and thanked her. But he could see she had her eye on the books which covered half the dining table. He was sure she was looking for the peacock. He repeated his thanks in as dismissive a tone as he could manage and she turned at once and left the room. The sandwiches she left him for lunch were tinned salmon and cucumber with a strawberry yogurt and a chocolate bar. Bernard fancied the standard was less high than it had been.

It was a relief to be without her as he always was on Thursdays. On Friday her face was once more the way it had been that first week, one eye black and swollen, her cheek bruised, her mouth cut. But he said nothing about it. He could see her gazing at all the books on the table, and after she had left the room he went quietly to the door and through the crack watched her slowly move the stacked volumes to dust the surface of a cabinet. By now it must have registered with her that he disliked the bookmark and had no intention of using it. It was, of course, a mistake to be too friendly with these people, to put them on a level with oneself. He wasn't used to servants and that was the trouble. Who was, these days? Returning to work, he felt a flash of envy for his poet who, though comparatively poor, had nevertheless kept a man and two maids to look after him.

She spoke to him, as in the old days, when she brought his coffee. Tentatively, as if she thought him in a bad mood and she was placating him, she said, "I've been in the wars a bit."

He glanced up, took in once again that awful damaged eye. How could he once have thought her pretty? The notion came to him that she was trying to tell him something, appeal to him. Was she perhaps going to ask yet again if he liked the bookmark? He put up his eyebrows and made a rueful face. "Close the door after you, will you, Judy?"

Still, he had been wrong about the standard of lunch, having no fault to find with pastrami sandwiches, watercress salad, and a slice of pineapple. Ann's advice was sound. By not yielding, he had shown the woman that imposing her atrocious taste on him wasn't on. But he hadn't bargained for what happened on the Tuesday.

She didn't come.

For a little while, when eleven was past and he was sure she wasn't coming, he felt awe at himself, at the stand he had taken. He had been strong and he had driven her away. Then he was pleased, he was relieved. Wasn't it absurd, a woman coming in three times a week to clean up after someone who didn't even sleep there, who scarcely ate there? Of course, she would probably come back when Peter returned in three weeks' time. It was he she was ostracizing. She had taken offense because he wouldn't give in to her and use her hideous gift.

He had worked himself up a bit over her defection by the time he got home. "She could at least have phoned and made some excuse."

"They don't," said Ann. "Those people don't."

✸

ANY QUALMS HE MIGHT HAVE HAD about Judy's turning up later were soon allayed. It was clear she wasn't coming back. Bernard got into the way of buying himself something for his lunch on his way to the flat. He went without coffee. It wasn't as if he was used to it, as if Ann had ever made it for him. He left his books lying about all over the floors, face-downward or with pieces of paper inserted between the pages. Of course he hadn't finished the life of his poet by the time Peter was due back, he wasn't even a quarter of his way through, but he had made such a good start he felt he could continue at home in spite of Jonathan and Jeremy, in spite of chaos and noise. He had broken the back of it.

Peter phoned the morning before he was due to leave New York. They talked about the weather, the heavy snowstorms which had been sweeping the East Coast of America. Then Peter said, "That was terrible about Judy."

A strong word to use, but Peter was inclined to be intense. "How did you know?" Bernard said.

"I saw it in the paper, of course. I do make a point of seeing English newspapers while I'm here."

They were at cross-purposes. "What did you see in the paper?"

Peter sounded astonished. "That he killed her, of course. I shouldn't have been surprised, I used to tell her he'd do it one day. I told her to leave him, but she wouldn't. She must have talked to you about him, surely? I can't believe she came in all that time without a mark on her from what he was doing to her. They've charged him with murdering her. Don't you read your newspaper?"

He hadn't known her name, Bernard said, he hadn't known where she lived or anything about her.

"What did you talk about? Didn't you ask?"

Bernard said goodbye and slowly let the receiver slide into

its rest. What had they talked about, he and Judy? His work, English literature, books, his past career. He had talked and she had listened. Raptly, he thought now, her battered face lifted, her damaged eyes watching him. Why hadn't she said what happened to her at home? Why, instead of giving him that ridiculous tasteless thing, hadn't she thrown herself on his mercy, confided in him, offered herself to him?

He didn't say a word about it to Ann. "What happened to the peacock bookmark?" he asked instead.

"The children were playing with it and Jeremy kept putting it in his mouth, so I threw it out."

He wanted to hit her, he wanted to strike her in the face, and he clasped his hands together to keep himself from that.

PENELOPE WALLACE

The World According to Uncle Albert

MY UNCLE WAS MAD ABOUT Sherlock Holmes.

Sometimes I just thought he was mad.

He had this enormous magnifying glass and, when he wasn't rereading The Master, he was cantering around the ample grounds of his country estate, waving it around. "A big dog's been through this thicket," he said.

"Yes, a Great Dane called Hound. *Your* Great Dane. You walked him through here this morning."

His embarrassment was fleeting. "I'd have known anyway, from the paw marks," he said scathingly.

"If you use that great thing in the afternoon sun, you'll start a fire," I told him. I'd just snagged my pantihose and I reflected for the hundredth time that the proper apparel for a stroll through Uncle Albert's underbrush was slacks.

Uncle Albert was against slacks. Women should look feminine and behave in a feminine way—preferably in high necks and long skirts as in dear old Sherlock's day. He didn't want an Irene Adler in the family.

I'd once pointed out to him that there were other crime writers. It was like telling a religious bigot that there were other churches.

I always explain to any visitors who my uncle means when he speaks of The Master. We'd had a nasty interlude when one of my old school friends thought he was referring to Noel Coward.

I should, perhaps, explain that I live by myself in London,

but Uncle Albert is my only living relative and, despite what he calls my aggressive modernity, he seems to like me, so I come down most weekends.

This Friday afternoon was particularly hot and, after my remarks about starting a fire, he reluctantly agreed that we retrace our steps.

He always wears an inverness for these walks—just like you-know-whose—and he stowed the magnifying glass away in a large pocket. "About the party—" I began. But he bent suddenly over a thorny bush, dragging out his "eye of God" and peering intently.

"That's not Hound's hair," he announced. "It's some fine shreds and—yes, by Jove, it's blood!"

"Group 'O'," I told him. "Rhesus positive."

He turned, amazed.

"How—?"

I pointed to my leg. "My blood," I told him. "And shreds of my pantihose."

He put away the magnifying glass and walked with me, rather huffily, back to the house.

I wondered whether I should apologize for scratching my leg or if I should have left a little notice: "Here lies the fine blood of Frances Stephen—wounded while on lawful pursuits."

Uncle relented when we were back in the drawing room. "Tea now, I think," he said, and rang the bell by the fireplace. "After tea I think I'll dip into *The Hound of the Baskervilles*."

The Great Dane uncurled himself at the sound of his name and ambled over to see if he was missing anything—like tea, I thought, the way that dog eats.

Poor Uncle. Mrs. Hubbard, the housekeeper, had refused to let him buy a mastiff and, although Hound was large enough, he didn't have at all the temperament of his namesake.

Once I'd pointed out to Uncle Albert that the Great Man hadn't owned a dog and had, on occasions, employed a tracking dog called Toby, who was an ugly lop-eared mixture of spaniel and Labrador. Uncle had become frosty and Hound had looked sad. He wasn't actually the kind of dog who carries the burglar's torch—he was too lazy even for that.

"Uncle," I said firmly. "Not too much reading after tea. Remember, you're giving a party; the guests will start arriving about seven."

Uncle mumbled crossly, but I knew that he actually liked

parties. It gave him a chance to quote The Master and recall a few occasions when he himself—in his humble way, as he put it—had made some startling discoveries and deductions.

"You're giving the party for me," I reminded him. "My nineteenth birthday party—although I'm not actually nineteen until the week after next. Roger and his wife will be coming from London. They'll be staying the weekend, and John Canning will be here for the night."

"Where's he coming from?"

"Six miles away, but you asked him when you met him last May. You said he was an unusually sensitive and perceptive young man."

"Oh, yes. I remember the boy. Reads The Master and congratulated me on some of my own achievements. Who else is coming?"

"Don's driving down from London with his sister and various others."

"Long-haired layabout."

"He's not a layabout; he works at the BBC."

Uncle Albert muttered something about Lord Reith and inquired whether they were all staying the night.

"They'll drive back to London after it's over," I told him.

"So few people," he said mournfully.

"I thought *you'd* asked some guests as well."

"The vicar and his wife and Dr. Spence and the Paynes and Mrs. Caxton, but they won't stay long after dinner. Oh, yes, and an author fellow I met last weekend—he lent me one of his books—I can't say I think much of it, but he seems a decent chap. Quite young too.

"I've got your mother's jewelry in the safe—you will wear some of it, won't you? I remember when your mother wore it at her parties."

He'd said the same at my last birthday party and the one before and the one before that. Then, as now, I agreed.

"I'll get it out now," he said, and I followed him through the connecting door to his study—an indescribably untidy room, since Mrs. Hubbard was allowed to do no more than vacuum the carpet. The safe was large, solid-looking, and very old. Uncle Albert started spinning dials. Usually he supported himself on the top while he did so, but on this occasion he kept well clear, with his left hand behind his back.

"Is it that dirty?" I asked him.

He hesitated. "Not dirty exactly," he said gruffly and I went forward to investigate. "Don't touch the door!"

I looked carefully at the safe door. "It's shinier," I said. "What have you done to it?"

"I suppose I might as well tell you. In fact, I'm rather proud of the idea. It's covered with a special fine grease. For finger-prints," he explained. "Of course, there are burglar alarms at the windows and doors and there's Hound, but someone might gain admittance by day when the alarms are off."

I recalled that they had been, at one time, left on by day— until one memorable occasion when the vicar, waiting for my uncle in the drawing room and presumably stifled by the heat, had flung open the French windows—and all hell had broken loose. Mrs. Hubbard, relating the event, said that even Hound had entered into the spirit of the thing, and fascinated villagers had seen the vicar running down the main street with his hands clapped to his ears and his bony legs clearly visible through the rips in his cassock.

The safe was filled with envelopes and packages—rare first editions and what Uncle referred to as "memorabilia and ephemera." My jewelry was in a strong cardboard box on the top shelf. Normally, covered with oceans of sealing wax, it was held at the bank. Only for my birthday was it brought to this temporary home. As usual I chose to wear a small dia-mond pendant and, also as usual, I refused to bedeck myself with various rings and bracelets or to take the box back to London to "bring an aura of gracious living," as he put it into my bed-sitter.

✳

I HAD REFERRED TO MY "BIRTHDAY PARTY" because that's how Uncle Albert thought of it, but it was really his evening. Some of his cronies, some of my more respectable friends—the others couldn't afford the fare or petrol from London—came in for a few drinks, dinner, and the birthday cake. Then, after a decent interval for coffee and recovery, the older guests would depart and Uncle would take himself off to the study and, as he said, "Leave the young people to enjoy themselves." Not surpris-ingly, the proceedings which followed lost spontaneity.

I was dutifully dressed, wearing the pendant, and down-stairs by six-thirty. Roger and Jane arrived a few minutes later. Roger's father had been a friend of my father's; they were in their late thirties but determined to be young or, as Roger said, "with it." Jane was small and slim, but Roger's spread was definitely middle-aged. I had a standing invitation to visit them in London and felt rather guilty that I so rarely did. Roger's publishing house was reputedly going through a difficult time. Soon after they joined me in the drawing room for a drink, a tap on the door revealed John Canning. Apparently he had arrived when I was changing and had been shown to his room by Batty Annie, who came from the village to help Mrs. Hubbard on special occasions.

I had only met John Canning twice before, and he didn't improve with the third meeting. He had impressed Uncle Albert with his knowledge of Sherlock Holmes and, when he heard that Roger was a publisher, he launched into the Meaning and Significance of the Modern Novel and the particular significance of Roger's publications.

Roger was puffing up nicely when Batty Annie flung open the door and let in the vicar and Mrs. Vicar and Mr. and Mrs. Payne. The Paynes were in their seventies; they had known my mother when she was a child and I was very fond of them. I couldn't say the same of Mrs. Caxton, who followed them in. She was a predatory forty-fiver, a widow whose target, I felt sure, was Uncle Albert. I didn't think she'd have any luck, noticing that when he joined the throng he had the wary look he usually has when she's around.

Dr. Spence arrived next, as untidy as usual, with his neat sparrow wife. I wondered where Don had got to, and then Batty Annie brought in Uncle Albert's author—who turned out to be Simon Lantern—and I rather forgot about Don. I could see John Canning bestowing himself on one group after another and, during lulls in the conversation, I heard him discussing heart surgery with Dr. Spence and God with the vicar. Predictably, he soon turned his attention on Simon.

"Mr. Lantern," he said. "You have given a new dimension to crime fiction."

Simon gave an enigmatic smile and I hoped the subject would change, because although, of course, I'd heard of the great Simon Lantern I'd never read any of his books. In fact, I don't like crime books, although it seems terribly disloyal to Uncle Albert to mention it.

I was saved by Batty Annie announcing dinner. She wasn't

really mad—I should explain—but had acquired the adjective as a result of a passing interest in spiritualism.

Uncle Albert had the problem of rudeness to my friends from London if we started dinner without them and offending Mrs. Hubbard if we didn't. I assured him that Don's car had probably broken down and we certainly shouldn't wait.

Dinner was somewhat formal, with Uncle Albert at one end of the long table and myself at the other. I firmly put Simon on my right, the chair on my left was tacitly left empty for Don, and a block of four were left empty below Simon. It turned out they weren't all needed, because Don arrived soon after the soup with apologies—they *had* broken down—and with him were only his sister Susan and one other. Susan was wearing a scarlet blouse and purple slacks; I could see Uncle shuddering in the distance, but he should have seen the jeans she normally wore. With Susan was a new friend of hers named Sammy—I hadn't met him before, but Susan believed in variety. Sammy had a scrubbed look and I suspected that Susan had bathed him for the occasion; my suspicion was later confirmed when I passed to windward and was rewarded by the unmistakable smell of Pink Lilac talc.

"Only the three of you?" asked Uncle.

"Yes," said Don. "The other two fell out at the first roundabout."

There was a stunned silence, and I feebly explained that Don was joking. Nobody laughed.

Simon asked Don what kind of car he had and they immediately entered into the kind of dialogue which is common to males of all ages and races—I suspect it's what they beat out on African drums, and maybe those streams of little flags my naval friends refer to as "making signals" don't actually carry stirring messages about "England expecting" or instructions to "Form line of battle," but really read, "I'd just been passed by this Lotus Elan—"

Anyway, it gave me a chance to look around the table. Uncle Albert was debating, as usual, with Dr. Spence. Mrs. Spence was chatting demurely with the vicar. Susan and Sammy were holding hands, which meant that Susan had to hold the soup spoon in her left hand. And John Canning was using what he thought was charm on Mrs. Caxton, who was smiling and nodding. He certainly worked hard. Jane was working hard too, conversing with Sammy, but whereas I thought John Canning had ulterior motives I knew that Jane was just pursuing her affection for, and hopeful affinity with, the young.

The car conversation seemed to have petered out, or maybe Don and Simon had remembered whose party it was. "So how are you, Frankie?" asked Don.

I hoped Uncle hadn't heard—and I loathed it too. "I'm fine, thank you, Donnie."

I was happy to see that he winced slightly.

Dinner proceeded smoothly with Mrs. Hubbard, as always, giving of her best. Her crowning effort was the birthday cake. The lights were turned out as she brought it in, firing on all nineteen candles, and put it in front of me with a large cake knife. Uncle Albert always insisted on champagne for my birthday dinner and, as the candles flickered, I began to wonder if I had let my glass be filled rather too often.

I stood up and thanked Uncle and Mrs. Hubbard before starting to blow at the flames and it was while I was leaning forward, puffing, that someone remarked on the beauty of the pendant— I couldn't tell who it was in the dark. I heard a murmur of assent, and by the time the candles were out and the lights back on, Uncle Albert was holding forth about the beauty of my mother's jewelry and my inexplicable behavior in refusing to take it to London and wear it. There were assents and reminiscences from the older members of the party and a tactful silence from the younger until Sammy, whom I had thought incapable of conversation, suddenly said that he thought I was right; that the trappings of wealth were no longer acceptable.

He didn't actually say, "Come the Revolution," but I could see Uncle Albert heating up—he has a low boiling point—and then Simon Lantern was coming to my rescue by pointing out the responsibility involved with valuable jewelry and the risk of theft. Someone mentioned the recent loss of a film star's emeralds and soon the conversation had generalized into talk of burglaries in general and of jewelry in particular, with Uncle quoting The Master's cases at appropriate moments.

Uncle Albert had a hankering for the port-and-nuts-for-the-boys segregation but I had talked him out of it the preceding year, so after we had finished the cake we all trooped into the drawing room for coffee.

By about ten the locals started to leave—but not, I was happy to see, Simon Lantern.

At 10:30, Uncle Albert retired to his study and the rest of us sat around talking—except for Susan and Sammy, who sat on the sofa still holding hands and apparently oblivious of all but each other. It was when Don got into a political argument with Jane aand Roger—with John Canning agreeing with both sides—that Simon said, "You haven't read any of my books, have you?" I admitted that I hadn't and apologized for the fact that I never read crime fiction. "There's one I think you would like," he told me. "May I send you a copy?"

I said I'd be delighted and he wrote down my London address, adding, as an afterthought, that perhaps I could dine with him the next time he visited his publisher and he could give me the book in person.

He was an undeniably attractive man—mid-forties, I thought, with black hair greying at the temples. It occurred to me that perhaps I should keep the diamond pendant, because I was sure he'd take me to dine at that sort of place. While I was telling him that I'd like that, I thought how part of his charm lay in the way he actually listened when people were speaking, his head held slightly on one side.

When the telephone rang about 11:30, I didn't bother to answer it because I knew that Uncle Albert had an extension in the study and would deal with it there. It was a call for Simon, and Uncle invited him to take it in the study. Don took advantage of his absence to remark unkindly on him and suggest that he practiced his air of attentive listening in the mirror each morning.

Simon wasn't long on the phone. We heard him speaking to Uncle Albert and Uncle saying, "Nonsense, my boy, no trouble at all," then he returned to explain that the call was from his sister. All the lights had failed and the electricity people had told her it was a cable fault that couldn't be mended until the following day. She was going to spend the night in the nearest hotel and advised him to do likewise but Uncle Albert had pressed him to stay the night here.

I thought his sister was taking rather drastic action but I only said that I had no idea he had a sister and asked why he hadn't brought her to the party. He replied that his sister wasn't good at parties, whereupon Don gave a baleful look at Susan and Sammy and said, "Nor's mine."

Around midnight Don said they'd better start back. It was a warm night and we all went out to wave them goodbye.

It was a dead loss, waving goodbye, because the car wouldn't start, and although Don and Simon both poked around under the bonnet it appeared that the problem couldn't be repaired without spares from the local garage. That meant three more besides John Canning, Roger, and Jane staying the night.

Proprieties had to be observed and Don and Sammy were given a twin-bedded room, Susan a smallish single room down the corridor. Uncle Albert doled out toothbrushes and pajamas, and I gave Susan a nightdress. Uncle Albert then took the reluctant Hound for a short walk while I busied myself with sheets and towels and offers of help in making beds.

While I was thus skivvying, I heard Uncle return and the clanking of bolts as he locked up for the night. He always locked the doors from the passage to the drawing room and study and took the respective keys to bed with him. When I heard his footsteps on the stairs, I left Don to finish making his own bed. Uncle Albert has some old-fashioned ideas, and I hate to shock him unnecessarily.

My bedroom was in the middle of the corridor and there was a certain amount of traffic during the night which I took to be guests en route to the bathroom or Sammy en route to Susan. I didn't sleep particularly well and sometime in the early hours I remembered that I should have given the pendant to Uncle Albert so he could lock it away in the safe. Instead, I had left it on the dressing table by the window. Remembering the tales of robbery earlier in the evening, I got up and actually leaned out of the window to check for drainpipes and other furtive access to my room but I couldn't see anything that would help a would-be thief. My room overlooked the drive and I peered anxiously at the trees which flanked it but I didn't see any suspicious shadows. I could hear owls hooting sadly and, somewhere to the front of the house, a faint hissing. For a moment I thought it was rain; then I remembered the Speckled Band Uncle Albert had insisted I read about in my early youth—but neither seemed applicable, so I went back to bed and, finally, to sleep.

⁂

WHEN I WOKE, IT WAS HALF PAST NINE and there was a lot of noise outside my window. I looked out and saw Don and the man from the local garage peering into the guts of Don's car while Simon sat in the driver's seat using the starter when requested. The car burst into noisy life for brief periods while the garage man poked about with an enormous screwdriver and Don watched anxiously.

I had a quick bath and dressed. My final look at the scene outside showed Don at the wheel—and no sign of Simon. I hoped he hadn't left.

I was halfway down the stairs when I saw Uncle Albert at the open study door.

"Frances," he called to me, and I followed him in. Simon was there. "I said I'd show Mr. Lantern some of my treasures," Uncle told me darkly, "and when I opened the safe, I found that all your jewelry is missing. We've had a burglary."

I wasn't particularly upset for myself. I seldom wore it and had no doubt that it was well insured. But Uncle Albert was very unhappy.

"Come and see this, Frances," he said, and Simon and I followed him to the drawing room.

The French windows were open—apparently Mrs. Hubbard had assumed that Uncle had opened them before she cleaned the room, since the alarm seemed to be switched off. "However," said Uncle, brightening visibly now that he could start deducting, "the alarm was *not* switched off, someone disconnected it. And look there"—he pointed to the earth outside the window, which bore strange marks, fairly deep and spade-shaped—"you will remember," he said, "how in 'The Adventure of the Priory School' The Master realized the cow hoofprints were actually made by horses?"

Simon said he remembered it well.

"*I* deduce that those prints were made by a man walking on his toes."

"Why?" I asked.

"Because," he explained, "it would give less guidance to the man's size of shoe than would a full footprint. You can see the tracks he made coming in—and going out."

"So," I said with some relief, "it could have been any thief for miles around."

"I'm afraid not, Frances. I told you the alarm on this window had been disconnected. That could only be done from inside the room. and it was done yesterday, because I tested the alarm on Thursday evening when I brought your jewelry home from the bank."

"Anyone could have come in yesterday. The windows were

open and we were out on the grounds. We wouldn't have seen anything."

"One thing we do know from the size of those footprints is that the robber returned to force open the French doors after it started to rain: the ground was very wet, which made the prints wide and deep."

"But," said Simon, "it didn't rain last night—or, if it did, it was a very light shower. I've been out in front trying to help Don with his car, and the ground's bone dry."

"Have you called the police?" I asked Uncle Albert.

He looked hurt. Simon persuaded me to do so. I've called the C.I.D. at Midhampton. I think I'll just go and have a quick look outside before they arrive. They have to travel sixteen miles." He scooted through the open French windows, more or less avoiding the footprints, and disappeared behind some nearby bushes. He didn't ask Simon to go with him; maybe he just didn't see him as an obedient Watson.

✳

WE SAW UNCLE ALBERT EMERGE from the bushes holding something white, and as he came back through the windows we could see it was a pair of gloves.

"Look," he said proudly. "The fingers of the right glove are covered with grease. The burglar was left-handed. The left glove is quite clean and is obviously the one that came in contact with the dial." He turned to Simon. "Who else aside from you is left-handed?" he asked.

Simon looked surprised. "I'm right-handed," he said.

Uncle was disappointed. "You picked up the telephone receiver with your left hand last night."

"I'm deaf in my right ear," Simon told him.

Uncle turned to me. "Your friend Susan," he said. "She held her soup spoon in her left hand at dinner."

I explained that Sammy had been holding her right one, and Uncle tutted a bit. "Anyway," I pointed out, "who's to say it's one of us? There are probably hundreds of left-handed burglars in the county."

A local bobby arrived at that moment. P.C. Brown was a keen gardener and, after one look at the footprints, opined that something funny had been going on, because it hadn't rained for three weeks and if someone had been using a hose it was strictly illegal.

"Of *course*," I said. "The hissing noise last night—it was either the hose or the garden sprinkler!" I explained why I'd been looking out of the window and Uncle Albert beamed at me.

"Excellent," he told me.

Don came in at that moment to say goodbye and P.C. Brown explained that Don and his party must wait for the Inspector from Midhampton. Uncle told Don about the burglary. P.C. Brown frowned at Uncle and Don swore. Reluctantly, the P.C. allowed him to telephone his excuses to London.

"Who else is staying in the house," Mr. Brown asked us afterward, "and where are they?"

Don had seen Roger and Jane heading toward the village, Sammy and Susan were packing—packing what? I wondered—and nobody had seen John Canning. "His car's still outside," offered Don.

P.C. Brown could never have played poker. Over his face there flitted the go-seek-and-round-up-suspects look, closely followed by a baleful stare at Uncle laced with the obvious thought—based perhaps on previous experience—that if he left the room Uncle would be off clue-hunting and Midhampton would be very displeased with the results. To his evident relief, Midhampton itself showed up at this point. The party consisted of a rather elderly and cynical Inspector, a sergeant who reminded me of a vicious terrier I'd once had, and a horde of experts who proceeded to search the grounds, take photographs, make casts of the footprints, and dust surfaces with grey powder.

The Inspector turned to Uncle Albert. "Have you found any evidence?" he asked in a sad voice. Evidently Uncle's fame *had* spread. Uncle pointed out the footprints outside the French windows. The Inspector peered out, looked for rather a long time at those on the periphery, and opined that Mr. Holmes would have used a mat.

A convert!

Uncle beamed. He realized he couldn't always be as perfect as The Master. With a flourish he produced the white cotton gloves. The sergeant yapped, whipped a polythene bag out of his case, and dropped them in.

P.C. Brown, who was being upstaged, told the Inspector of the hissing noise I'd heard in the night.

"Not the Speckled Band," I interrupted and got a half smile

from the Inspector and a rather hurt look from P.C. Brown, who battled on and was then sent to round up those of the party who could be located. The sergeant left with him and Mrs. Hubbard appeared with coffee and biscuits, followed by the still-clasped Sammy and Susan, who sat together on the sofa.

We all heard a sharp yelp through the French windows. It wasn't the call of Hound. I suspected it was the terrier-sergeant hot on the trail. The Inspector departed in its direction and Uncle Albert said he must wash his hands. He reappeared some ten minutes later with a smug expression, a pair of binoculars, and Hound.

He hadn't been able to observe much from the downstairs loo—cloakroom, as he insists on calling it—even with the binoculars, because the window glass is opaque and the window is small and high, but he'd had a good view of the sergeant's back, and heard him refer to faint scuffmarks at the foot of the drainpipe and yelp a second time when he spied some threads of material caught partway up the pipe.

A man had been dispatched for a ladder and Uncle had had to step away so that the climber wouldn't see him.

"It's definitely an inside job," he said. "Someone in the house climbed down the drainpipe after everyone was asleep, forced open the French windows—having earlier disconnected the burglar alarm—opened the safe, took the jewelry, and climbed back up the drainpipe to his room."

"Clasping the jewelry," I asked, "until such time as the police would arrive to take it from him?"

"He may have had an accomplice on the grounds," said Uncle, "or he may have concealed it in the house. In 'The Naval Treaty'—"

Jane and Roger came in at that point and Jane, wearing a well cut trouser suit which had Uncle tutting under his breath, helped herself and Roger to coffee. Uncle brought them up to date on the facts and on his deductions. Midway through his dissertation John Canning came in and explained that he'd been reading in his room until the police had turned him out to conduct their search. I gave him a cup of coffee.

Uncle moved to the window, his binoculars in hand.

"They've found something!" he said.

And Hound, who'd been lying peacefully on Sammy and Susan, obeyed some atavistic call, leaped to his feet, bounded through the windows, and was off at a speed I'd never credited him with. I could see that Uncle was as surprised as I was, but he was very loyal.

"They've found something!" he repeated. "They're holding it up—some sort of bundle—and Hound—yes, Hound's got the scent!"

I suppose I was the only other person in the room who knew that Hound could no more follow a scent than I could fly to the moon. Uncle retained his optimism.

"Yes," he cried, "and now he's coming back here!"

Hound came bounding back and sank, panting and exhausted, at Uncle's feet.

A few minutes later, the Inspector came in with a rolled-up bundle tied with garden twine. From it he drew a pair of loud check trousers. I'd always thought they were hideous since the day Uncle bought them.

"These are yours also?" asked the Inspector, holding up a pair of overshoes. "And the gardening gloves?"

"Yes," admitted my uncle. "I keep them in the garden room for when I do the garden."

"The garden room," I explained, "is the one with the cracked sink and the broken lawnmower next to the—the cloakroom."

"And the room is not locked?"

My uncle looked sad and shook his head.

"I assume," he said, "that the thief wore my clothing to protect his own whilst climbing up and down the drainpipe— and then threw it out of the landing window."

"It would be one hell of a throw," I pointed out.

"Yes," agreed the Inspector. "It seems more likely that your uncle's clothes were hidden in the bushes sometime later, possibly early this morning."

"And why the hose?" I persisted.

"You will remember," said Uncle Albert, "that The Master could calculate the weight and possibly the height of a man from his footprints, but a man standing on very wet ground in someone else's overshoes—" A faraway look came into his eyes and I knew he was on the track—or, as he would have said, "deducting."

I tried to pull him back to the present. "Surely it would have been even more difficult if the ground had been bone dry."

Uncle responded with a proud smile. "I always keep that

patch of ground slightly wet," he said. "Damp enough to hold footprints in the event of a burglary."

I saw Don looking at Uncle Albert and then at me. Well, I'm not the only person in the world with an eccentric relation.

"It's very interesting," said Don. "But may I ask when we shall be allowed to leave, Inspector?"

"You're all free to go now" was the answer.

Don galvanized Susan and Sammy and then his car into action. In minutes, they were speeding dangerously down the drive. Then John Canning made his polite departure, followed by Simon Lantern.

Our weekend guests, Jane and Roger, remained.

The Inspector agreed to join us for a pre-lunch drink. Uncle Albert looked portentous and frustrated until both Jane and Roger decided to tidy up before lunch. As the door closed behind them, Uncle launched into his theory.

"Of course it was them," he said. "Very sad, but Roger's firm is in need of money and the jewelry would fetch a very good price." He shook his head sadly and continued. "They are both familiar with the house. They knew where I kept my gardening clothes and where the hose was. They went out for a walk quite early, hiding my clothes in the bushes on the way. They're great walkers so no one would remark on the fact that they strode out to the village. No doubt they met an accomplice there. Of course it was Jane who came down the drainpipe—Roger's a little stout for a maneuver of that sort—and she had to make the ground really wet to disguise her lack of weight and inches. It all fits," he added. "And I hope that you will be able to apprehend them and trace the jewelry before the accomplice sells it."

He said it with a look which would have made Lestrade quail, but it didn't have that effect on the Inspector.

"We certainly hope to recover the jewelry," he said. "My men are watching the thief at this moment and they will see when he makes contact with his accomplice. In fact, we pretty well know who that will be, because he usually works with the same man."

"Usually?" My uncle was shocked. "You mean this isn't their first offense?"

"It won't be the thief's first offense—but the thief is neither of your two friends."

"I'm glad of that," I said with feeling, "but who is it?"

"I'll tell you that as soon as we're able to make the arrest," the Inspector promised.

✻

IT WAS A STICKY WEEKEND, with Uncle having to admit failure to himself and pretending like mad he'd never suspected Jane and Roger—who didn't make the situation any easier by constantly asking Uncle for his opinion on the theft. It was quite a relief when they left on Sunday afternoon, and even more pleasant when the Inspector rang in the evening and asked if he could call around. I'd refused a lift from Jane and Roger and decided to stay over and take an early train in the morning in case there was any news.

The Inspector brought my jewelry along for formal identification.

"Who was it?" I asked.

"Mr. Canning."

"How did you know?" Uncle asked.

"It was quite simple. Canning had several convictions under other names and it was his style. He fit the general description. His fingerprints clinched it. Of course, the fact that he is a jewel thief didn't prove he'd stolen Miss Stephen's jewelry— we had to wait until he collected it from his accomplice."

"But how could you know?" I asked. "How could you know his style, what he looked like, who his accomplice was?"

"I didn't need to, Miss Stephen. Scotland Yard has a fine Criminal Records Office. A man with a police radio has a great advantage over a man with a magnifying glass."

Uncle Albert was very unhappy in the hours that followed the Inspector's departure and I was considering phoning the office in the morning to say my uncle was ill when he suddenly perked up.

"It was entirely solved by the fingerprints," he said. "Entirely. And, of course, The Master was one of the very first to realize their importance."

LAWRENCE BLOCK

With a Smile for the Ending

I HAD ONE DEGREE FROM TRINITY, and one was enough, and I'd
had enough of Dublin, too. It is a fine city, a perfect city, but
there are only certain persons that can live there. An artist will
love the town, a priest will bless it, and a clerk will live in it
as well as elsewhere. But I had too little of faith and of talent
and too much of a hunger for the world to be priest or artist
or pen warden. I might have become a drunkard, for Dublin's
a right city for a drinking man, but I've no more talent for
drinking than for deception—yet another lesson I learned at
Trinity, and equally a bargain. (Tell your story, Joseph Cameron Bane would say. Clear your throat and get on with it.)

I had family in Boston. They welcomed me cautiously and
pointed me toward New York. A small but pretentious publishing house hired me; they leaned toward foreign editors and
needed someone to balance off their flock of Englishmen. Four
months was enough, of the job and of the city. A good place
for a young man on the way up, but no town at all for a
pilgrim.

He advertised for a companion. I answered his ad and half
a dozen others, and when he replied I saw his name and took
the job at once. I had lived with his books for years: *The Wind
At Morning, Cabot's House, Ruthpen Hallburton, Lips That Could
Kiss*, others, others. I had loved his words when I was a boy
in Ennis, knowing no more than to read what reached me, and
I loved them still at Trinity where one was supposed to care

only for more fashionable authors. He had written a great many books over a great many years, all of them set in the same small American town. Ten years ago he'd stopped writing and never said why. When I read his name at the bottom of the letter I realized, though it had never occurred to me before, that I had somehow assumed him dead for some years.

We traded letters. I went to his home for an interview, rode the train there and watched the scenery change until I was in the country he had written about. I walked from the railway station carrying both suitcases, having gambled he'd want me to stay. His housekeeper met me at the door. I stepped inside, feeling as though I'd dreamed the room, the house. The woman took me to him, and I saw that he was older than I'd supposed him, and next saw that he was not. He appeared older because he was dying.

"You're Riordan," he said. "How'd you come up? Train?"

"Yes, sir."

"Pete run you up?" I looked blank, I'm sure. He said that Pete was the town's cab driver, and I explained that I'd walked.

"Oh? Could have taken a taxi."

"I like to walk."

"Mmmmm," he said. He offered me a drink, I refused, but he had one. "Why do you want to waste time watching a man die?" he demanded. "Not morbid curiosity, I'm sure. Want me to teach you how to be a writer?"

"No, sir."

"Want to do my biography? I'm dull and out of fashion, but some fool might want to read about me."

"No, I'm not a writer."

"Then why are you here, boy?"

He asked this reasonably, and I thought about the question before I answered it. "I like your books," I said finally.

"You think they're good? Worthwhile? Literature?"

"I just like them."

"What's your favorite?"

"I've never kept score," I answered.

He laughed, happy with the answer, and I was hired.

There was very little to do that could be called work. Now and then there would be a task too heavy for Mrs. Dettweiler, and I'd do that for her. There were occasional errands to run, letters to answer. When the weather turned colder he'd have me make up the fire for him in the livingroom. When he had a place to go, I'd drive him; this happened less often as time passed, as the disease grew in him.

And so, in terms of the time allotted to various tasks, my job was much as its title implied. I was his companion. I listened when he spoke, talked when he wanted conversation, and was silent when silence was indicated. There would be a time, his doctor told me, when I would have more to do, unless Mr. Bane would permit a nurse. I knew he would not, any more than he'd allow himself to die anywhere but in his home. There would be morphine shots for me to give him, because sooner or later the oral drug would become ineffective. In time he would be confined, first to his home and then to his room and at last to his bed, all a gradual preparation for the ultimate confinement.

"And maybe you ought to watch his drinking," the doctor told me. "He's been hitting it pretty heavy."

This last I tried once and no more. I said something foolish, that he'd had enough, that he ought to take it with a little water; I don't remember the words, only the stupidity of them, viewed in retrospect.

"I did not hire a damned warden," he said. "You wouldn't have thought of this yourself, Tim. Was this Harold Keeton's idea?"

"Well, yes."

"Harold Keeton is an excellent doctor," he said. "But only a doctor, and not a minister. He knows that doctors are supposed to tell their patients to cut down on smoking and drinking, and he plays his part. There is no reason for me to limit my drinking, Tim. There is nothing wrong with my liver or with my kidneys. The only thing wrong with me, Tim, is that I have cancer.

"I have cancer, and I'm dying of it. I intend to die as well as I possibly can. I intend to think and feel and act as I please, and go out with a smile for the ending. I intend, among other things, to drink what I want when I want it. I do not intend to get drunk, nor do I intend to be entirely sober if I can avoid it. Do you understand?"

"Yes, Mr. Bane."

"Good. Get the chessboard."

For a change, I won a game.

✳

THE MORNING AFTER RACHEL AVERY WAS FOUND DEAD in her bath-tub I came downstairs to find him at the breakfast table. He had not slept well, and this showed in his eyes and at the corners of his mouth.

"We'll go into town today," he said.

"It snowed during the night, and you're tired. If you catch cold, and you probably will, you'll be stuck in bed for weeks." This sort of argument he would accept. "Why do you want to go to town, sir?"

"To hear what people say."

"Oh? What do you mean?"

"Because Rachel's husband killed her, Tim. Rachel should never have married Dean Avery. He's a man with the soul of an adding machine, but Rachel was poetry and music. He put her in his house and wanted to own her, but it was never in her to be true, to him or to another. She flew freely and sang magnificently, and he killed her.

"I want to learn just how he did it, and decide what to do about it. Perhaps you'll go to town without me. You notice things well enough. You sense more than I'd guessed you might, as though you know the people."

"You wrote them well."

This amused him. "Never mind," he said. "Make a nuisance of yourself if you have to, but see what you can learn. I have to find out how to manage all of this properly. I know a great deal, but not quite enough."

Before I left I asked him how he could be so sure. He said, "I know the town and the people. I knew Rachel Avery and Dean Avery. I knew her mother very well, and I knew his parents. I knew they should not have married, and that things would go wrong for them, and I am entirely certain that she was killed and that he killed her. Can you under-stand that?"

"I don't think so," I replied. But I took the car into town, bought a few paperbound books at the drugstore, had an un-necessary haircut at the barber's, went from here to there and back again, and then drove home to tell him what I had learned.

"There was a coroner's inquest this morning," I said. "Death by drowning induced as a result of electrical shock, accidental in origin. The funeral is tomorrow."

"Go on, Tim."

"Dean Avery was in Harmony Falls yesterday when they finally reached him and told him what had happened. He was completely torn up, they said. He drove to Harmony Falls the day before yesterday and stayed overnight."

"And he was with people all the while?"

"No one said."

"They wouldn't have checked," he said. "No need, not when it's so obviously an accident. You said the funeral was tomorrow. You'll go to it."

"Why?"

"Because I can't go myself."

"And I'm to study him and study everyone else? Should I take notes?"

He laughed, then chopped off the laughter sharply. "I don't think you'll have to. I didn't mean that you would go in my place solely to observe, Tim, though that's part of it. But I would want to be there because I feel I ought to be there, so you'll be my deputy."

I had no answer to this. He asked me to build up the fire, and I did. I heard the newspaper boy and went for the paper. The town having no newspaper of its own, the paper he took was from the nearest city, and of course there was nothing in it on Rachel Avery. Usually he read it carefully. Now he skimmed it as if hunting something, then set it aside.

"I didn't think you knew her that well," I said.

"I did and I didn't. There are things I do not understand, Tim; people to whom I've barely spoken, yet whom I seem to know intimately. Knowledge has so many levels."

"You never really stopped writing about Beveridge." This was his fictional name for the town. "You just stopped putting it on paper."

He looked up, surprised, considering the thought with his head cocked like a wren's. "That's far more true than you could possibly know," he said.

He ate a good dinner and seemed to enjoy it. Over coffee I started aimless conversations but he let them die out. Then I said, "Mr. Bane, why can't it be an accident? The radio fell into the tub and shocked her, and she drowned."

I thought at first he hadn't heard, or was pretending as

much; this last is a special privilege of the old and the ill. Then he said, "Of course, you have to have facts. What should my intuition mean to you? And it would mean less, I suppose, if I assured you that Rachel Avery could not possibly be the type to play the radio while bathing?"

My face must have showed how much I thought of that. "Very well," he said. "We shall have facts. The water in the tub was running when the body was found. It was running, then, both before and after the radio fell into the tub, which means that Rachel Avery had the radio turned on while the tub was running, which is plainly senseless. She wouldn't be able to hear it well, would she? Also, she was adjusting the dial and knocked it into the tub with her.

"She would not have played the radio at all during her bath—this I simply *know*. She would not have attempted to turn on the radio until her bath was drawn, because no one would. And she would not have tried tuning the set while the water was running because that is sheerly pointless. Now doesn't that begin to make a slight bit of sense to you, Tim?"

❈

THEY PUT HER INTO THE GROUND on a cold gray afternoon. I was part of a large crowd at the funeral parlor and a smaller one at the cemetery. There was a minister instead of a priest, and the service was not the one with which I was familiar, yet after a moment all of it ceased to be foreign to me. And then I knew. It was Emily Talstead's funeral from *Cabot's House*, except that Emily's death had justice to it, and even a measure of mercy, and this gray afternoon held neither.

In that funeral parlor I was the deputy of Joseph Cameron Bane. I viewed Rachel's small body and thought that all caskets should be closed, no matter how precise the mortician's art. We should not force ourselves to look upon our dead. I gave small words of comfort to Dean Avery and avoided his eyes while I did so. I sat in a wooden chair while the minister spoke of horrible tragedy and the unknowable wisdom of the Lord, and I was filled with a sense of loss that was complete in itself.

I shared someone's car to the cemetery. At graveside, with a wind blowing that chilled the edge of thought, I let the gloom slip free as a body into an envelope of earth, and I did what I'd come to do; I looked into the face of Dean Avery.

He was a tall man, thick in the shoulders, broad in the fore-

head, his hair swept straight back without a part, forming
upon his head like a crown. I watched his eyes when he did
not know that anyone watched him, and I watched the curl of
his lip and the way he placed his feet and what he did with
his hands. Before long I knew he mourned her not at all, and
soon after that I knew the old man was right. He had killed
her as sure as the wind blew.

They would have given me a ride back to his house, but I
slipped away when the service ended, and spent time walking
around, back and forth. By the time I was back at her grave,
it had already been filled in. I wondered at the men who do
such work, if they feel a thing at all. I turned from her grave
and walked back through the town to Bane's house.

I found him in the kitchen with coffee and toast. I sat with
him and told him about it quickly, and he made me go back
over all of it in detail so that he could feel he had been there
himself. We sat in silence awhile, and then went to the livingroom. I built up the fire and we sat before it.

"You know now," he said. I nodded, for I did; I'd seen for
myself and knew it and felt it. "Knowing is most of it," he
said. "Computers can never replace us, you know. They need
facts, information. What's the term? Data. They need data. But
sometimes men can make connections across gaps, without
data. You see?"

"Yes."

"So we know." He drank, put down his glass. "But now we
have to have our data. First the conclusion, and then backward
to the proof."

My eyes asked the question.

"Because it all must round itself out," he said, answering
the question without my giving voice to it. "This man killed
and seems to have gotten away with it. This cannot be."

"Should we call the police?"

"Of course not. There's nothing to say to them, and no reason they should listen." He closed his eyes briefly, opened
them. "We know what he did. We ought to know how, and
why. Tell me the men at the funeral, Tim, as many as you
remember."

"I don't remember much before the cemetery. I paid them
little attention."

"At the cemetery, then. That's the important question,
anyway."

I pictured it again in my mind and named the ones I knew. He listened very carefully. "Now there are others who might have been there," he said, "some of whom you may not know, and some you may not remember. Think, now, and tell me if any of these were there."

He named names, five of them, and it was my turn to listen. Two were strangers to me and I could not say if I'd seen them. One I remembered had been there, two others had not.

"Get a pencil and paper," he told me. "Write these names down: Robert Hardesty, Hal Kasper, Roy Teale, Thurman Goodin. Those will do for now."

The first two had been at the funeral, and at the cemetery. The other two had not.

"I don't understand," I said.

"She had a lover, of course. That was why he killed her. Robert Hardesty and Hal Kasper should not have been at that funeral, or at least not at the cemetery. I don't believe they're close to her family or his. Thurman Goodin and Roy Teale should have been at the funeral, at the least, and probably should have been at the cemetery. Now a dead woman's secret love may do what you would not expect him to do. He may stay away from a funeral he would otherwise be expected to attend, for fear of giving himself away, or he might attend a funeral where his presence would not otherwise be required, out of love or respect or no more than morbid yearning. We have four men, two who should have been present and were not, and two who should not have been present but were. No certainty, and nothing you might call data, but I've a feeling one of those four was Rachel Avery's lover."

"And?"

"Find out which one," he said.

"Why would we want to know that?"

"One must know a great many unimportant things in order to know those few things which are important." He poured himself more bourbon and drank some of it off. "Do you read detective stories? They always work with bits and pieces, like a jigsaw puzzle, find out trivia until it all fits together."

"And what might this fit into?"

"A shape. How, why, when."

I wanted to ask more, but he said he was tired and wanted to lie down. He must have been exhausted. He had me help him upstairs, change clothes, and into bed.

I knew Hal Kasper enough to speak to, so it was his shop I started with that night. He had a cigar store near the railroad terminal and sold magazines, paperbound books, candies and stationery. You could place a bet on a horse there, I'd heard. He was thin, with prominent features—large, hollow eyes, a long, slim nose, a large mouth with big gray-white teeth in it. Thirty-five or forty, with a childless wife whom I'd never met, I thought him an odd choice for a lover, but I knew enough to realize that women did not follow logic's rules when they committed adultery.

He had been at the funeral. Joseph Cameron Bane had found this a little remarkable. He had no family ties on either side with Rachel or Dean Avery. He was below them socially, and not connected through his business. Nor was he an automatic funeral-goer. There were such in the town, I'd been told, as there are in every town; they go to funerals as they turn on a television set or eavesdrop on a conversation, for entertainment and for lack of something better to do. But he was not that sort.

"Hi, Irish," he said. "How's the old man?"

I thumbed a magazine. "Asleep," I said.

"Hitting the sauce pretty good lately?"

"I wouldn't say so, no."

"Well, he's got a right." He came out from behind the counter, walked over to me. "Saw you this afternoon. I didn't know you knew her. Or just getting material for that book of yours?"

Everyone assumed I was going to write a novel set in the town, and that this was what had led me to live with Mr. Bane. This would have made as much sense as visiting Denmark in order to rewrite *Hamlet*. I'd stopped denying it. It seemed useless.

"You knew her?" I asked.

"Oh, sure. You know me, Irish. I know everybody. King Farouk, Princess Grace—" He laughed shortly. "Sure, I knew her, a lot better than you'd guess."

I thought I'd learned something, but as I watched his face I saw his large mouth quiver with the beginnings of a leer, and then watched the light die in his eyes and the smile fade from his lips as he remembered that she was dead, cold and in the ground, and not fit to leer over or lust after. He looked ever so slightly ashamed of himself.

"A long time ago," he said, his voice pitched lower now. "Oh, a couple of years. Before she got married, well, she was a pretty wild kid in those days. Not wild like you might think; I mean, she was free, you understand?" He groped with his hands, long-fingered, lean. "She did what she wanted to do. I happened to be there. I was a guy she wanted to be with. Not for too long, but it was honey-sweet while it lasted. This is one fine way to be talking, isn't it? They say she went quick, though; didn't feel anything, but what a stupid way, what a crazy, stupid way."

So it was not Hal Kasper who had loved her; not recently, at least. When I told all this to Joseph Cameron Bane he nodded several times and thought for some moments before he spoke.

"Ever widening circles, Tim," he said. "Throw a stone into a still pool and watch the circles spread. Now don't you see her more clearly? You wouldn't call Kasper a sentimental man, or a particularly sensitive man. He's neither of those things. Yet he felt that sense of loss, and that need to pay his last respects. There's purpose in funerals, you know, purpose and value. I used to think they were barbaric. I know better now. He had to talk about her, and had also to be embarrassed by what he'd said. Interesting."

"Why do we have to know all this?"

"Beginning to bother you, Tim?"

"Some."

"Because I am involved with mankind," he quoted. "You'll learn more tomorrow, I think. Get the chessboard."

I did learn more the next day. I learned first to forget about Roy Teale. I had not recognized his name, but when I found him I saw that he was a man who had been at the funeral, as he might have been expected to be. I also learned, in the barber shop, that he was carrying on a truly passionate love affair, but with his own wife. He sat in a chair and grinned while two of the men ragged him about it.

I left, knowing what I had come to learn; if I'd stayed much longer I'd have had to get another haircut, and I scarcely needed one. I'd taken the car into town that day. It was colder than usual, and the snow was deep. I got into the car and drove to Thurman Goodin's service station. Mr. Bane usually had me fill the car at the station a few blocks to the north, but

I did want to see Goodin. He and Robert Hardesty were the only names left on our list. If neither had been the woman's lover, then we were back where we'd started.

A high school boy worked afternoons and evenings for Goodin but the boy had not come yet, and Thurman Goodin came out to the pump himself. While the tank filled he came over to the side of the car and rested against the door. His face needed shaving. He leaned his long hard body against the car door and said it had been a long time since he'd put any gas into the car.

"Mr. Bane doesn't get out much any more," I said, "and I mostly walk except when the weather's bad."

"Then I'm glad for the bad weather." He lit a cigarette and inhaled deeply. "Anyway, this buggy usually tanks up over to Kelsey's place. You had better than half a tankful; you could have made it over there without running dry, you know."

I gave him a blank look, then turned it around by saying, "I'm sorry, I didn't hear you. I was thinking about that woman who was killed."

I almost jumped at the sight of his face. A nerve twitched involuntarily, a thing he could not have controlled, but he might have covered up the other telltale signs. His eyes gave him away, and his hands, and the movements of his mouth.

"You mean Mrs. Avery," he said.

His wife was her cousin, Mr. Bane had told me. So he should have been at her funeral, and now should have been calling her Rachel or Rachel Avery. I wanted to get away from him!

"I was at the funeral," I said.

"Funerals," he said. "I got a business to run. Listen, I'll tell you something. Everybody dies. Fast or slow, old or young, it don't make a bit of difference. That's two twenty-seven for the gas."

He took three dollars and went into the station. He came back with the change and I took it from him. My hand shook slightly. I dropped a dime.

"Everybody gets it sooner or later," he said. "Why knock yourself out about it?"

When I told all of this to Joseph Cameron Bane he leaned back in his chair with sparkle in his eyes and the ghost of a smile on his pale lips. "So it's Thurman Goodin," he said. "I knew his father rather well. But I knew everybody's father, Tim, so that's not too important, is it? Tell me what you know."

"Sir?"

"Project, extend, extrapolate. What do you know about Goodin? What did he tell you? Put more pieces into the puzzle, Tim."

I said, "Well, he was her lover, of course. Not for very long, but for some space of time. It was nothing of long standing, and yet some of the glow had worn off."

"Go on, Tim."

"I'd say he made overtures for form's sake and was surprised when she responded. He was excited at the beginning, and then he began to be frightened of it all. Oh, this is silly, I'm making it all up—"

"You're doing fine, boy."

"He seemed glad she was dead. No, I'm putting it badly. He seemed relieved, and guilty about feeling relieved. Now he's safe. She died accidentally, and no one will ever find him out, and he can savor his memories without shivering in the night."

"Yes." He poured bourbon into his glass, emptying the bottle. Soon he would ask me to bring him another. "I agree," he said, and sipped at his whiskey almost daintily.

"Now what do we do?"

"What do you think we should do, Tim?"

I thought about this. I said we might check with persons in Harmony Falls and trace Dean Avery's movements there. Or, knowing her lover's name, knowing so much that no one else knew, we might go to the police. We had no evidence, but the police could turn up evidence better than we, and do more with it once they had it.

He looked into the fire. When he did speak, I thought at first that he was talking entirely to himself and not to me at all. "And splash her name all over the earth," he said, "and raise up obscene court trials and filth in the newspapers, and pit lawyers against one another, and either hang him or jail him or free him. Ruin Thurman Goodin's marriage, and ruin Rachel Avery's memory."

"I don't think I understand."

He spun quickly around. His eyes glittered. "Don't you? Tim, Timothy, don't you truthfully understand?" He hesitated, groped for a phrase, then stopped and looked pointedly at his empty glass. I found a fresh bottle in the cupboard, opened it, handed it to him. He poured a drink but did not drink it.

He said, "My books always sold well, you know. But I had a bad press. The small town papers were always kind, but the real critics . . . I was always being charged with sentimentality. They used words like *cloying* and *sugary* and *unrealistic*." I started to say something but he silenced me with an upraised palm. "Please, don't leap to my defense. I'm making a point now, not lamenting a misspent literary youth. Do you know why I stopped writing? I don't think I've ever told anyone. There's never been a reason to tell. I stopped, oh not because critics were unkind, not because sales were disappointing, I stopped because I discovered that the critics, bless them, were quite right."

"That's not true!"

"But it is, Tim. I never wrote what you could honestly call sentimental slop, but everything always came out right, every book always had a happy ending. I simply *wanted* it to happen that way, I wanted things to work out as they *ought* to work out. Do you see? Oh, I let my people stay in character, that was easy enough. I was a good plot man and could bring that off well enough, weaving intricate webs that led inexorably to the silver lining in every last one of the blacker clouds. The people stayed true but the books became untrue, do you see? Always the happy ending, always the death of truth."

"In *Cabot's House* you had an unhappy ending."

"Not so. In *Cabot's House* I had death for an ending, but a death is not always an occasion for sorrow. Perhaps you're too young to know that, or to feel it within. You'll learn it soon enough. But to return to the point, I saw that my books were false. Good pictures of this town, of some people who lived either in it or in my mind or in both, but false portraits of Life. I wrote a book, then, or tried to; an honest one, with loose threads at the end and—what was that precious line of Salinger's? Yes. With a touch of squalor, with love and squalor. I couldn't finish it, I hated it."

He picked up the glass, set it down again, the whiskey untouched. "Do you see? I'm an old man and a fool. I like things to come out right, neat and clean and sugary, wrapped with a bow and a smile for the ending. No police, no trials, no public washing of soiled underwear. I think we are close enough now. I think we have enough of it." He picked up his glass once more and this time drained it. "Get the chessboard," he said.

I got the board. We played, and he won, and my mind spent

more of its time with other pawns than the ones we played with now. The image grew on me. I saw them all, Rachel Avery, Dean Avery, Thurman Goodin, carved of wood and all of a shade, either black or white; weighted with lead, and bottomed with a circlet of felt, green felt, and moved around by our hands upon a mirthless board.

"You're afraid of this," he said once. "Why?"

"Meddling, perhaps. Playing the divinity. I don't know, Mr. Bane. Something that feels wrong, that's all."

"Paddy from the peat bog, you've not lost your sense of the miraculous, have you? Wee folk, and gold at the rainbow's end, and things that go bang in the night, and man a stranger and afraid in someone else's world. Don't move there, Tim, your queen's *en prise*, you'll lose her."

We played three games. Then he straightened up abruptly and said, "I don't have the voice to mimic, I've barely any voice at all, and your brogue's too thick for it. Go up to the third floor, would you, and in the room all the way back, there's a closet with an infernal machine on its shelf—a tape recorder. I bought it with the idea that it might make writing simpler. Didn't work at all; I had to see the words in front of me to make them real. I couldn't sit like a fool talking at a machine. But I had fun with the thing. Get it for me, Tim, please."

It was where he'd said, in a box carpeted with dust. I brought it to him, and we went into the kitchen. There was a telephone there. First he tested the recorder, explaining that the tape was old and might not work properly. He turned it on and said, "Now is the time for all good men to come to the aid of the party. The quick brown fox jumped over the lazy dog." Then he winked at me and said, "Just like a typewriter; it's easiest to resort to formula when you want to say something meaningless, Tim. Most people have trouble talking when they have nothing to say. Though it rarely stops them, does it? Let's see how this sounds."

He played it back and asked me if the voice sounded like his own. I assured him it did. "No one ever hears his own voice when he speaks," he said. "I didn't realize I sounded that old. Odd."

He sent me for bourbon. He drank a bit, then had me get him the phone book. He looked up a number, read it to himself a time or two, then turned his attention again to the recorder.

"We ought to plug it into the telephone," he said.

"What for, sir?"

"You'll see. If you connect them lawfully, they beep every fifteen seconds, so that the other party knows what you're about, which hardly seems sensible. Know anything about these gadgets?"

"Nothing," I replied.

He finished the glass of whiskey. "Now what if I just hold the little microphone to the phone like this? Between my ear and the phone, hmm? Some distortion? Oh, won't matter, won't matter at all."

He dialed a number. The conversation, as much as I heard of it, went something like this:

"Hello, Mr. Taylor? No, wait a moment, let me see. Is this 4215? Oh, good. The Avery residence? Is Mrs. Avery in? I don't . . . Who'm I talking with, please? . . . Good. When do you expect your wife, Mr. Avery? . . . Oh, my! . . . Yes, I see, I see. why, I'm terribly sorry to hear that, surely . . . Tragic. Well, I hate to bother you with this, Mr. Avery. Really, it's nothing . . . Well, I'm Paul Wellings of Wellings and Doyle Travel Agency . . . Yes, that's right, but I wish . . . Certainly. Your wife wanted us to book a trip to Puerto Rico for the two of you and . . . Oh? A surprise, probably . . . Yes, of course, I'll cancel everything. This is frightful. Yes, and I'm sorry for disturbing you at this—"

There was a little more, but not very much. He rang off, a bitter smile on his pale face, his eyes quite a bit brighter now than usual. "A touch of macabre poetry," he said. "Let him think she was planning to run off with Goodin. He's a cold one, though. So calm, and making me go on and on, however awkward it all was. And now it's all ready on the tape. But how can I manage this way?"

He picked up a phone and called another number. "Jay? This is Cam. Say, I know it's late, but is your tape recorder handy? Well, I'd wanted to do some dictation and mine's burned out a connection or something. Oh, just some work I'm doing. No, I haven't mentioned it, I know. It's something different. If anything ever comes of it, then I'll have something to tell you. But is it all right if I send Tim around for your infernal machine? Good, and you're a prince, Jay."

So he sent me to pick up a second recorder from Jason Falk. When I brought it to him, he positioned the two machines side by side on the table and nodded. "I hate deception," he said, "yet it seems to have its place in the scheme of things. I'll need half an hour or so alone, Tim. I hate to chase you away, but I have to play with these toys of mine."

I didn't mind. I was glad to be away from him for a few moments, for he was upsetting me more than I wanted to admit. There was something bad in the air that night, and more than my Irish soul was telling me so. Joseph Cameron Bane was playing God. He was manipulating people, toying with them. *Writing* them, and with no books to put them in.

It was too cold for walking. I got into the car and drove around the streets of the town, then out of the town and off on a winding road that went up into the hills beyond the town's edge. The snow was deep but no fresh snow was falling, and the moon was close to full and the sky cluttered with stars. I stopped the car and got out of it and took a long look back at the town below, his town. I thought it would be good right now to be a drinking man and warm myself from a bottle and walk in the night and pause now and then to gaze at the town below.

※

"YOU WERE GONE LONG," he said.

"I got lost. It took time to find my way back."

"Tim, this still bothers you, doesn't it? Of course it does. Listen to me. I am going to put some people into motion, that is all. I am going to let some men talk to one another, and I am going to write their lines for them. Do you understand? Their opening lines. They wouldn't do it themselves. They wouldn't start it. I'll start it, and then they'll help it play itself out."

He was right, of course. Avery could not be allowed to get away with murder, nor should the dead woman's sins be placed on public display for all to stare at.

"Now listen to this," he said, bright-eyed again. "I'm proud of myself, frankly."

He dialed a number, then poised his index finger above one of the buttons on the recorder. He was huddled over the table so that the telepone mouthpiece was just a few inches from the recorder's speaker. The phone was answered, and he pressed a button and I heard Dean Avery's voice. "Goodin?"

A pause. Then, "This is Dean Avery. I know all about it,

Goodin. You and my wife. You and Rachel. I know all about it. And now she's dead. An accident. Think about it, Goodin. You'll have to think about it."

He replaced the receiver.

"How did you . . ."

He looked at my gaping mouth and laughed aloud at me. "Just careful editing," he said, "Playing from one machine to the next, back and forth, a word here, a phrase there, all interwoven and put together. Even the inflection can be changed by raising or lowering the volume as you bounce from one machine to the other. Isn't it startling? I told you I have fun with this machine. I never got anything written on it, but I had a good time fooling around with it."

"All these phrases—you even had his name."

"It was *good* of you to call. And the tail syllable of some other word, *happen*, I think. The two cropped out and spliced together and tossed back and forth until they fit well enough. I was busy while you were gone, Tim. It wasn't simple to get it all right."

"Now what happens?"

"Goodin calls Avery."

"How do you know?"

"Oh, Tim! I'll call Goodin and tell him how my car's broken down, or that he's won a football pool, or something inane, and do the same thing with his voice. And call Avery for him, and accuse him of the murder. That's all. They'll take it from there. I expect Avery will crack. If I get enough words to play with, I can have Goodin outline the whole murder, how it happened, everything."

His fingers drummed the table top. "Avery might kill himself," he said. "The killers always do in that woman's stories about the little Belgian detective. They excuse themselves and blow their brains out in a gentlemanly manner. There might be a confrontation between the two. I'm not sure."

"Will it wait until morning?"

"I thought I'd call Goodin now."

He was plainly exhausted. It was too late for him to be awake, but the excitement kept him from feeling the fatigue. I hated playing nursemaid. I let him drink too much every day, let him die as he wished, but it was not good for him to wear himself out this way.

"Goodin will be shaken by the call," I told him. "You'll

probably have trouble getting him to talk. He may have closed the station for the night."

"I'll call and find out," he said.

He called, the recorder at the ready, and the phone rang and went unanswered. He wanted to wait up and try again, but I made him give it up and wait until the next day. I put him to bed and went downstairs and straightened up the kitchen. There was a half inch of whiskey in a bottle, and I poured it into a glass and drank it, a thing I rarely do. It warmed me and I'd needed warming. I went upstairs and to bed, and still had trouble sleeping.

There were dreams, and bad ones, dreams that woke me and set me upright with a shapeless wisp of horror falling off like smoke. I slept badly and woke early. I was downstairs while he slept. While I ate toast and drank tea, Mrs. Dettweiler worried aloud about him. "You've got him all worked up," she said. "He shouldn't get like that. A sick man like him, he should rest, he should be calm."

"He wants the excitement. And it's not my doing."

"As sick as he is . . ."

"He's dying, and has a right to do it his own way."

"Some way to talk!"

"It's his way."

"There's a difference."

The radio was playing, tuned to a station in Harmony Falls. Our town had one FM station but the radio did not get FM. Mrs. Dettwiler always played a radio unless Mr. Bane was in the room, in which case he generally told her to turn it off. When she was upstairs in her own room, the television was always on, unless she was praying or sleeping. I listened to it now and thought that he might have used it for his taping and editing and splicing. If you wished to disguise your voice, you might do it that way. If Dean Avery had never heard Thurman Goodin's voice, or not well enough to recognize it, you could work it well enough that way. With all those words and phrases at your disposal. . . .

Halfway through the newscast they read an item from our town, read just a brief news story, and I spilled my tea all over the kitchen table. The cup fell to the floor and broke in half.

"Why, for goodness. . . ."

I turned off the radio, thought better and reached to pull its plug. He never turned it on, hated it, but it might occur to him to tape from it, and I didn't want that. Not yet.

"Keep that thing off," I said. "Don't let him hear it, and don't tell him anything. If he tries to play the radio, say it's not working."

"I don't. . . ."

"Just do as you're told!" I said. She went white and nodded mutely, and I hurried out of the house and drove into town. On the way I noticed that I held the steering wheel so tightly my fingers had gone numb. I couldn't help it. I'd have taken a drink then if there'd been one about. I'd have drunk kerosene, or perfume—anything at all.

I went to the drugstore and to the barbershop, and heard the same story in both places, and walked around a bit to relax, the last with little success. I left the car where I'd parked it and walked back to his house and breathed cold air and gritted my teeth against more than the cold. I did not even realize until much later that it was fairly stupid to leave the car. It seemed quite natural at the time.

He was up by the time I reached the house, wearing robe and slippers, seated at the table with telephone and tape recorder. "Where'd you go?" he wanted to know. "I can't reach Thurman Goodin. Nobody answers his phone."

"Nobody will."

"I've half a mind to try him at home."

"Don't bother."

"No? Why not?" And then, for the first time, he saw my face. His own paled. "Heavens, Tim, what's the matter?"

All the way back, through snow and cold air, I'd looked for a way to tell him—a proper way. There was none. Halfway home I'd thought that perhaps Providence might let him die before I had to tell him, but that could only have happened in one of his novels, not in this world.

So I said, "Dean Avery's dead. It happened last night; he's dead."

"Great God in Heaven!" His face was white, his eyes horribly wide. "How? Suicide?"

"No."

"How?" he asked insistently.

"It was meant to look like suicide. Thurman Goodin killed him. Broke into his house in the middle of the night. He was going to knock him out and poke his head in the oven and put the gas on. He knocked him cold all right, but Avery came to on the way to the oven. There was a row, and Thurman Goodin beat him over the head with some tool he'd brought along. I believe it was a tire iron. Beat his brains in, but all the noise woke a few of the neighbors and they grabbed Goodin on his way out the door. Two of them caught him and managed to hold him until the police came, and of course he told them everything."

I expected Bane to interrupt, but he waited without a word. I said, "Rachel Avery wanted him to run away with her. She couldn't stand staying with her husband, she wanted to go to some big city, try the sweet life. He told the police he tried to stop seeing her. She threatened him, that she would tell her husband, that she would tell his wife. So he went to her one afternoon and knocked her unconscious, took off her clothes and put her in the bathtub. She was still alive then. He dropped the radio into the tub to give her a shock, then unplugged it and checked to see if she were dead. She wasn't, so he held her head under water until she drowned, and then he plugged the radio into the socket again and left.

"And last night he found out that Avery knew about it, about the murder and the affair and all. So of course he had to kill Avery. He thought he might get away with it if he made it look like suicide, that Avery was depressed over his wife's death and went on to take his own life. I don't think it would have washed. I don't know much about it, but aren't the police more apt to examine a suicide rather carefully? They might see the marks on the head. Perhaps not. I don't really know. They've put Goodin in jail in Harmony Falls, and with two bloody murders like that, he's sure to hang." And then, because I felt even worse about it all than I'd known, "So it all comes out even, after all, the way you wanted it, the loose ends tied up in a bow."

"Good heavens!"

"I'm sorry." And I was, as soon as I'd said the words.

I don't think he heard me. "I am a bad writer and a bad man," he said, and not to me at all, and perhaps not even to himself, but to whatever he talked to when the need came. "I thought I created them, I thought I knew them, I thought they all belonged to me."

So I went upstairs and packed my bags and walked all the way to the station. It was a bad time to leave him and a heartless way to do it, but staying would have been worse, even impossible. He was dying, and I couldn't have changed that, nor made the going much easier for him. I walked to the station and took the first train out and ended up here in Los Angeles, working for another foolish little man who likes to hire foreigners, doing the same sort of nothing I'd done in New York, but doing it at least in a warmer climate.

Last month I read he'd died. I thought I might cry but didn't. A week ago I re-read one of his books, *Lips That Could Kiss*. I discovered that I did not like it at all, and then I did cry. For Rachel Avery, for Joseph Cameron Bane. For me.